iculture

Handbook
Series
Book 6

Building a Sustainable Business

A Guide to Developing a Business Plan for Farms and Rural Businesses

Developed by:
the Minnesota Institute for Sustainable Agriculture
Saint Paul, MN

Co-published by:
The Sustainable Agriculture Network
Beltsville, MD

Project Coordinators
Gigi DiGiacomo, Economic Consultant
Debra Elias Morse, Consultant
Robert King, University of Minnesota

Authors
Gigi DiGiacomo, Economic Consultant
Robert King, University of Minnesota
Dale Nordquist, University of Minnesota

Contributors
Vern Eidman, University of Minnesota
Debra Elias Morse, Consultant
Susan McAllister, Marketing Consultant
Kenneth Thomas, Professor Emeritus, University of Minnesota

Farmer Business Plan Participants and Reviewers
Nancy Aspelund
Mabel Brelje
Mary Doerr, Dancing Winds Farms
Frank Foltz, Northwind Nursery and Orchards
Dave and Florence Minar, Cedar Summit Farm
Greg Reynolds, Riverbend Farm

Technical Reviewer
Damona Doye, Oklahoma State University

Editor
Beth Nelson, Minnesota Institute for Sustainable Agriculture

Production
Nancy Goodman, copy editor
Karol Keane, cover
Jim Kiehne, layout
Valerie Berton, Sustainable Agriculture Network

Cover photo collage: top, Greg Reynolds; right, Frank Foltz's son; lower left, Florence and Dave Minar; upper left, Mary Doerr

This publication was developed by the Minnesota Institute for Sustainable Agriculture in cooperation with the Center for Farm Financial Management, with funding from the Minnesota State Legislature.

This publication was co-published by the Sustainable Agriculture Network (SAN), under a cooperative agreement with USDA's Cooperative State Research, Education, and Extension Service.

To order copies of this book ($14.00 plus $3.95 shipping and handling), contact (802) 656-0484, sanpubs@uvm.edu, (800) 9096472, or misamail@umn.edu. This publication can be viewed on-line at www.misa.umn.edu/publications/bizplan.html.

Library of Congress Cataloging In Publication Data

Building a sustainable business : a guide to developing a business plan for farms and rural businesses / by the Minnesota Institute for Sustainable Agriculture.
p. cm. – (Sustainable Agriculture Network handbook series ; bk. 6)
Includes bibliographical references.
ISBN 1-888626-07-0 (pbk.)
1. Farm management. I. Minnesota Institute for Sustainable Agriculture. II. Sustainable Agriculture Network. III. Series.
S561.B84 2003
630'.68–dc21

2003005514

Sustainable Agriculture Information Exchange

This publication was developed through the Sustainable Agriculture Information Exchange, a clearinghouse of sustainable agriculture information and materials in Minnesota. The Information Exchange is a program of MISA, the Minnesota Institute for Sustainable Agriculture. MISA is a partnership between the University of Minnesota's College of Agricultural, Food and Environmental Sciences and the Sustainers' Coalition, a group of individuals and community-based, nonprofit organizations. MISA's purpose is to bring together the agricultural community and the University community in a cooperative effort to develop and promote sustainable agriculture in Minnesota and beyond.

To ensure that all of the Information Exchange's publications are applicable and user-friendly, they are developed by teams and reviewed by individuals who will use the material, including farmers, researchers, extension educators and other agricultural community members.

Other publications in the Sustainable Agriculture Information Exchange series (available through the University of Minnesota Extension Service Distribution Center) include:

Collaborative Marketing: A Roadmap & Resource Guide for Farmers (BU-07539-S)
Discovering Profits in Unlikely Places: Agroforestry Opportunities for Added Income (BU-07407)
Hogs Your Way: Choosing a Hog Production System in the Upper Midwest (BU-07641)
Minnesota Soil Management Series (PC-07398-S)
Organic Certification of Crop Production in Minnesota (BU-07202)
Whole Farm Planning: Combining Family, Profit, and Environment (BU-06985)

For more information on this series, the Information Exchange, or MISA, contact: Minnesota Institute for Sustainable Agriculture, 411 Borlaug Hall, 1991 Buford Circle, St. Paul, MN 55108-1013; (612) 625-8235, or toll-free (800) 909-MISA (6472); Fax (612) 625-1268; misamail@umn.edu; www.misa.umn.edu.

Center for Farm Financial Management

The Center for Farm Financial Management at the University of Minnesota cooperated in the development of this publication. The Center's mission is to improve the farm financial management abilities of agricultural producers and the professionals who serve them through educational software and training programs. Contact: Center for Farm Financial Management, University of Minnesota, 130 Classroom Office Building, 1994 Buford Avenue, St. Paul, Minnesota 55108; (612) 625-1964 or toll-free (800) 234-1111; cffm@cffm.agecon.umn.edu; www.cffm.umn.edu.

Sustainable Agriculture Research and Education (SARE) Sustainable Agriculture Network (SAN)

SARE is a program of USDA's Cooperative State Research, Education, and Extension Service. For more information about SARE grant opportunities and informational resources, go to www.sare.org. SAN publishes information about sustainable agriculture under a cooperative agreement with CSREES. For more information about SAN, or other SAN publications, contact: Andy Clark, SAN Coordinator, Sustainable Agriculture Network, 10300 Baltimore Ave., Bldg. 046 BARC-West, Beltsville, MD 20705-2350; (301) 504-5236; Fax (301) 504-5207; san@sare.org

Funding for this project was approved by the Minnesota State Legislature and the Energy and Sustainable Agriculture Program of the Minnesota Department of Agriculture.

Preface

Business planning is an important part of owning and managing a farm. Producers traditionally go through the business planning process to:

- Evaluate production alternatives;
- Identify new market opportunities; and
- Communicate their ideas to lenders, business partners and family.

As agricultural entrepreneurs define and create themselves away from more "conventional" farming models, business planning has become more important than ever.

Producers considering innovative management practices and immature markets use business plans to map out strategies for taking advantage of new opportunities such as organic farming, on-farm processing, direct marketing and rural tourism. A business plan helps producers demonstrate that they have fully researched their proposed alternative; they know how to produce their product, how to sell what they produce, and how to manage financial risk.

"Building a Sustainable Business: A Guide to Developing a Business Plan for Farms and Rural Businesses" was conceived in 1996 by a planning team for the Minnesota Institute for Sustainable Agriculture (MISA), to address the evolving business planning needs of beginning and experienced rural entrepreneurs. From the onset, the planning team envisioned a truly useful guidebook that would be relevant to the alternative farm operations and rural businesses of today. There are certainly more detailed business planning, strategy building, succession planning, marketing and financial planning resources available. It was not our intention to replace these materials. Many of these existing resources are listed in an extensive "Resources" section at the end of this Guide. Instead, our objective was to compile information from all available resources, including farmers and other business experts, that could be used to create a business planning primer—a guide that will help today's alternative agriculture entrepreneurs work through the planning process and to begin developing their business plans.

This Guide was developed over a period of seven years by a team of University of Minnesota faculty and staff, individual farmers and consultants. Two formal reviews were conducted by MISA throughout the 1998–2000 period to test and refine this Guide. During these reviews, six farmers were asked to develop their own business plans using the draft materials. This Guide incorporates recommendations on content, language and organization from the review process as well as examples from five of the review team's business plans. We are grateful to them for their assistance and their willingness to share their business planning efforts. This Guide was originally targeted toward Upper Midwest producers and entrepreneurs, hence the "Resources" section is weighted toward Midwest organizations. As the project evolved, we realized that the material is applicable to a variety of operations throughout the United States; the basic business planning process is universal. The Sustainable Agricultural Network agreed that this information should reach a national audience and graciously agreed to co-publish this material. This Guide benefited greatly from a careful review by Damona Doye, Extension Economist, Oklahoma State University, and we are grateful for her suggested revisions. Parallel to the development of this Guidebook, a business planning software package was developed by the Center for Farm Financial Management at the University of Minnesota. This Guide and software are complementary.

Ultimately, this Guide is as much about the planning process as it is about the creation of a final business plan. MISA followed one of the farm reviewer families, Cedar Summit Farm owners Dave and Florence Minar and their family, throughout their planning process. The Minars' planning experience—their initial exploration of values, brainstorming of goals, and research into on-farm milk processing, markets and financing—is incorporated throughout this Guide's text and Worksheets. A completed business plan for the Minars' Cedar Summit Creamery is attached in Appendix A. This enabled us to "put a face" on the business planning process, and we thank the Minars for their openness in sharing so much of their story. Armed with their business plan, the Minars were able to obtain financing. We are happy to report that as we go to press, Cedar Summit Creamery is up and running.

We hope this Business Planning Guide will assist today's alternative and traditional business owners alike with the creation of a holistic business plan rooted firmly in personal, community, economic and environmental values. With a business plan in hand, today's farmers and rural entrepreneurs will be able to take that first step toward the creation of a successful and sustainable business.

Table of Contents

Task Four: Strategic Planning and Evaluation–What Routes Can You Take to Get Where You Want to Go? 103

List of Figures

INTRODUCTION

"Business planning is a critical component to any operation. Even though a 'seat-of-the-pants' approach to farming might work, it takes too long to figure out if a decision is a poor one; you can waste years doing the wrong thing when you could have been doing the right thing."

—Greg Reynolds, Riverbend Farm owner/operator.

Regardless of whether you are a beginning entrepreneur who has recently inherited a business, an experienced farmer who is considering on-farm processing, or a retiring business owner who is looking to pass on the farm, business planning is important. It is an ongoing process that begins with the identification of values and ends with a strategic plan to address critical management functions.

Like many rural entrepreneurs, you may have a strong sense of the values that drew you to the land or inspired you to begin a business. You may also have a clear set of personal and business goals that you would like to pursue "when the time is right." But, if you're like most farmers and rural business owners, you run into problems when trying to incorporate values and goals into day-to-day business decisions. How can you build a balanced and sustainable business—one that reflects your values and is successful—in the long run?

Unlike most other business planning tools, *Building a Sustainable Business: A Planning Guide for Farmers and Rural Business Owners* takes a whole-farm approach. You will consider traditional business planning and marketing principles as well as your personal, economic, environmental and community values—those less tangible things that are a part of your thoughts every day, but which often don't become a planned part of your business. You will be asked to integrate values with business management practices throughout this Guide.

Planning Tasks

- One: Identify Values
  What's Important to You?
- Two: Review History and Take Stock of Your Current Situation
  What Have You Got?
- Three: Clarify Your Vision, Develop a Mission Statement and Identify Goals
  Where Do You Want to Go?
- Four: Strategic Planning and Evaluation
  What Routes Can You Take to Get Where You Want to Go?
- Five: Present, Implement and Monitor Your Business Plan
  Which Route Will You Take and How Will You Check Your Progress Along the Way?

Structure of This Guide

This Guide is divided into five chapters—each reflecting a critical "planning task."

- Task One: Identify Values—What's Important to You?
- Task Two: Review History and Take Stock of Your Current Situation—What Have You Got?
- Task Three: Clarify Your Vision, Develop a Mission Statement and Identify Goals—Where Do You Want to Go?
- Task Four: Strategic Planning and Evaluation—What Routes Can You Take to Get Where You Want to Go?
- Task Five: Present, Implement and Monitor Your Business Plan—Which Route Will You Take and How Will You Check Your Progress Along the Way?

Within each Planning Task, the four key functional planning areas are addressed: *marketing, operations, human resources* and *finances*. In Planning Task One, you and your planning team (family, business partners, lenders) will identify the values that bring each of you to the table. Planning Task Two asks you and your team to document business history and take stock of your current situation. In Planning Task Three, you will clarify a future vision for your business as well as develop goals and a mission statement that reflect the values you identified in Planning Task One. Planning Task Four addresses the crux of your business plan: the development and evaluation of strategic marketing, operations, human resources and financing alternatives. Finally, in Planning Task Five you will pull everything together into a written business plan.

Within each task, you'll find examples of completed worksheets from five of the farmers who completed business plans for their enterprises using this guide.

To print a complete set of blank worksheets, go to ***www.misa.umn.edu/publications/bizplan.html***

These icons let you know which of the four key management areas is being discussed in each Planning Task.

The Four Key Management Areas:
- **Marketing**
- Operations
- Human Resources
- Finance

The Four Key Management Areas:
- Marketing
- **Operations**
- Human Resources
- Finance

The Four Key Management Areas:
- Marketing
- Operations
- **Human Resources**
- Finance

The Four Key Management Areas:
- Marketing
- Operations
- Human Resources
- **Finance**

Mabel Brelje: Certified organic small grain, corn, and soybean grower located in Glencoe, Minnesota. Mabel began the planning process shortly after receiving organic certification in 1998. At that time, her planning needs were three-fold and revolved around human resources, operations and marketing issues. Her primary planning issues concerned: (1) chronic labor and equipment shortages; (2) lack of established, reliable markets; and (3) the need to find a buyer for the farm.

Mary Doerr, Dancing Winds Farm: On-farm goat cheese producer and bed and breakfast operator located in Kenyon, Minnesota. Mary had been operating her farm business for 14 years prior to developing her business plan as part of the MISA review process. At the time, Mary's planning objectives included improving financial management, increasing the number of B&B guests, and developing an apprenticeship cheese-making program on the farm.

Frank Foltz, Northwind Nursery and Orchard: Edible landscape nursery stock grower and marketer located in Princeton, Minnesota. Frank had operated his family business for 17 years when he drafted a business plan to ready the catalogue portion of his business for sale to an outside buyer and to map out a long-term plan for on-farm nursery stock sales, tourism, and homesteading education.

Dave and Florence Minar, Cedar Summit Farm: Large-scale dairy graziers located in New Prague, Minnesota. They operated the farm together for 30 years before preparing a business plan in 1999-2001. The Minars' primary planning objective was to evaluate on-farm milk processing as a strategy to reduce year-to-year income volatility and to create permanent work for several of their adult children. Dave and Florence shared their worksheets and business plan with MISA. You will see examples from their planning experience and their final business plan for the newly created Cedar Summit Creamery throughout this Guide.

Greg Reynolds, Riverbend Farm: Organic Community Supported Agriculture (CSA) vegetable grower and marketer located in Delano, Minnesota. Greg was in his fourth growing season when he sat down to write a business plan as part of the MISA review process. His critical planning issues were human resources and finance related. Greg struggled with seasonal labor and cash-flow constraints. Throughout the planning process, Greg considered two strategy alternatives: hiring labor and purchasing labor-saving equipment to address his seasonal shortages.

Using This Guide

This Guide is intended to be user-friendly—written so that anyone should be able to walk through the business planning process by following the Planning Tasks.

As you begin the planning process, try to work through the tasks as they are ordered and to consider all four of the functional areas within each task, since these aspects of business management are interrelated. However, it is equally important to work through this Guide in a way that makes sense given your needs and time constraints. You may not be able to address all of your planning needs the first time through this Guide. It may be more important to simply begin the process of planning and to recognize that it will be an ongoing project.

Some of the Planning Tasks are quite involved, such as Task Four, in which you develop alternative business strategies. As you go through each consideration for each of the marketing and finance alternatives, it can be easy to forget where you are! We've provided a flow diagram that we'll repeat at the beginning of each section, to help you keep track of where you are in the planning process and show you how it relates to the big planning picture.

The Table of Contents includes a list of completed Worksheet samples and the page number where they can be found in the text. This will allow you to find them more easily when you begin working on your own Worksheets. Blank Worksheets for you to use are found at the end of each Planning Task.

Each Planning Task also ends with a section about which parts of your work from that Planning Task should be included in a final business plan. You can also use the FINPACK Business Planning Software to help you assemble the final plan, and use the data directly from financial Worksheets.

Before You Begin: Why Develop a Business Plan and Who Should Be Involved in the Planning Process?

New and experienced business owners, regardless of history or current situation, can benefit from business planning. As an experienced producer, you may develop a business plan to: map out a transition from conventional to organic production management; expand your operation; incorporate more family members or partners into your business; transfer or sell the business; add value to your existing operation through product processing, direct sales or cooperative marketing. It's never too late to begin planning! If you are a first-time rural land owner or beginning farmer who may be considering the establishment of a bed and breakfast or community supported agriculture (CSA) enterprise, business planning can help you identify management tasks and financing options that are compatible with your long-term personal, environmental, economic, and community values.

Business planning is an on-going, problem-solving process that can identify business challenges and opportunities that apply to your marketing, operations, human resources and finances, and develop strategic objectives to move your business beyond its current situation toward your future business vision.

Once developed, your business plan can be used as a long-term, internal organizing tool or to communicate your plans to others outside your business. Use your business plan to:

- Make regular or seasonal marketing, operations, human resources and finance decisions.
- Pursue long-term personal, economic, environmental and community goals.
- Develop a business profile for communicating within or outside your family to potential business partners, lenders and customers.

Before you begin working through this Guide, take a few moments to consider where you are in the business life cycle and why you are developing a business plan. Are you just beginning? Ready for growth? Planning to consolidate and transfer out of the business?

Figure 1. The Business Life Cycle[1]

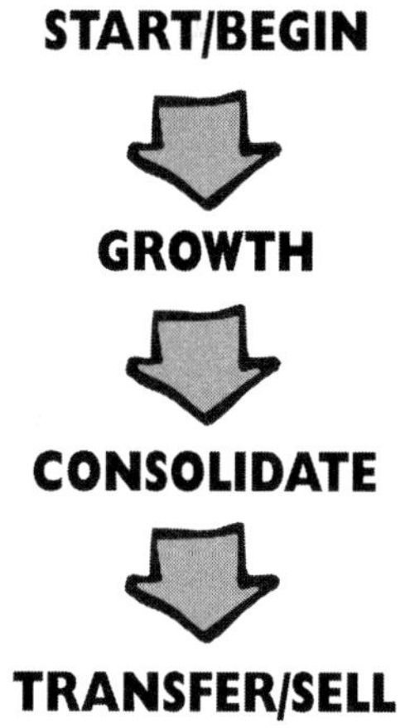

START/BEGIN

↓

GROWTH

↓

CONSOLIDATE

↓

TRANSFER/SELL

Based on your position in the business life cycle, what do you want to accomplish? Do you need to explore a critical finance- or operations-related challenge that you currently face? Research a perceived marketing opportunity? Prepare for an anticipated internal change in human resources? Most likely you have several, interdependent planning motives. This Guide is designed to help you work through many of them. Be aware, however, that retirement and farm transfer issues are not treated directly in the text or Worksheets. If retirement and business transfer are your critical planning issues, you may benefit by working through the first few tasks (identifying values, reviewing your history and current situation, and identifying your vision and goals), before talking with an attorney or financial consultant to help you develop specific business liquidation or transfer strategies.

Once you've identified why you're developing a business plan, you need to decide who will be involved in developing your plan. Your planning should ideally be done as a team—this will not only enrich brainstorming, but will also secure support for your plan by those who are involved in the operation. Your planning team can be thought of as business "stakeholders"—those people who

1 *Financial Management in Agriculture*, 7th ed., Barry et al., 2002.

This symbol will appear wherever we encourage you to fill in your own worksheet or business plan.

play a key role in your operation or who will be involved in business and personal decisions. Stakeholders often include family members, employees, partners, renters, other producers, landlords, customers, resource organizations, input dealers, lenders, community members, and veterinarians or other technical experts. These critical stakeholders should be considered your "planning team."

Use the **Why Are You Developing a Business Plan? Worksheet** to think about your specific business planning issues and to help you identify your planning team. If you are feeling overwhelmed and unsure about where to begin in the planning process, try narrowing your initial planning focus to one critical management area. For example, in the Worksheet at right, Cedar Summit Farm owner Dave Minar began the planning process by identifying a critical issue related to his dairy farm's long-term human resources availability. Minar considers his desire to employ more family members through the farm business his critical planning issue; it is his motivation behind the idea for on-farm milk processing which Dave and his wife, Florence, explore and present in their business plan (Appendix A).

Once you've identified the critical planning issues that you would like to address with your plan, think about how your plan will be used. If you intend to use the plan as a guide to seasonal operations, you will want to focus on the practical aspects of implementation. If your primary planning objective is to attract a potential business partner or financing, you will need to devote more time and space to fleshing out your business vision, its financial feasibility, and a marketing description of your final product or service.

Worksheet Introduction **Why Are You Developing a Business Plan?**

Spend a few moments thinking about your planning needs. Be clear about which issues you would like to address with your plan and consider how you will use the final plan. This Worksheet is for your eyes only.

What key issues are motivating you to plan?

We have several adult children who want to continue farming. We would like to add jobs to our farm without increasing our milking herd. We would like to explore the feasibility of building and operating an on-farm creamery to add value to our milk, increase profitability and support more family members financially. We would also like to begin to map out a retirement plan that includes turning over the business to our children.

1. Who is your business planning team? Who should be involved in your planning process?

First and foremost, our planning team includes all five of our adult children and their spouses. We also consider our local farm business management instructor and other experienced processors as members of the planning team who can provide information and feedback on some of our ideas.

2. How will you use your business plan? Will it serve as an internal organizing tool, be used to communicate outside your business, or both?

Initially our plan will be used to communicate outside our business with a lender to secure financing. Our plan will also be used as an internal organizing tool to develop job descriptions, a production and processing schedule, a marketing and delivery plan, and cash flow projections.

**Figure 2.
Example from Cedar Summit Farm—Introduction Worksheet: Why Are You Developing a Business Plan?**

Spend a few moments thinking about your planning needs. Be clear about which issues you would like to address with your plan and consider how you will use the final plan. This Worksheet is for your eyes only.

What key issues are motivating you to plan?

1. **Who is your business planning team? Who should be involved in your planning process?**

2. **How will you use your business plan? Will it serve as an internal organizing tool, be used to communicate outside your business, or both?**

Identify Values – What's Important to You?

Your values are critical to the business planning process. They will guide you through business management choices and personal decisions as you dream a future vision, set goals, consider strategic alternatives, and develop monitoring checkpoints.

Planning Task One

- ✔ Discuss values: What are they and how do they affect business planning and management decisions?
- ✔ Identify your own values.
- ✔ Identify common values among your planning team.
- ✔ Prepare the Values section of your Business Plan.

Values: What Are They and How Are They Important to the Planning Process?

Values are the standards, beliefs or qualities that you consider worth upholding or pursuing. They are not goals, but instead can be thought of as something that reflects your view on life or a judgment about what you find important.

Your values will directly shape your business strategy and whole farm management choices. The excerpt from the Cedar Summit Farm business plan that follows demonstrates how the Minars' values have affected management choices and how these values continue to influence their operating decisions.

See pages 24–25 for a complete set of blank worksheets for Task One.

TASK 1

To print a complete set of blank worksheets, go to ***www.misa.umn.edu/publications/bizplan.html***

"Because our health is directly tied to the health of the environment, we strive to produce healthy dairy and meat products by utilizing sustainable methods in their production. . . . We put all of our land in permanent pasture grasses to let the cows harvest their own feed and to stop erosion. This can also improve animal health as well as the water and mineral cycles. . . . Our community values the esthetic beauty of seeing farm animals on the land."

Similarly, the values identified by Greg Reynolds of Riverbend Farm had a big impact on his choice of production system. Greg believes that agriculture should be both labor and knowledge intensive, thus *"involving more people in production agriculture to create a healthy rural economy."* These values or beliefs have led him toward the establishment of a labor-intensive organic vegetable business.

Value identification becomes critically important if you are planning collectively with other business stakeholders such as family, formal partners and community members. Awareness of the different values held by each planning team member will make goal setting and conflict resolution easier down the road. A clear understanding of core values can help expose the personal biases that you have and make it easier to come to more objective business decisions.

You may ultimately decide to share your values with future stakeholders as they join your business or hold on to them privately to serve as internal yardsticks throughout the business planning process.

Identify Your Own Values

Take time now to explore your own values. Begin by asking yourself and members of your planning team what being "successful" means or recall a critical turning point in your life when you were faced with a serious tradeoff. What values guided you?

Which of the following statements ring true for you?

To me, being "successful" in farming means:

- Paying down our expenses.
- Putting money away for the future.
- Farming full time.
- Taking pride in the products we produce.
- Creating a place for the next generation to farm.
- Taking time to rest, vacation.
- Being able to save for down times.
- Having a surplus to share with others in need.
- Working together as a family.

- Helping neighbors who are farming.
- Creating a beautiful landscape and environment.
- Working outdoors with livestock.
- Generating ____ % of my income from the farm.

Or, try to identify specific personal, economic, environmental and community values. Ask yourself:

- What type of life do I want to lead? (personal)
- What do I consider financially important? (economic)
- What role does the environment play in my life? (environmental)
- How do I define community and why is it important? (community)

Goat-cheese producer Mary Doerr of Dancing Winds Farm, for example, thoroughly explored her values in the context of personal, economic, environmental and community sustainability. She included a full values description in her business plan.

Use **Worksheet 1.1: My Values** to think about and define your values. You may decide to write a comprehensive

Figure 3.
Example from Dancing Winds Farm—Worksheet 1.1: My Values

TASK 1

Worksheet 1.1 My Values

Think about your values and list them in the space below. Consider what it means for you to be "successful" in farming, or try distinguishing between personal, economic, environmental, and community values. If you are having trouble putting values onto paper, try drafting a brief essay. Begin by recalling a critical turning point in your life when you were faced with a serious tradeoff: What values guided you?

Personal Values:

I value good health - physical, emotional and spiritual - and work to keep those in good balance. One's health is truly a very precious commodity. I live with allergies and asthma, and it may sound obvious, but if can't breath nothing else matters. It's important for me to get good nourishment (mind, body and soul), exercise regularly, and get enough rest. I value my relationships with people: family, loved ones, friends and community. I believe that it is important to be authentic, honest, and understanding with others and to try to help make a positive difference in this world. I want to continue to grow and learn, respect life, value its diversity and work for justice, equality, environmental protection, and a safe, affordable food system. I value travel - it is always good to explore and see how others live. It is an education unto itself. I value the philosophy of letting others live as they will. It is a basic human right, I believe, to be free to live and love as you choose ... without fear of persecution or discrimination.

Economic Values:

I value living modestly. I try to practice wise management of my financial resources and carry no debt-load beyond my mortgage at this time. I want to make an honest living. I enjoy producing and promoting quality goat products and providing friendly hospitality to my guests.

Environmental Values:

I believe in leaving my environment better than how I found it. I strive to be a good steward of the land, trying to help maintain and enhance soil, water, and air quality through sustainable farming practices. I plant trees every year on the farm. My philosophy is to take the long view when making business decisions that will impact the farm's environment - trying to imagine that impact seven generations into the future ... We need to pay attention to our actions and care about all forms of life on this planet, even the forms we cannot readily see.

Community Values:

It's important for me to try to be part of the solution, not part of the problem. I want to make a positive difference in my community and be a good role model for other young women who may have an interest in sustainable farming. I will support the local economy as much as I can, realizing that this effort, in itself, helps sustain the community.

description of your values and their potential effect on management decisions as Mary Doerr did, or simply list your values as was done by Dave and Florence Minar on their Common Values Worksheet (Figure 4).

TASK 1

Identify Common Values

Next, it's a good idea to share your values with other planning team members. Identify those values that you, as a team, hold in common and to become aware of the different values held by each planning team member. This will make goal setting and conflict resolution easier down the road. Ideally, by gaining an understanding of what motivates each member of your planning team, you will be able to develop goals that everyone can commit to and support.

Dave and Florence Minar had family members identify values individually. Each family member was then asked to rank their values in order of personal importance and to share their top five values. When the family came together, *"we found that nearly everyone had identified and prioritized the same core values,"* Dave recalls. From these core values, Dave and Florence were able to develop a values statement for inclusion in their final business plan. This statement is reproduced as Dave Minar's answer to question two in Worksheet 1.2.

By gaining an understanding of what motivates each member of your planning team, you will be able to develop goals that everyone can commit to and support.

Complete **Worksheet 1.2: Common Values** to identify the values shared by your planning team members.

Worksheet 1.2 Common Values

Use the space below to identify common or shared values among your planning team members. You may want to begin by simply listing the values identified by each team member and then determine what values you share as a team. If you are uncomfortable sharing personal values, focus on the environmental, finance and community values that you share.

Values Identified by Individual Planning Team Members:

- *Human health*
- *Animal health*
- *Christianity*
- *Financial stability*
- *Open communication*
- *Healthy soil and water*
- *Beautiful landscape*
- *Community relationships*

Values That We Share as a Planning Team:

We value health, Christian values, trust, and open communication. Because our health is directly tied to the health of the environment, we strive to produce healthy dairy and meat products by utilizing sustainable methods in their production. We value preserving our forests and grasslands for future generations to enjoy. It is important to be a contributing member of the community both socially and economically. Our community values the esthetic beauty of seeing farm animals on the land.

Figure 4.
Example from Cedar Summit Farm—
Worksheet 1.2: Common Values

Preparing the Values Section of Your Business Plan

Values are very personal statements about you, your family and other planning team members. If this plan is for internal use, then it may be important to include a good description of your values, like that of Dancing Winds Farm owner Mary Doerr, in your final written plan. If your plan is primarily for external use, however, then you probably want to include a succinct values statement, like that written by Dave and Florence Minar, in your business plan.

The most important thing to remember is to write about what you feel is important. You can always trim or revise your values statement to use in a written plan once you've settled on a whole farm business strategy and outline.

Worksheet 1.1 My Values

Think about your values and list them in the space below. Consider what it means for you to be "successful" in farming, or try distinguishing between personal, economic, environmental, and community values. If you are having trouble putting values onto paper, try drafting a brief essay. Begin by recalling a critical turning point in your life when you were faced with a serious tradeoff: What values guided you?

TASK 1

Personal Values:

Economic Values:

Environmental Values:

Community Values:

Worksheet 1.2 Common Values

Use the space below to identify common or shared values among your planning team members. You may want to begin by simply listing the values identified by each team member and then determine what values you share as a team. If you are uncomfortable sharing personal values, focus on the environmental, finance and community values that you share.

Values Identified by Individual Planning Team Members:

Values That We Share as a Planning Team:

TASK 1

TASK 1

PLANNING TASK TWO

Farm History and Current Situation—What Have You Got?

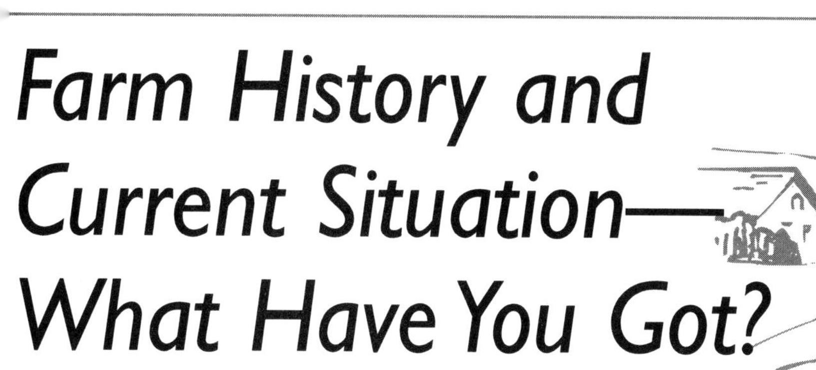

TASK 2

A clear understanding of your farm operation's history and current situation is the second building block in the foundation for your business plan. Your evaluation of alternative strategies for your farm and your efforts to persuade others that the strategy you ultimately propose is workable must be based on a comprehensive, realistic assessment of your current situation.

The materials in this chapter guide you through the development of such an assessment. This task requires time and effort—which will pay off later in the planning process. You'll begin by preparing a brief history of your family, farm, and business. Next, you'll systematically assess your operation in terms of the four key management areas: marketing, operations, human resources and finances. Finally, you'll summarize your operation's history and current situation to include in your business plan.

Planning Task Two

- ✔ Prepare a brief history of your family, farm and business
- ✔ Assess your current situation in:
  - **Marketing:**
    - Product
    - Customers
    - Unique Features
    - Distribution
    - Pricing
    - Promotion
    - Anticipated Marketing/Industry Changes
  - **Operations:**
    - Physical Resources
    - Production Systems
    - Management Systems
  - **Human Resources:**
    - Work Force
    - Unique Skills
    - Anticipated Changes in Work Force
  - **Finances:**
    - Needs
    - Performance
    - Risk
    - Financial Environment and Anticipated Changes
- ✔ Conduct a whole farm SWOT analysis
- ✔ Prepare the History and Current Situation section of your Business Plan

See pages 67–86 for a complete set of blank worksheets for Task Two.

To print a complete set of blank worksheets, go to ***www.misa.umn.edu/publications/bizplan.html***

TASK 2

A Brief History of Your Business

Before jumping into a summary of your current situation, it's important to look back to important events and decisions from the past one, five or ten years—whatever time frame can best describe why and how you've arrived at your current business situation.

If you're an experienced farmer or business owner, think about the different phases you have gone through in terms of marketing, operations, human resources and finances. Identify your most important successes and failures as well as the key opportunities and challenges you have encountered. Reflect on what you've learned from your experiences. Consider how your values have shaped the choices you've made.

If you're a beginning farmer or rural entrepreneur, focus on previous personal, economic, environmental, and community experiences that triggered your current desire to begin a business. Also, take time to learn about the history of the land you'll farm, the markets you'll serve and the industry you plan to enter. Understanding and developing strategies to serve viable markets is a key aspect of the business planning process and a critical ingredient for the success of your business plan. It's important to look beyond your own operation to its economic environment as you review the history of your business.

This review of your business and personal history, as well as market and industry trends, will be valuable as you develop a business plan, particularly as you begin to consider alternative strategies. The circumstances and ultimate decisions leading up to previous business successes and failures will provide insights as you choose between future strategic business options. Keep your history, as well as the values driving previous decisions, in mind as you continue to plan.

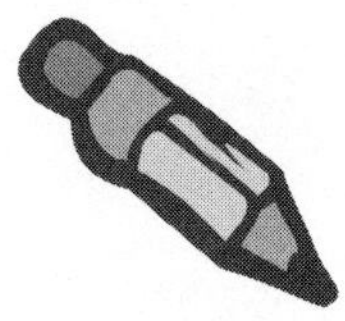

Use **Worksheet 2.1: A Brief History of Our Farm Operation** as a guide for writing your farm history. For now, you and other planning team members are the intended audience, so don't be too concerned about length or writing style. The important thing is to document key events and key decisions and to reflect on how these have shaped not only your current situation, but also your dreams for the future.

Dave Minar's history of Cedar Summit Farm shows one method that can be used to review your business and personal history (Figure 5). He simply chose to describe key events in the nearly forty years he and his wife, Florence, have been farming together. During that time, both their family and their farm

Figure 5. Example from Cedar Summit Farm—Worksheet 2.1: A Brief History of Our Farm Operation

Worksheet 2.1 A Brief History of Our Farm Operation

Write a brief history describing the important events and decisions in your life and operation. Why did you make the choices you did? What have been the most important outcomes resulting from the interaction of your own choices and external circumstances? What key lessons have you learned? Include planning team members in this review. Use whatever time frame (one, five, ten years) best describes why and how you've arrived at your current business situation.

My Grandfather purchased what is now Cedar Summit Farm in 1935. When my parents married in 1938, they moved onto the farm. I was born and raised there. Florence and I met at the University of Minnesota where we were both students. I graduated in 1963 with a BS in Ag. Econ. & Dairy Science, and in 1964 we were married. I farmed with my father after service in the US Army and in 1966 accepted a position with Minn. Valley Breeders as an A. I. technician. Our family grew fast–Lisa was born in 1965, Chris in 1966 and Mike in 1967.

In 1969 we made the decision to return to the farm full time. Having been raised there, I knew what we were getting into. I was the only son and felt an obligation to return to what my Grandfather started. We built a new sixty-cow tie stall barn in 1971. Over the years we developed a registered Holstein herd that had received state and national recognition. We showed our animals at many shows and fairs.

The farm was originally 120 acres. We purchased an additional 80 acres in 1972, and another 18 acres more recently. We lease an additional 65 acres that adjoin our property. We also own a 160-acre farm at McGrath, MN that consists of 90 acres of improved pasture for young stock. In 1974 we discontinued the use of pesticides, and started exploring alternative ways to combat pests. We knew it could be done, because it had been done in the past.

In 1977, we started our second family when Laura was born. Dan was to follow in 1980. In this time period more changes were made in our family. My father, who was my main source of help, died in 1979. Chris and Mike, who were 13 and 12, were now my main source of labor. We managed to get the work done with the help of Dan Kajer, a part-time helper, and still allow them time for sports and 4-H. In the mid-80's the older children graduated from high school and went to college. In 1986, our Dan was starting school and Florence found a full time job in town. We hired Paul Kajer, Dan Kajer's younger brother who was still in school, to help. Paul stayed with us until 1991, when he left to start farming on his own. Laura and our Dan were old enough to help now, and we also hired John Nelson full time.

By the late 1980's, we began to realize that we weren't making the progress that we should be making, and started asking ourselves some serious questions. Our debt load had remained static through the years because of equipment replacement costs and herd turnover. We were intrigued with the idea of improving animal health by allowing them to harvest their own feed for 7 months of the year. The idea, which we found exciting, was that all of our land, some of which adjoins Sand Creek, would be in permanent pasture grasses and thus would stop erosion. This would also improve the water and mineral cycles. We could see how it would improve our quality of life with less feed to harvest. We sold our milking herd and bred heifers in 1993 and started grazing with our young stock. This sale allowed us to pay off almost all of our loans. In 1994, we built a new milking parlor and started milking again.

Paul Kajer joined our operation again in 1997 and brought with him the nucleus of his herd. Paul is paid a percentage of the gross check with a bonus at the end of the year. He retains ownership of the growth of his herd.

We were told when we started grazing that there was a 7-year learning curve. This seems to be true, because after a few years of struggling, in 1999 we were able to significantly reduce our debt load.

In 1994 we started a direct marketing retail meat business with pasture-raised chicken. We had some underutilized areas where we could raise chickens and the chickens we had been buying in the grocery store were becoming less and less appealing. We knew others felt the same way. We hired a marketing consultant to help us with a brochure and we raised 900 chickens. Our chickens sold out and we were on our way. This venture has evolved into a significant sideline. In 1998 Florence quit her job to help more at home. Over the past 5 years we have also included turkeys, hogs and steers.

It is a good feeling to be able to supply our community with high quality food and hope we can continue to do so in the future.

TASK 2

operation have grown. They have made important choices that have shaped their current situation and the strategies they are considering for the future. These include the decision to stop using pesticides in 1974, the shift to grazing in 1993, and the addition of a direct marketing meat business in 1994. This history clarifies the context for the Minars' desire to add on-farm milk processing and direct marketing of dairy products to their farm business.

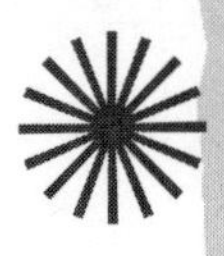

Evaluate Your Current Situation for:

S = Strengths
W = Weaknesses
O = Opportunities
T = Threats

TASK 2

Assess Your Current Situation

The current circumstances surrounding your life and business can create unique opportunities as well as obstacles. This section guides you through a description of your current situation for each of four business management functions: **marketing, operations, human resources and finances**. This is a chance to inventory your resources and assess how well you are using them.

In each management area, you'll collect facts and figures that will help you evaluate your operation in terms of *Strengths, Weaknesses, Opportunities and Threats (SWOT)*. The *SWOT* analysis is a planning tool used by businesses and organizations of all sizes and types. Strengths and weaknesses refer to factors that are internal to your business. Opportunities and threats refer to your business' external environment. Ultimately, your plans for the future should help you build on your strengths and overcome your weaknesses. Your plan should help you take advantage of opportunities or ward off threats offered by your environment. Keep a running list of strengths, weaknesses, opportunities and threats in each management area as you work through the text and Worksheets in this section. Finally, you'll summarize that information and make an overall SWOT analysis for your business that you can include in your final business plan.

Involve members of your planning team and other business stakeholders in this process. Assessing your current situation from several points of view can help you gain perspective on the issues and alternatives that your business plan will address.

The Four Key Management Areas:
- **Marketing**
- Operations
- Human Resources
- Finance

Marketing Situation

When you ask another farmer to describe his or her operation, the response will usually begin with information on the number of acres farmed, the type of crops grown, and livestock raised. This made sense for the "old agriculture" when focus was on selling undifferentiated commodities to anonymous buyers. More and more, we are moving toward a "new agriculture" where farmers sell differentiated products and are in direct contact with their customers.

You can begin with any of the four management areas as you develop a description of your operation, but we encourage you to consider starting with an assessment of the markets you serve and your strategies for serving them. These are the key questions you'll need to answer:

- **Product:** What is our product?
- **Customers:** What markets do we serve?
- **Unique Features:** What are the unique features that distinguish our products?

Worksheet 2.2 Current Market Assessment

Complete this worksheet for each of your major products or services. Be as specific as you can and, where relevant, include numeric facts and figures. These will be the basis for projections you'll make later on for the strategies that you consider.

Product/Service: *Meat products*

Markets Served: Geographic/Customer Segments
Answer the following questions for each major market segment (geographic and/or customer type) you serve. Use additional sheets if this product has more than three major market segments.

Segment	1. *On-farm sales*	2. *New Prague farmers market*	3.
Potential Number of Customers	a. *?*	a. *?*	a.
Current Number of Customers	b. *400*	b. *25*	b.
Current Sales Volume	c. *$43,600*	c. *$1500*	c.
Current Sales per Customer (c / b)	d. *$109*	d. *$60 /year*	d.
Potential Sales Volume (a x d)	e. *?*	e. *?*	e.

Unique Characteristics
What are the unique features that distinguish this product or service? For which customer segments are they important? How easily can they be imitated by competitors?

Characteristic 1: *Grass fed*
Appeals to which segments? *Both segments*
Easy for competitors to imitate? ____Yes _x_ No

Characteristic 2: *Locally produced*
Appeals to which segments? *Both segments*
Easy for competitors to imitate? _x_ Yes ____ No

Distribution
Describe the current distribution channels for this product.

Logistics: *Customers come to farm; we deliver to farmers market once each week.*

Market Locations: *On-farm and in New Prague – all local*

Market Intermediaries: *None*

Marketing Costs (transportation, labor, spoilage, price discounts for intermediaries):
Farmers market stall space fee = $25/year
Labor for market-related travel and staffing = 8 hours/week
Labor for on-farm sales = 2 hours/week

CONTINUED

TASK 2

Figure 6. Example from Cedar Summit Farm—Worksheet 2.2: Current Market Assessment (side 1)

- **Distribution:** How do we distribute our products?
- **Pricing:** How do we price our products?
- **Promotion:** How do we promote our products?
- **Market and Industry:** How is our market changing?

Use **Worksheet 2.2: Current Market Assessment** to record your answers as you work through this section. The Minars' Current Market Assessment Worksheet for their meat products (beef, pork, chickens and turkeys) is reproduced as Figure 6.

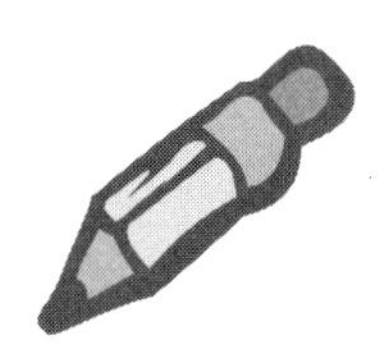

Page 5

FALL APPLES

CHESTNUT⊙: A small apple perfect for your child's lunch box! Firm, crisp, fine-grained and juicy.
Often considered the best-tasting apple grown in our area. Fruit hangs well and ripens over a long
period. Annual bearer. Productive. Z-3, H-3, DR-1 (L, XL)
CORTLAND: This apple has proven itself over a wide area of the country and has become a standard
of excellence. Large, red, crisp, tart, tangy flavor. Excellent for eating, cooking, cider, and salads as
the pure white flesh does not brown readily when cut. Annually productive, long lived. Z-3b, H-3 (S,M)
DAKOTA: Very productive. Wealthy x Whitney from N. Dakota. Med. size red over yellow fruit good
for fresh eating and cooking and keeps two months. Z-3. (M, XL)
HONEYCRISP®⊙: (PP-7197) Exciting new apple from the U. of Mn. that is explosively crisp and
juicy. Promising variety for commercial & home orchards. Exceptional flavor and texture. We have
kept this apple until July forth in our root cellar. Add $1 to reg. price for royalty. Z-3b, H-3 (XS,S,M)
LAKELAND: Open-pollinated seedling of Malinda. Mild, pleasant flavor, medium red apple. Good
all-purpose apple for home orchards. Z-3, H-2. (M, L,XL)
MANDAN: Red with firm, juicy flesh. Good eating and extremely hardy. Z-3, H-2, DR-2 (M,XL)
RED BARON⊙: Attractive red fruit is crisp, juicy and tasty. Good for pie, sauce, cider and fresh
eating. Moderately resistant to fireblight and cedar-apple rust. One of our favorite all-purpose fall
apples. Z-3b, H-3, DR-2 (All sizes)
SWEET SIXTEEN⊙: Open-pollinated Malinda x Northern Spy. U of MN 1978. Excellent all-purpose
apple. Red, med. size, aromatic, spicy flavor, crisp & juicy. Annually productive, disease-resistant &
very hardy. Great keeper. Z-3b, H-3, DR-3 (ALL)
WHITE MCMAHON: Originated about 1860 in Richland Co., Wisconsin and thought to be a seedling
of Alexander. We are re-introducing this variety due to it's adaptability to our harsh, northern climate.
It bears large, round apples of high quality for a home or specialty orchard. Z-3b (M,L,XL)
WODARZ: Sweet apple of good quality from N. Dakota. Z-3. (M,L,XL)
WOLF RIVER: Old cooking variety from Wisconsin. Very large red over yellow fruit. Good for drying
& apple butter. Z-3, H-3. (M)

Northwind Notes - Apple Growing

Apples, due to their long ripening season and incredible storage ability under common homesteading conditions, can provide most of your family's fresh fruit needs. They can tolerate some shade but 6 to 8 hours of full sun in soil that is well drained is best. Avoid frost pockets or low lying areas. Eliminate grass and weed competition for the first few years until fully established. Spread compost, worm castings, well rotted manure, or organic fertilizer around the drip line in the spring but never in the fall.

Every serious homestead should have at least three apple trees, five to tèn or more for larger families or if you want to sell, barter, or share a few with the neighbors. Choose some early, mid season and late bearing varieties to spread out your harvest season. Your varieties should include some that keep well such as Honeycrisp, Keepsake, Haralred, Haralson, Northwest Greening, etc. Disease resistance is important with apples, especially if you plan on marketing them.

Cultural practices are also important to minimize insect and disease damage. Diversify your orchard and homestead to encourage a balanced eco-system and provide important habitat for beneficial predators. Poultry can be used to great advantage for insect and even weed control if managed properly. Good pruning practices to allow air and sun penetration throughout the tree can go a long way in preventing fungal diseases. For more information on organic cultural practices, see our book section.

DEER APPLE SPECIAL

CRAB APPLE: (Malus ranetka, antonovka, etc.) Used for wildlife plantings to attract deer, birds, etc. or to lure them away from your other valuable crops. Z-3
PRICES: Med. - 2 to 5' $5.00, Large - 5 to 6' $6.00, Ex. Large - 6' up $8.00
(Large and Ex. Large sizes cannot be shipped)

Figure 7. "Northwind Notes—Apple Growing" from Northwind Nursery Catalogue

Product: What is our product?

This is usually an easy question—but it's sometimes useful to step back and think about what it is that you produce. What is a product? For example, Frank Foltz of Northwind Nursery and Orchard produces edible landscaping plants that are well-adapted to northern winters. Yet, he also provides knowledge and information in the form of "Northwind Notes" (Figure 7) and annual workshops to help educate his customers about fruit production and other homesteading skills. Is this service component of his business something that's simply "bundled" with the plants he sells, or does it have the potential to be a separate product? For each product you produce, fill out a copy of **Worksheet 2.2: Current Market Assessment.** As you ponder the question What is our product? you may identify products that have great potential. For practical purposes, *products* are defined as *commodities, final consumer goods, and services.*

Customers: What markets do we serve?

We often think of a market as a place, but it's more useful to think of your markets in terms of the potential buyers for your products. Some examples will help illustrate this concept of a market:

- Greg Reynolds of Riverbend Farm sells fresh, organically produced vegetables to restaurants, food cooperatives, and Community Supported Agriculture (CSA) customers in the Twin Cities metropolitan area.
- Mary Doerr of Dancing Winds Farm sells goat cheese made on her farm to shoppers at the St. Paul Farmers' Market. She also offers visitors to southeast Minnesota an opportunity to enjoy her farm and to learn about cheese making by staying in her bed and breakfast.
- Dave and Florence Minar sold milk to their local cooperative and pasture-raised poultry, beef and pork to customers from the greater Twin Cities metropolitan area who visit Cedar Summit Farm.

Each of these short market descriptions indicates not only *where* products are sold—the geographic scope of the market—but also *to whom* they are sold. [Note that it is common to serve more than one market and that the customers in a market can often be segmented into several distinct groups.]

Once you have a basic description of the market or markets you currently serve, you'll need to gather more detailed information on the segmentation, size and scope of your market, as well as who is already serving the market. Are there distinct segments in your customer base—for example, households and businesses? How many potential customers are there in each segment in the area you serve? How many customers do you have in each segment and how much do they buy? Use the **"Markets Served" section of Worksheet 2.2** to answer these basic questions for each of the markets you serve. This will help you identify the most attractive market opportunities.

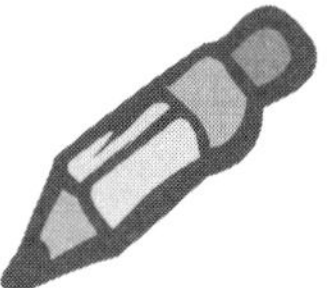

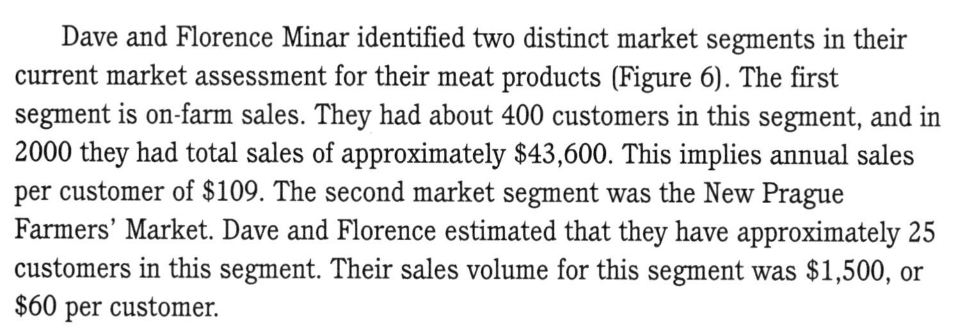

Dave and Florence Minar identified two distinct market segments in their current market assessment for their meat products (Figure 6). The first segment is on-farm sales. They had about 400 customers in this segment, and in 2000 they had total sales of approximately $43,600. This implies annual sales per customer of $109. The second market segment was the New Prague Farmers' Market. Dave and Florence estimated that they have approximately 25 customers in this segment. Their sales volume for this segment was $1,500, or $60 per customer.

It's not unusual to have some question marks in this segment of the Worksheet, as the Minars do. These point to areas where it may be important to gather information as you begin to look ahead to expanding sales within a particular segment or to entering a new market segment.

Unique Features: What are the unique features that distinguish our products?

Unique characteristics differentiate your product and make it more attractive to your customers. For example, Riverbend Farm owner Greg Reynolds' vegetables are known by restaurant owners and food cooperative produce buyers for freshness and high quality. As a result, these customers prefer to buy from Riverbend Farm whenever possible. Similarly, the milk Dave and Florence Minar produce is unique because their cows are pasture-fed. Many consumers who have tried graziers' milk prefer the taste, and there is some evidence that it may have health benefits that are not present in conventional milk. Some consumers also prefer graziers' milk because they want to support and encourage this production method. When Dave and Florence Minar began the business planning process in 1998, they recognized these distinctive features of the milk they produced, but were unable to capitalize on these differences since they sold it to a cooperative where it was blended with milk from other farms.

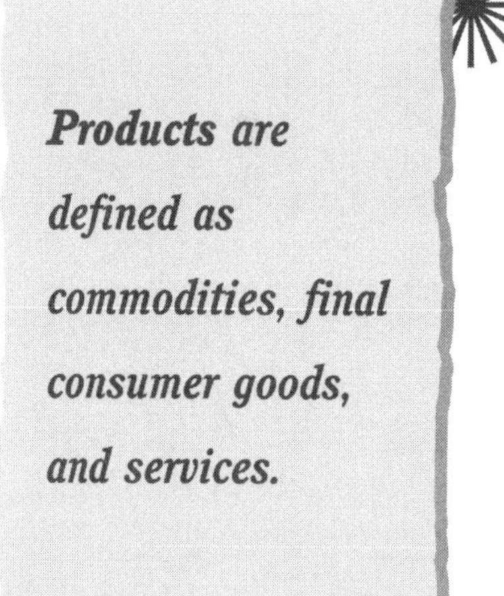

Dave and Florence identified two distinguishing features of their meat products—the animals are grass-fed and locally produced. These characteristics appeal to their retail customers in both market segments. The grass-fed characteristic is difficult for competitors to imitate, but other producers in their area can offer locally produced meat products.

As you complete the **"Unique Characteristics" section of Worksheet 2.2**, ask whether the unique characteristics of your products appeal equally to all the market segments you serve. A product attribute that is important to one group of customers may be irrelevant to others. This is a good time to think about product features that appeal most to each customer segment. Even if your product or service is not strong in delivering those features, your business plan may focus on ways you can improve your operation to make your product more appealing to market segments with good growth potential.

Distribution: How do we distribute our products?

Distribution is the work of getting products from your farm to your customers. A distribution system is described in terms of the logistics—processes used to store and transport the product, the places where the product is sold, and the market intermediaries that help facilitate the flow of your product. In broad terms, most farm product distribution systems can be grouped into three categories:

- Sale of a commodity product to a first handler or processor—for example, sale of grain to a local elevator, milk to a creamery, or hogs to a slaughter plant.
- Sale through a grocery wholesaler or retailer—for example, sale of processed, packaged chickens through a local retailer, sale of a branded pancake mix through a natural foods distributor, or sale of fresh vegetables through a natural foods cooperative.
- Direct marketing—for example, sale of fresh produce at a roadside stand, sale of farm-produced cheese at a farmers' market, or catalog sales of bare-root nursery stock.

Of course, within each of these categories there is an endless range of variation for specific products.

Dave and Florence use direct marketing for their meat products, with simple logistics and no intermediaries. Their direct costs for market access and travel to the farmers' market are modest, but it's important to note that they also use about 10 hours of valuable labor time each week. It's also interesting to note that most of their distribution costs are linked to sales at the farmers' market, while most of their sales appear to be on-farm. Of course, their presence at the farmers' market may be their best way to make first contact with potential customers for on-farm sales.

As you describe the distribution systems you currently use for your operations, think about how well they help you preserve the unique characteristics of your product. The Minars preserve the unique qualities of their grass-fed meat by direct marketing their meat products. However, by selling their milk to the local cooperative, the Minars were losing the opportunity to reach customers who were willing to pay a premium for graziers' milk. It's also important to think about the costs and cost savings associated with your current system. The Minars' distribution system for their milk was less costly than a system that involves on-farm processing and sale through local retailers or home delivery.

In general, commodity distribution systems are the least expensive, but they also offer the fewest opportunities for establishing close contacts with consumers and for adding value through unique characteristics. Direct marketing systems offer the greatest opportunity for customer contact and product differentiation, but they are often the most expensive when costs for time and transportation are added. Selling through a wholesaler or retailer—that is, connecting with your ultimate customer through market intermediaries—is sometimes an attractive alternative to the other two distribution systems. You can often keep a strong link with your customers by using distinct packaging or by doing regular in-store product demonstrations. Also, there are clear cost savings in sharing storage, transportation, and product display costs. Most of those cost savings, however, will go to the wholesaler or retailer. In other words, when you work through an intermediary, you will need to share the proceeds of the sale to the final consumer with the retailer or wholesaler.

As you complete the **"Distribution" section of Worksheet 2.2** for each of your major products, think about the advantages and disadvantages of current systems. Are there significant opportunities for reducing costs or increasing revenues by improving your current distribution system or shifting to something new? If there are, this is an area to revisit later in the planning process when you begin developing strategies for more effectively meeting the goals you set for your operation.

Pricing: How do we price our products?

The prices you charge for your products are influenced by production costs (yours and your competitors') and by your customers' willingness to pay. From a farmer's perspective, it would be great to set product prices at levels that cover all costs and include a "fair" profit. However, your ability to do this will depend on the actions of your competitors and on the strength of your customers' demand for the characteristics that make your product or service unique. You've almost certainly seen these market forces at work on any visit to a farmers'

TASK 2

market. When there are several producers selling the same product, with no significant differences among them in quality, the price will quickly converge to a single level. Originally, this may be at a level that covers all costs and yields a profit, at least for the most efficient producers. By the end of the market day, though, the price for a perishable product may drop well below production costs if several producers still have a large supply of product that will be wasted if not sold. In this same situation, if customers perceive one producer's product as higher quality, that producer will be able to charge a higher price. As the price of the higher quality product increases, though, the least loyal customers will opt for lower price over higher quality. Competition sets a ceiling on the price the market will bear for any product. The more intense the competition, the more difficult it will be to charge a premium price. In this example we have focused on competition at the same farmers' market. It's important to recognize that the relevant competition may be the local supermarket or some other product altogether.

Dave and Florence Minar used their 2000 financial analysis (created with FINPACK software[2]) to calculate average prices they receive for each of the four meat categories they market. The prices for beef and pork reflect retail sales per pound of live weight. They are, of course, much lower than prices for retail cuts of meat, but they are well above prices farmers receive for "commodity" steers and hogs. Similarly, the prices for chickens and turkeys are on a per bird basis, and they are well above retail prices for "commodity" chickens and turkey. The Minars note that they have a high level of power in setting prices for these products, but they also face some demand sensitivity to price changes.

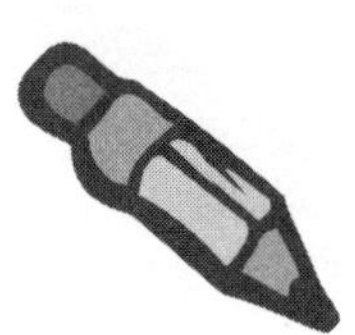

As you complete the **"Pricing" section of Worksheet 2.2** for each of your products, record the typical price level (or range of price levels if there is significant variation) and the size of the premium, if any, that your product receives over a typical competitor's price. Also, comment on your ability to set the price and the sensitivity of demand to price increases. For example, if you are the only seller of a truly unique product, you have a high degree of power in setting the price. You may have no power if you are selling into a highly competitive market with many other sellers. Regardless of your ability to establish a price, the quantity you sell may or may not be sensitive to price increases. Demand for a unique, high-quality cheese may hardly be affected by a significant price increase, while buyers of free-range chickens may switch to grass-fed beef if the price of chickens rises dramatically relative to that of beef.

2 *FINPACK* software, Center for Farm Financial Management, University of Minnesota, updated annually.

Promotion: How do we promote our products?

Effective product promotion is critical for successful marketing. We often think of advertising when we hear the term product promotion. This may take the form of brochures, posters or a web site. Of course, there are many other ways you can inform potential customers about your products. For example, many producers offer taste tests for their products in retail stores and at farmers' markets. Other producers rely on promotional efforts by a commodity group or collaborative marketing group. A good example of this kind of promotional strategy is "eco-labelling." Several organizations throughout the country have certification programs to recognize food that is produced according to specified ecological or sustainability standards.

Worksheet 2.2 Current Market Assessment

CONTINUED

Pricing

What price do you receive for this product or service, and how does it compare to the price of a typical competitor? How much power do you have to set the price for this product or service? How sensitive is demand to price changes?

Typical Price and Price Range:

Varies by product- $0.95/lb for steers, $1.07/lb for hogs $9.50/chicken, $41.00/turkey

Price Relative to Competitor:

Our Power to Set Prices: ___ Low ___ Some _x_ High

Demand Sensitivity to Price Changes: ___ Low _x_ Some ___ High

Promotions

Describe the strategies you use to promote consumer awareness of this product or service. How effective are they in reaching your most important potential customers? How costly are they?

We promote our meat products through brochures, advertisements in the local newspaper, and word-of-mouth. We think that these have all been very effective. All advertising (not including labor) costs us $1,125/year – this includes the cost of printing and mailing brochures as well as fees charged for newspaper advertisement space.

Changing Market Conditions

Describe important trends of the supply and demand side of the market for this product or service. Are there important new competitors or competing products? Is demand expanding?

As food scares occur and as people become more concerned with food safety, we think that demand will increase for our products– for products that consumers purchase directly from the farmer that they know and trust. Also, as conservation becomes more important to society as a whole, we feel that more and more consumers will turn to environmentally-friendly products from animals that have been grass-fed. Our current and future competition will likely be other farmers who supply locally-produced meat products. Even now, however, these competitors do not necessarily produce products from grass-fed animals and do not supply convenient meat cuts – they typically sell meat in halves or quarter [carcasses].

TASK 2

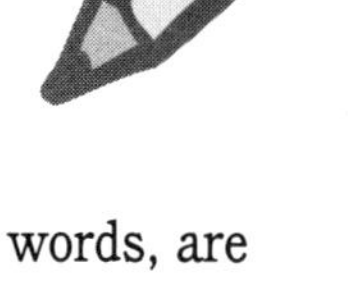

Figure 6. Example from Cedar Summit Farm—Worksheet 2.2: Current Market Assessment (side2)

Dave and Florence Minar use a combination of brochures, advertisements and word-of-mouth to promote their meat products. They estimate their annual costs for promotions, excluding labor, to be $1,125—approximately 2.5 percent of their annual sales of these products.

In completing the **"Promotions" section of Worksheet 2.2** for each of your products, list all the promotional strategies you use. Then assess how effective they are in reaching potential customers (or in retaining current customers) and how much they cost. In other words, are your current strategies "paying their way"?

Market and Industry: How is our market changing?

Markets rarely stand still. On the supply side, new competitors might enter, while old rivals go out of business. On the demand side, the introduction of new substitute products might reduce demand for your product or new research might make it possible for you to make a health claim that helps you expand demand for your product. In the longer term, broad trends in customer and competitor demographics, technology and government policy can transform the size and structure of your market. The last step in assessing your current marketing strategies and activities is to look ahead to evaluate their potential for change.

TASK 2

Dave and Florence Minar observed that growing concerns over food safety and interest in more environmentally friendly farming practices should have positive impacts on the market for their meat products. They also noted that price premiums for locally produced meat products are attracting competitors. Still, Dave and Florence believed their grass-based production system and their attention to supplying convenient products would help them sustain their competitive advantage.

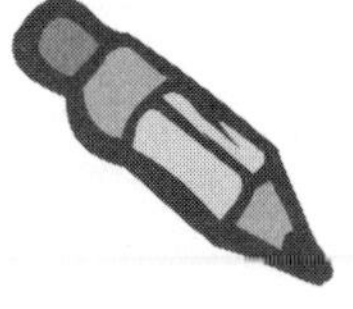

Be sure to consider a wide range of potential changes to your market as you complete the **"Changing Market Conditions" section of Worksheet 2.2** for each of your products. Often when we look back after experiencing a sudden, unexpected change, we realize that we could have seen it coming. Questioning even the most long-held assumptions about your markets can help you identify issues that need to be addressed as you develop a business plan for the future.

The Four Key Management Areas:
- Marketing
- **Operations**
- Human Resources
- Finance

Operations Situation

Before planning for the future, it's important to step back and assess the resources available to your farm operation and the enterprises in which you use those resources. In this section the focus is on physical resources. Later, you'll assess the human and financial resources of your business.

The assessment of physical resources and farm operations should answer the following questions:

- Resources: What physical resources are available for our business?
- Production: What production systems are we using?
- Management: What management systems do we have in place to support our business?

You'll use Worksheets 2.3 through 2.6 to record your answers as you work through this section. These Worksheets are designed for use in a farm business, but the fundamental questions are the same for any business and can be adapted for use by nonfarm rural businesses.

What physical resources are available for our farm business?

Physical resources include land, buildings and other structures, machinery and equipment, and breeding livestock and poultry. These are the tangible assets that you use to produce the products you market. Clearly the quantity and quality of the resources you control affect your current operations and influence your future opportunities. In addition to listing your physical resources, it is also important to note institutional restrictions on their use, including long-term leases, easements, conservation agreements, and other arrangements that must be honored in future years.

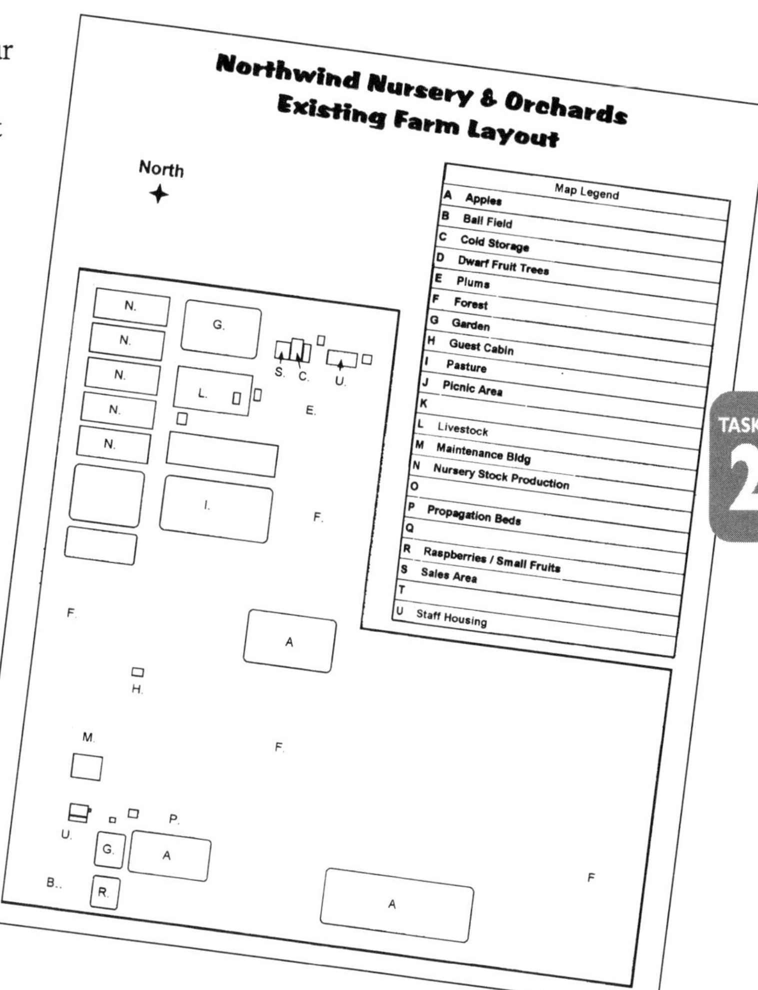

Figure 8.
Farm map: the Foltzes' Northwind Nursery and Orchards

A *farm map* can be a good tool to use to describe your land resources. For example, Frank Foltz used a map (Figure 8) to describe the existing layout of Northwind Nursery at the start of his business planning process.

Your map should be drawn approximately to scale showing the size and configuration of important physical features on your farm, including fields used for crop production, pastures, woodlands, lakes, ponds and streams. Contact your local United States Department of Agriculture Natural Resources Conservation Service (USDA-NRCS) agent (see "Resources") for help in locating a good map of your land. The map should also show the location of man-made features, including the farmstead, permanent fence lines, the contours, grass waterways and irrigation wells. It may also be useful to show the location of crops currently on the farm, including perennial crops, such as alfalfa, vineyards and orchards. This provides a basis for planning the sequence of crops in rotation. Finally, if you rent land, draw a similar map for each rental tract. Then draw a smaller scale map that shows the location of your home farm and all the other parcels you farm.

Worksheet 2.3 Tangible Working Assets

Use this worksheet to describe the non-land physical assets used in your current farm operation. Be as specific as you can be about size, capacity and condition.

	ITEM	SIZE	CAPACITY	CONDITION	VALUE
Buildings/Permanent Structures	1. Milking Parlor	34 x 160	160 animals	good	
	2. Calving/hog shed	60 x 50	80 cows	good	
	3. Machine shed	48 x 96	–	good	
	4. Sales shed	40 x 64	–	good	
	5. Brooder	30 x 30	500 chicks	good	
Machinery and Equipment	1. Tractor	JD4030	80 hp	good	
	2. Tractor	JD4010	90 hp	good	
	3. Four 4-wheelers	—	—	fair	
	4. Swather	Hesston	12-foot	good	
	5. Cooler	2 x 4 x 5	40 cub.ft.	good	
	6. Freezer	6 x 8 x 6	288 cub.ft.	good	
	7. Pick-up	350 Chev	3/4 ton	fair	
	8. Drill				
	9. Disc Mower				
Livestock Equipment	1. Trailer	—	300 bu	good	
	2. Manure spreader	NH 665	—	good	
	3. Skid loader	—	—	fair	
	4. Freezer truck	16 foot	—	good	
Breeding Livestock	150 dairy cows	Good (average annual production is 13,311 pounds per cow, which is good for grass-based dairy production)			

Figure 9. Example from Cedar Summit Farm—Worksheet 2.3: Tangible Working Assets

Use **Worksheet 2.3: Tangible Working Assets** to list the remaining physical assets on your farm. Buildings and permanent structures, machinery and equipment, livestock equipment and breeding livestock are the major categories. Focus your efforts on describing the major tangible assets that are important for your current operations or for activities you may consider in the future. Be specific in noting size, capacity, and condition when relevant.

As noted in their farm history, Dave and Florence own 218 acres and lease another 65 acres that adjoin their property in New Prague, MN. They also own a 160-acre farm in McGrath, MN that they use for young stock production. The Minars' list of machinery and equipment is smaller than that of most farms, since they do not raise row crops.

Laws and regulatory policies affect business operations. In addition, opportunities to market through long-term contracts and value-added cooperatives may represent important institutional considerations in planning your operations. Use **Worksheet 2.4: Institutional Considerations** to record the important existing institutional restrictions that must be considered in developing your operations plan. These include long-term leasing arrangements for land and other real estate, as well as any leases in effect with state and federal agencies. It is also important to note any long-term contracts for marketing crop and livestock products, whether they represent an opportunity to market or a commitment that must be fulfilled.

Dave and Florence Minar used Worksheet 2.4: Institutional Considerations, to record information about their lease for 65 acres of neighboring cropland and the 30-year living snow fence easement they recently signed. They also noted that they have a temporary feedlot permit that will be good until 2010. Since these institutional considerations will be in effect for many years to come, the Minars didn't need to be concerned about being forced to make major changes in their grass-based dairy operation in the near future.

Worksheet 2.4 Institutional Considerations

Describe institutional factors that currently affect your ability to use and manage physical resources. Include any long-term leasing arrangements, conservation easements, permit requirements, legal restrictions, production or marketing contracts.

Long-term Leasing Arrangements for Real Estate
(specify whether items are leased in for your use or leased out for the use of others)

We have a ten-year lease on 65 acres of neighboring cropland planted to hay.

Long-term Agreements and Easements

We signed a 30-year living snow fence easement in the winter of 2001 with the Scott County Highway Department and the local Soil and Water Conservation Service office. The land will be planted in trees provided by the SWCS office.

Permit and Legal Restrictions
(specify the agency responsible for issuing permits, conditions and compliance factors, fees, and your ability to meet these conditions)

We have a temporary feedlot permit from the Minnesota Pollution Control Agency. It is good for ten years and was obtained in 2000.

Long-term Production Contracts and Marketing Agreements

None – we do not have a legal contract with our milk cooperative.

Figure 10. Example from Cedar Summit Farm—Worksheet 2.4: Institutional Considerations

TASK 2

Crop Enterprise Checklist

- ❑ **Seed, seed stock, plants, seedlings, etc.**
- ❑ **Fertilizer used (by blend or by total N, P, K, etc.)**
- ❑ **Chemicals (by type; application costs must be separable)**
  - Herbicide
  - Insecticide
  - Fungicide
  - Growth regulators
  - Harvest aids
- ❑ **Custom services (by type)**
  - Conservation consulting
  - Dues
  - Freight
- ❑ **Machinery**
  - Fuel and lube
  - Repairs
- ❑ **Irrigation**
  - Water (consider system efficiency)
  - Water district charges, taxes, and other expenses
  - Fuel and lube
  - Repairs
- ❑ **Utilities (enterprise-specific)**
- ❑ **Labor**
- ❑ **Miscellaneous crop-specific supplies**
- ❑ **Crop insurance**
- ❑ **Costs of accessing market**
- ❑ **Checkoff/assessment (involuntary)**
- ❑ **Shipping/transportation**
- ❑ **Storage/processing**

Figure 11.
Crop Enterprise Checklist

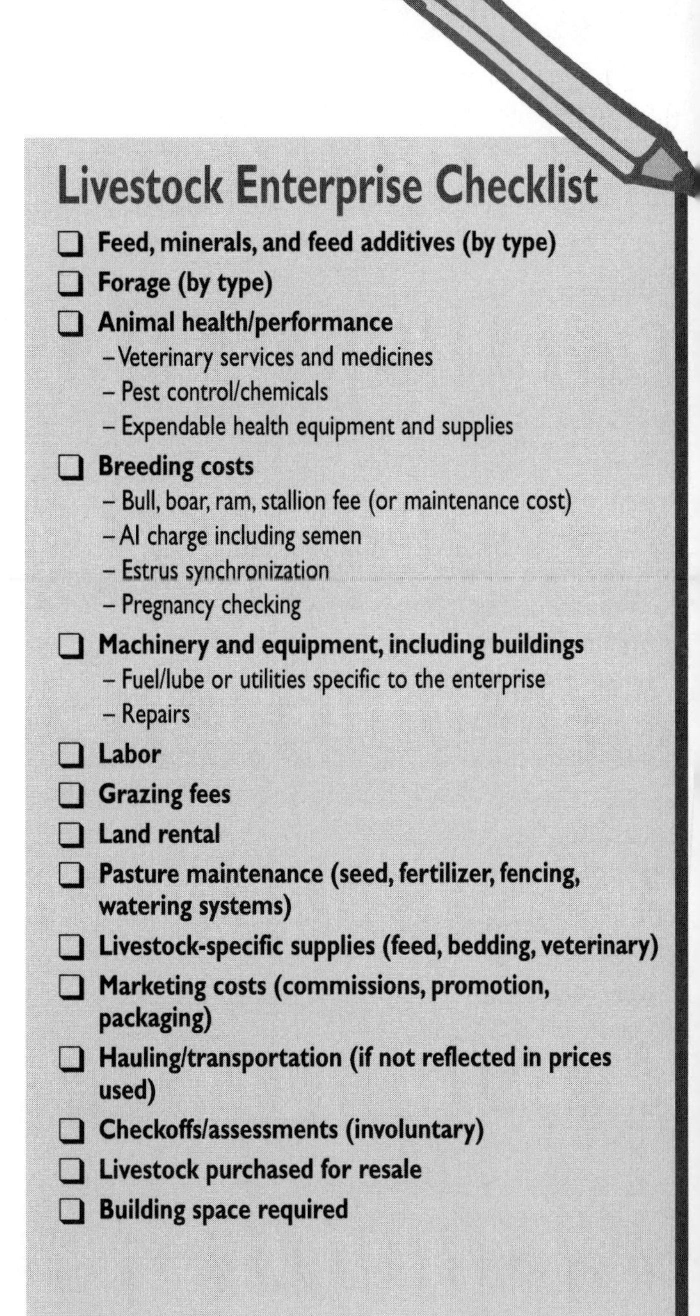

Livestock Enterprise Checklist

- ❑ **Feed, minerals, and feed additives (by type)**
- ❑ **Forage (by type)**
- ❑ **Animal health/performance**
  - Veterinary services and medicines
  - Pest control/chemicals
  - Expendable health equipment and supplies
- ❑ **Breeding costs**
  - Bull, boar, ram, stallion fee (or maintenance cost)
  - AI charge including semen
  - Estrus synchronization
  - Pregnancy checking
- ❑ **Machinery and equipment, including buildings**
  - Fuel/lube or utilities specific to the enterprise
  - Repairs
- ❑ **Labor**
- ❑ **Grazing fees**
- ❑ **Land rental**
- ❑ **Pasture maintenance (seed, fertilizer, fencing, watering systems)**
- ❑ **Livestock-specific supplies (feed, bedding, veterinary)**
- ❑ **Marketing costs (commissions, promotion, packaging)**
- ❑ **Hauling/transportation (if not reflected in prices used)**
- ❑ **Checkoffs/assessments (involuntary)**
- ❑ **Livestock purchased for resale**
- ❑ **Building space required**

Figure 12.
Livestock Enterprise Checklist

What production systems are we using?

Now that you have described the physical resources you use in your current operation, the next task is to describe the current production systems in which you use those resources. This involves describing the crop rotations, timing of operations, the machinery and other inputs used, the quantity of production, and how your production is stored, processed and delivered to the market.

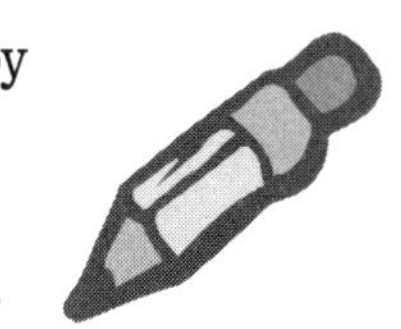

For crop production, this process can usually be accomplished most easily by thinking through the sequence of activities involved and carefully noting the machinery used, operational inputs such as seed and fertilizer applied, and the labor requirements. Refer to the Crop Enterprise Checklist (Figure 11) for items that should be included. Use **Worksheet 2.5: Describing Crop Production Systems** for each of the major crop enterprises in your current operation.

TASK 2

The **Worksheet 2.5: Describing Crop Production Systems** (Figure 13) Dave and Florence Minar completed for pasture shows that maintaining 240 acres of pasture (the primary source of feed for their cows) requires one hour of labor per acre each year, as well as 20 pounds of seed, three gallons of fuel and seasonal access to the tractor, drill, disc mower and manure spreader.

Figure 13. Example from Cedar Summit Farm—Worksheet 2.5: Describing Crop Production Systems

Worksheet 2.5 Describing Crop Production Systems

Complete this worksheet for each major crop enterprise. Be as specific and accurate as you can be, since this information will be the basis for projections you'll make later for the strategies that you consider.

Crop Enterprise: *pasture* Current Acreage: *240 acres*

Month	Machinery Operations: Operation	Hrs/ Acre	Machine 1	Machine 2	Operating Input: Item	Quantity/ Acre	Units	Price/ Unit	Labor: Hrs/ Acre	Type
April	*Seeding (40 acres)*	*0.25*	*Tractor*	*Drill*	*Seed and fuel*	*20 pounds*	*50 lb bags*	*$80/bag*	*0.25*	*In-house; family*
June	*Clipping (40 acres)*	*0.25*	*Tractor*	*Disc Mower*	*Fuel*	*1 gallon*			*0.25*	*In-house; family*
Aug	*Clipping*	*0.25*	*Tractor*	*Disc Mower*	*Fuel*	*1 gallon*			*0.25*	*In-house; family*
Sept	*Fertilize*	*0.25*	*Tractor*	*Manure Spreader*	*Fuel*	*1 gallon*			*0.25*	*In-house; family*

Worksheet 2.6 Describing Livestock Production Systems

Complete this worksheet for each major livestock enterprise. Be as specific and accurate as you can be, since this information will be the basis for projections you'll make later for the strategies that you consider. Specify diets on a separate sheet if appropriate.

Livestock/Poultry Production System: *dairy* Current Number of Units: *150 cows*

Month or Period	Facility Space Req.	Labor		Feed Required	Vet & Medications Items & Amounts	Machinery & Equipment Req.	Other Inputs
		Hours	Type				
Jan	*Dry lot, parlor*	*120/month* *40/month*	*Milking* *Herd mgmt.*	*Corn/distillers grain (9 pounds/day/cow), silage, legume-grass balage*	*$137/month*	*Skid loader*	
Feb	*Dry lot, parlor*	*120/month* *40/month*	*Milking* *Herd mgmt.*	*Corn/distillers grain (9 pounds/day/cow), silage, legume-grass balage*	*$137/month*	*Skid loader*	
March	*Dry lot, parlor, calving shed*	*120/month* *40/month*	*Milking* *Herd mgmt.*	*Corn/distillers grain (9 pounds/day/cow), silage, legume-grass balage*	*$137/month*	*Skid loader*	
April	*Dry lot, parlor, calving shed*	*120/month* *40/month*	*Milking* *Herd mgmt,* *Calving*	*Corn/distillers grain (9 pounds/day/cow), silage, legume-grass balage*	*$137/month*	*Skid loader*	
May	*240 acres of pasture, parlor, calving shed*	*140/month* *40/month* *20/month*	*Milking* *Herd mgmt.* *Calving Rotation*	*Corn/distillers grain (6 pounds/day/cow), pasture, plus access to hay after milking*	*$137/month*	*Skid loader*	
June	*240 acres of pasture, parlor*	*140/month* *40/month* *20/month*	*Milking* *Herd mgmt.* *Calving Rotation*	*Corn/distillers grain (6 pounds/day/cow), pasture, plus access to hay after milking*	*$137/month*	*Skid loader*	
July	*240 acres of pasture, parlor*	*140/month* *40/month* *20/month*	*Milking* *Herd mgmt.* *Rotation*	*Corn/distillers grain (6 pounds/day/cow), pasture, plus access to hay after milking*	*$137/month*	*Skid loader*	
Aug	*240 acres of pasture, parlor*	*140/month* *40/month* *20/month*	*Milking* *Herd mgmt.* *Rotation*	*Corn/distillers grain (6 pounds/day/cow), pasture, plus access to hay after milking*	*$137/month*	*Skid loader*	
Sept	*240 acres of pasture, parlor*	*140/month* *40/month* *20/month*	*Milking* *Herd mgmt.* *Rotation*	*Corn/distillers grain (6 pounds/day/cow), pasture, plus access to hay after milking*	*$137/month*	*Skid loader*	
Oct	*240 acres of pasture, parlor*	*140/month* *40/month*	*Milking* *Herd mgmt.*	*Corn/distillers grain (6 pounds/day/cow), pasture, plus access to hay after milking*	*$137/month*	*Skid loader*	
Nov	*240 acres of pasture, parlor*	*140/month* *40/month* *20/month*	*Milking* *Herd mgmt.* *Rotation*	*Corn/distillers grain (6 pounds/day/cow), pasture, plus access to hay after milking*	*$137/month*	*Skid loader*	
Dec	*Dry lot, parlor*	*120/month* *40/month*	*Milking* *Herd mgmt.*	*Corn/distillers grain (9 pounds/day/cow), silage, legume-grass balage*	*$137/month*	*Skid loader*	

Figure 14. Example from Cedar Summit Farm—Worksheet 2.6: Describing Livestock Production Systems

Describing a livestock production system is often more complicated than crops because labor and other inputs are required daily. You can simplify the task by describing the activities that take place by period of the year. The appropriate periods depend on the species of livestock or poultry and how frequently input levels are being changed throughout the year. For example, if raising market hogs, you could specify the production periods based on the time and weight at which changes in the ration are made. If four diets are fed as the pig goes from weaning to market weight, the length and the input requirements could be specified for each of the four periods. In breeding livestock, the year might be divided into periods representing major differences in housing and labor requirements. In each case, the length of the period should be determined by the period over which labor and other input requirements are relatively stable on a day-to-day basis. Now complete **Worksheet 2.6: Describing Livestock Production Systems** for each major livestock enterprise in your current operation. Use the livestock enterprise checklist shown here to help you remember the items that should be included.

As a livestock producer, particularly a grazier, this assessment may be a good opportunity to also evaluate the sustainability of your livestock operation.

You can use the Beef or Dairy Sustainability Checklists that are available free from the Appropriate Technology Transfer for Rural Areas Center (www.attra.org). Both resources provide a series of questions regarding herd health, nutrition, productivity and pasture composition. The questions are designed to help you evaluate your current operations (see "Resources").

While it is critical to describe each crop and livestock enterprise separately, it is also important to consider how they fit together. Otherwise, a change in one enterprise may have unintended consequences for other parts of the operation. Do you feed crops produced on your farm to livestock? Do you use manure from a livestock enterprise as an input in one or more of your crop enterprises? Are there significant bottleneck or slack periods in the annual calendar for your farm?

Worksheet 2.7 Enterprise/Calendar Matrix

Summarize and combine your crop and livestock production systems in this calendar. Look for bottlenecks or conflicts in timing of operations.

Enterprise and Tasks	Hours/Month											
	Jan	**Feb**	**Mar**	**Apr**	**May**	**June**	**July**	**Aug**	**Sep**	**Oct**	**Nov**	**Dec**
Dairy												
• *Milking, feeding, herd health*	*180*	*180*	*200*	*200*	*200*	*200*	*180*	*180*	*180*	*200*	*200*	*180*
• *Calving*				*100*	*100*	*100*			*60*	*100*		
Hogs												
• *Feeding, monitor health*						*30*	*30*	*30*	*30*	*30*	*20*	*20*
Broilers/Turkey												
• *Feeding, monitor health*				*10*	*15*	*15*	*15*	*15*	*15*	*6*		
Beef												
• *Feeding, monitor health*				*10*	*10*	*20*				*10*	*20*	*20*
Hay							*25*	*25*	*20*			
Pasture												
• *Seeding*				*80*								
• *Maintenance*					*55*	*38*	*30*	*30*	*30*	*20*	*10*	
Other												
• *General Mgmt.*	*10*	*10*	*10*	*10*	*10*	*10*	*10*	*10*	*10*	*10*	*10*	*10*
• *Marketing*	*6*	*6*	*25*	*6*	*10*	*36*	*32*	*36*	*32*	*36*	*50*	*20*
• *Bookkeeping*	*10*	*4*	*2*	*8*	*4*	*2*	*4*	*2*	*4*	*2*	*2*	*10*
Total Hrs/Month	*206*	*200*	*237*	*424*	*404*	*381*	*326*	*328*	*381*	*414*	*312*	*260*

Figure 15. Example from Cedar Summit Farm—Worksheet 2.7: Enterprise/Calendar Matrix

TASK 2

Use **Worksheet 2.7: Enterprise/Calendar Matrix** to describe the links among the major enterprises in your farm operation. In Figure 15, the Minars' peak labor demand months are April and May and September and October. Note that the hog, beef and poultry enterprises fit in well with their dairy operation, since most of the labor requirements for these enterprises are concentrated in months after calving when the dairy cows are out on pasture.

As you think about individual enterprises and the annual calendar of activities for your own operations, keep the big picture in mind and look at the synergies and conflicts between enterprises. Think hard about whether you are using your physical resources as efficiently as possible.

What management and management information systems do we have in place to support our farm operations?

The knowledge embodied in sound management practices and the information contained in good production records are also important resources for your farm operation. At the enterprise level, regular review of production records can help you spot problems before they become serious—helping you control costs and boost production. For example, the Minars regularly review milk quantity and quality reports from their local dairy cooperative to monitor their dairy enterprise. Through participation in a local Dairy Herd Improvement Association, they get more detailed information on each cow's production. At the whole farm level, familiarity with annual planning and analysis can be an invaluable asset for an operation that is poised for making a major change. Regular meetings and discussions involving everyone in the operation are also valuable. The Minars have experience with using FINPACK[3] for financial analysis and planning, and they have developed a habit of maintaining good communication among family members and their partner Paul Kajer. These skills—essential for dealing with the unexpected events that are sure to come with a significant business expansion—would be difficult to develop on an "as needed" basis.

The Four Key Management Areas:
- Marketing
- Operations
- **Human Resources**
- Finance

Human Resources Situation

People are an essential resource in any farm business. Those who plan, manage and do day-to-day work may well be the most important factor in determining a farm operation's success. The human resources base for your farm includes you and others in your family or household who contribute time and effort to the operation. It also includes full-time and part-time employees, interns, consultants you hire to provide specialized advice or expertise, and other resource providers such as local production specialists or neighbors.

Your assessment of your farm's human resources should answer the following questions:

- Current Work Force: Who is involved in our business and what roles do they play?
- Skills: What are our unique skills? What skills do we lack?
- Change: Will our labor situation change in the near future? Will someone enter or leave the operation?

Use Worksheets 2.8 and 2.9 to record your answers as you work through this section.

3 *FINPACK* software, Center for Farm Financial Management, University of Minnesota, updated annually.

Worksheet 2.8 Human Resources Matrix

Use this worksheet to identify the people involved in your operations and the roles they play.

Person	Enterprise: Dairy	Hogs	Broilers/Turkey	Beef	Hay	Pasture	General Management
Dave Minar (FT)	Order feed, manage dry cows	Production labor and management; marketing	Production labor and management; marketing	Production labor and management; marketing	Production labor and management	Production labor and management	Book-keeping and financial analysis
Florence Minar (FT)		Marketing	Marketing	Marketing			General customer comm.
Paul Kajer (FT)	Herd manager; milking and other labor				Production labor and management	Production labor and management	
Dan Minar (PT)					Production labor and management		General farm labor
Ryan Jirik (PT)	Milking, Tuesdays and weekends						
Summer student (FT)		Feed animals	Feed animals	Feed animals	Hauling		Other farm labor
Other Labor: Consultants Ira Beckman, FBM							Financial analysis
Cenex Coop Technician	Maintain milking equipment						

Figure 16. Example from Cedar Summit Farm—Worksheet 2.8: Human Resources Matrix

Current Work Force: Who is involved in our business and what roles do they play?

The best place to start an assessment of your current human resources situation is with a straightforward listing of all the people involved in your operation and the roles they play. This sounds simple, but it can provide some eye-opening insights on how you have organized decision making and work responsibilities. A simple matrix with a column for each major enterprise or activity and a row for each individual is an effective way to structure this information.

In their Worksheet 2.8: Human Resources Matrix (Figure 16), the Minars have drafted a brief description of duties and responsibilities in the cell for each enterprise in which that individual is involved. For example, Paul Kajer has major management and labor responsibilities for the dairy enterprise. He also works closely with Dave in the pasture enterprise and with Dave and Dan in the hay enterprise. Note that the Minars have included general management as a separate enterprise. In doing so, they recognize that there are important tasks associated with managing and coordinating the entire operation. Also note that they have included the dairy technician from their

local cooperative and their farm business management advisor in their human resources matrix. Though not employed directly by Cedar Summit Farm, both provide important expertise and advice.

A quick glance at this matrix indicates the degree of specialization and the extent of teamwork within the operation. Paul, Dave and Ryan specialize and work together in the dairy, pasture and hay enterprises. Dave and Florence work together in the meat marketing enterprises. Also, the fact that Dave is involved in all the enterprises means that he plays a key role in coordinating activities for the entire operation. Finally, note that this matrix can help identify enterprises that depend almost entirely on one person (a column with only one completed cell) and people who may be overloaded and spread too thin (almost every cell in a row has an entry).

Use **Worksheet 2.8: Human Resources Matrix** to sketch a clear picture of your current human resources. Also, look back to your completed Worksheet 2.7: Enterprise/Calendar Matrix to describe the seasonal pattern of activities across all your enterprises. Are there critical times of the year when more work could be shared? Are some people in your operation over- or under-employed? Looking back to the Minars' Enterprise/Calendar Matrix, April through November are busy months, as they are for most farm operations in the Upper Midwest. The Minars use a summer student worker to add labor during some of these peak months. Adding total labor hours from the enterprise/calendar matrix across all twelve months, the Minars estimate their total labor demand to be 3,873 hours. Assuming a full-time worker contributes 2,000 hours of labor per year (forty hours per week for fifty weeks), this translates to just under two "full-time equivalent" workers.

Skills: What are our unique skills? What skills do we lack?

Worksheet 2.8: Human Resources Matrix describes the current pattern of decision and work responsibilities, but it is also important to assess how well suited each individual is to the roles he or she plays in the operation. **Worksheet 2.9: Assessing Worker Abilities and Needs** guides you through a simple evaluation of an individual's abilities and needs. Fill out a copy of this Worksheet for each person in your operation. You may want to have some or all of your team members complete their own assessment form as a way of identifying untapped skills. You may not be aware of a particular talent or skill that someone on your team has developed. A completed Worksheet 2.9 for Ryan Jirik, the Minars' part-time milker, follows as an illustration. Note that Ryan's long-term goal is to own and operate his own dairy farm, and the Minars are considering hiring him as a full-time milker on Cedar Summit Farm when he graduates from high school.

As you review these Worksheets for people involved in your operation, ask whether there are people in your operation who have unique but untapped skills

Worksheet 2.9 Assessing Worker Abilities and Needs

Use this worksheet to describe the experience, skills and goals of each member of your workforce. Then estimate your average cost for this person and consider where this person ideally fits into your operation.

Name and Current Position: *Ryan Jirik, part-time milker*

1. What is the person's background-experience and education?

Ryan is a neighbor "city kid" who has no background in milking.

2. What particular abilities does this person have?

Hard worker

3. What are this person's strengths and weaknesses?

Ryan is very personable and reliable - these are strengths

4. What are the person's interests? What motivates them?

Ryan has a strong interest in learning about the farm and the dairy industry in general. We are training him as a milker on our farm.

5. What are the person's own personal goals in life?

To own and operate his own dairy farm.

6. What are we currently paying this person ($/hour)?

[Confidential]

7. Conclusion: Where might this person best fit in meeting our human resource needs?

We see Ryan fitting in as our full-time milker once he graduates from high school.

Figure 17. Example from Cedar Summit Farm—Worksheet 2.9: Assessing Worker Abilities and Needs

or critical skills that you are lacking. Also ask whether there are people who would be happier in other roles. These are opportunities or problems that can and should be addressed in developing your business plan.

Change: Will our labor situation change in the near future? Will someone enter or leave the operation?

A significant change in the lives of people involved in a farming operation is often the factor that motivates the development of a new business plan. Dave and Florence Minar were motivated to explore on-farm milk processing, in part, as a way to create opportunities for their children to join the operation. Frank Foltz

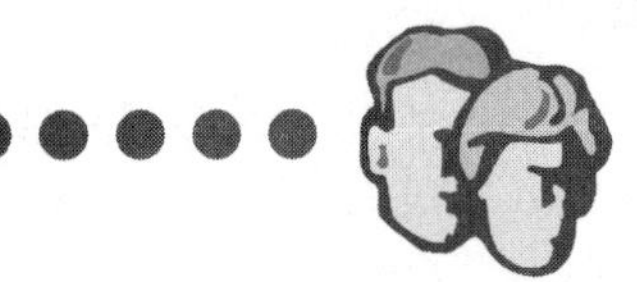

began to consider selling the catalog sales part of his business shortly after two daughters had married and moved away from home.

Now that you have described your current human resources situation, spend some time thinking systematically about how that situation may change in the next year, five years or ten years. **Worksheet 2.10: Likely Changes in Our Human Resources Situation** poses questions about three of the most common and most significant human resources changes in farm operations. The first two questions focus on people who will be leaving or joining the operation and the opportunities and challenges created by these changes. The third question focuses on a difficult issue in many family farming operations—the transfer of managerial responsibilities from one person to another. One or more of these questions may be relevant for your operation—or you may face some other important human resources change. Careful attention to potential changes, whatever they may be, will help you clarify the issues that need to be addressed by your business plan.

TASK 2

Worksheet 2.10 Likely Changes in Our Human Resources Situation

Use this worksheet to describe likely changes in your human resources situation over the next year, five years or ten years.

Current Workforce: Will anyone who currently works in our operation be leaving for other work or for personal reasons? What activities/enterprises will this affect?

We don't foresee anyone leaving the operation.

Future Workforce: Will any new people be joining our operation? What new knowledge and skills will they bring? Do we have enough physical and financial resources for them to be fully employed and appropriately paid?

Several of our children would like to join our operation. They are:

Mike Minar: has worked with processing equipment and is currently attending boiler operations school. He has excellent supervisory skills. He would like to become a full-time employee of the farm.

Dan Minar: has a business degree, good people skills and a general working knowledge of our current operation. He would like to become a full-time employee of our farm business.

Laura Ganske: has very good people skills and has worked with the public. She would like to work part-time on marketing and administrative issues.

Merrisue Minar: has professional bookkeeping experience and enjoys working with people. She would also like to work part-time on marketing and bookkeeping.

Future Management: Do we foresee a change in the allocation of decision-making and management responsibilities?

Currently, we do not have the financial resources to hire any of our children on a full- or part-time basis.

We would like to shift some of the general farm management to our current business partner. Paul Kajer, and eventually pass on all responsibilities to our children when we retire.

Figure 18. Example from Cedar Summit Farm—Worksheet 2.10: Likely Changes in Our Human Resources Situation

Financial Situation

The Four Key Management Areas:
- Marketing
- Operations
- Human Resources
- ➠ **Finance**

TASK 2

Detailed information on current finances is a key component of any business plan, particularly if it will be used to generate outside resources in the form of loans or equity investments. While many of your personal goals cannot be expressed in monetary terms, a certain level of financial planning is necessary for a farm operation to be viable in the long term. An accurate assessment of your current financial situation provides a comprehensive summary of the value of the physical resources available to your operation. It also shows you the income being generated by those resources in combination with human resources through your operations and marketing strategies. In addition, the strength of your financial position will determine your ability to access the capital resources you will need to add and use new resources in your operation.

Your assessment of your farm's financial resources should answer the following questions:

- Financial needs: What are our current family living expenses?
- Financial performance: How well has our business performed in the past, and how strong is our current financial position?
- Risk: What type of risk is our business currently exposed to?
- Financial environment: What is our current business environment, and how is it changing?

Use Worksheets 2.11 through 2.15 as a guide for recording your answers as you work through this section.

Financial Needs: What are our current family living expenses?

If you and your family rely on your farm business as your only source of income, or as a major source of income that is supplemented by earnings from off-farm work, your operation can only be sustainable in the long run if it provides enough income to meet your family's basic living expenses. For most people, then, making a realistic estimate of current family living expenses is the starting point for assessing the financial status of your current operation.

Use **Worksheet 2.11: Estimating Family Living Expenses and Income Needs** to estimate your annual family living expenses and your family's earnings from off-farm work. The difference between the two is the amount of income you need from your farm operation.

If you do not maintain current records that can be used to estimate your family's current and future living expenses, you may want to contact Minnesota's Center for Farm Financial Management (CFFM). The CFFM maintains a database, called FINBIN, which tracks personal and household expenses for thousands of Minnesota and North Dakota farm families. Average Minnesota household

Figure 19.

FINBIN Average Expenses for 2001 Farm Family in Minnesota and North Dakota

In the year 2001, family living expenses averaged $53,187 for 954 Minnesota and North Dakota farm families enrolled in the Farm Business Management Program. According the Center for Farm Financial Management's FINBIN database, the largest spending among farm households was for food and meals, medical care and health insurance, household supplies, personal care, recreation, nonfarm vehicle expenses, taxes, real estate and other capital purchases.

Household and Personal Expenses: 2001	
Number of farms	954
Family Living Expenses	**(in dollars)**
Food and meals expense	$ 5,590
Medical care and health insurance	4,886
Cash donations	1,337
Household supplies	3,673
Clothing	1,586
Personal care	2,781
Child / Dependent care	766
Gifts	1,631
Education	1,305
Recreation	2,253
Utilities (household share)	1,654
Nonfarm vehicle operating expense	2,489
Household real estate taxes	172
Dwelling rent	119
Household repairs	1,101
Nonfarm interest	873
Life insurance payments	1,538
Total cash family living expense	**33,754**
Family living from the farm	356
Total family living	**34,110**
Other Nonfarm Expenditures	
Income taxes	6,823
Furnishing & appliance purchases	635
Nonfarm vehicle purchases	3,320
Nonfarm real estate purchases	3,060
Other nonfarm capital purchases	2,901
Nonfarm savings & investments	2,695
Total other nonfarm expenditures	**19,433**
Total cash family living investment & nonfarm capital purchases	**53,187**

Example derived from FINBIN Database, Center for Farm Financial Management, University of Minnesota

Data Source(s): Minnesota Farm Business Management Education, 914 farms
Southwest Minnesota Farm Business Management Association, 131 farms
Southeast Minnesota Farm Business Management Association, 18 farms
North Dakota Farm and Ranch Business Management—Red River Valley, 8 farms

expenses for 2001 are listed in Figure 19. Use the database averages if you do not have reliable family living expenditure estimates and adjust them according to your family's needs. The FINBIN database is accessible through CFFM's website (www.cffm.umn.edu/) or by contacting the Center directly. See "Resources" for more information.

Financial Performance: How well has our business performed in the past, and how strong is our current financial position?

Your ability to assess the past financial performance of your farm will depend on the financial information that you have available. If you have access to detailed past financial information on your farm business, the process may be one of laying past years' information side by side in a trend analysis. If you do not have access to much past financial information, you may be limited to comparing information from past tax schedules. Although this approach of comparing tax records is widely used by financial institutions to assess financial performance, it violates one of the primary requirements of a complete financial analysis—that the analysis should be completed based on accrual, not cash, information.

Why accrual? Figure 20 compares financial results for a hypothetical operation based on tax information vs. accrual income information. This illustrates how easy it is to underestimate financial progress if you look only at the Schedule F (tax) information. One of the reasons for this is that U.S. farmers enjoy the unusual ability to report taxes on a

cash rather than accrual basis. Most farmers find ways of continuously pushing income forward, consistently building inventories and underrecognizing income on their tax statements. So, by using the traditional method of many financial institutions of laying several Schedule F's side by side, you are likely to underestimate the financial progress you have been making. On the other hand, you could be overestimating performance if assets are being used up and not replaced.

Looking ahead, the Minars' Worksheet 2.12: Income Statement (Figure 23) offers a real-life example of how tax information can underestimate financial performance. For 2000, they reported a net farm income of $28,147 on their Schedule F, but their net farm income calculated on an accrual basis was $65,083 (Numbers have been changed to protect confidentiality). So cash vs. accrual information is one of the first adjustments to consider when you begin to evaluate your past financial performance and consider accounting alternatives.

Figure 20.
Comparison of Financial Results Based on Tax and Accrual Information

	Schedule F	Accrual
Gross cash farm income	$ 123,720	$ 123,720
Cash farm operating expenses	–108,564	–108,564
Accrual adjustment		
Change in crop inventory		16,298
Change in livestock inventory		–3,656
Change in accounts receivable		1,950
Change in accounts payable		2,450
Total inventory change		17,042
Depreciation	–6,745	–6,745
Net farm income	8,411	25,453

Another concern is market vs. cost asset valuation. Agricultural lenders have traditionally evaluated farm financial performance based on the market value of farm assets. This gives the lender a basis for evaluating the risk faced by the lending institution and the collateral available in case a borrower defaults on a loan. Market valuation of assets provides the information demanded by external users of your financial information. What about your situation? Do market values give you the information you need for internal evaluation of progress? Using market values mixes net worth growth from farm earnings with growth from "paper changes" in the value of assets. So if you lay out your financial history using market values for assets, you can never be quite sure how profitable your farming operations have been, or even if your farm has been profitable at all.

Figure 21.
Comparison of Net Worth Based on Cost and Market Values for Assets

		Cost Valuation	Market Valuation
Total assets		$ 267,438	$ 358,590
Total liabilities		–105,367	–105,367
Contributed capital and retained earnings	(a)	162,071	
Net worth or owner's equity	(b)		253,223
Market valuation equity	(c) = (b – a)		91,152

Figure 21 shows a comparison of the net worth picture for a hypothetical farm using cost vs. market values on assets. The cost column values assets at their original purchase cost minus depreciation. This results in a cost net worth, which reflects only what has been invested from outside the farm (contributed capital) and what has been earned and retained over time (retained earnings).

TASK 2

Figure 22.

Defining Financial Performance Measurement Areas

Profitability: Profitability evaluates just what you would expect—whether your business is making money. This sounds pretty basic, but it is probably the most neglected part of the financial evaluation process by farmers. Traditionally, farmers have prepared their financial information for lenders instead of for their own purposes. How many times has your lender asked you for an accrual income statement? Even if you evaluate several years of tax schedules, you may be missing the mark on how profitable your business has been.

Liquidity: Your business is liquid if you have available funds or can easily access funds to meet ongoing or unforeseen cash requirements. You may have a very liquid farm business even though you do not have a lot of cash in the bank if you have assets that can be sold and turned into cash easily, without interrupting the flow of ongoing business.

Solvency: Your business is solvent if it has an adequate net worth to make your farm attractive to lenders and others who you might want to invest in your business. Lenders want to lend you money. That is how they make their living. But they won't be interested unless you have adequate assets relative to claims on the assets (debts). This makes lenders comfortable investing their assets in your farm business.

Repayment Ability: While liquidity evaluates the overall availability of liquid financial reserves, repayment ability looks more at whether your business generates enough cash to repay debt on time. It is closely related to profitability in that a profitable farm will usually generate sufficient funds for debt repayment. But repayment ability is also related to debt structure. If you have too much short-term debt, with high repayment requirements, even a profitable business may experience repayment problems. This is often a problem for farms that are growing rapidly. They may be very profitable, but they often need to plow their earnings right back into the farm during periods when debt repayment requirements are at their highest.

Efficiency: Efficiency is very closely related to the issues discussed in the section on operations. It measures how much income is being produced, how much it costs to produce it, and where the money is going. So, efficiency is where you should look if you are interested in evaluating cost control.

The net worth on the market value side includes these earnings, but it also includes the accumulated changes in market values of all assets over time (market valuation equity).

Look at the Minars' sample Worksheet 2.13: Balance Sheet for a real-life example of the difference between cost and market valuation. At the end of 2000, their net worth under cost valuation was $126,610, while it was $735,642 under market valuation (from Minars' Worksheet 2.10: Income Statement—not shown for privacy reasons).

Market valuation is important if your goals include looking for external funds. Yet you should consider adding cost information to your analysis for your own evaluation of financial progress. These concepts (and the following financial performance measurement concepts) are explained in greater detail in *Evaluating Financial Performance and Position*, available through the Oklahoma Cooperative Extension Service (see "Resources").

Before going into the tools used in financial analysis, it may be useful to discuss the basic financial performance measurement areas of most businesses. The Farm Financial Standard's Council (FFSC) has identified five financial measurement areas for farm businesses (Figure 22).[4] They are no different than those sought by nonfarm businesses. However, some of these performance measurement areas have not been systematically analyzed in farming as in other businesses.

The five recommended financial performance measurement areas are:

- Profitability
- Liquidity
- Solvency
- Repayment Ability
- Efficiency

To get a complete look at the past financial performance of your farm business, you should prepare the following statements to evaluate profitability, liquidity and solvency: the *income statement,* the *cash flow statement,* the

4 *Financial Guidelines for Agricultural Producers*, Recommendations of the Farm Financial Standards Council, 1995 (revised).

balance sheet, and the *statement of owner's equity.* We will discuss the income statement and balance sheet in detail, since these are probably the most important for farm business analysis.

Income Statement. The income statement is a basic tool used to determine farm income for the past year; it shows whether or not your business has generated sufficient income to cover family living and tax expenses.

Worksheet 2.12: Income Statement provides a basic structure for your income statement. Once again, the example provided here is based on the Minars' FINAN analysis for 2000, although some numbers have been changed to protect their confidentiality.

Use Worksheet 2.12 to develop historical net farm income statements from your available records. Begin by listing gross revenue from market livestock sales, crop sales, services, government payments, insurance claims, patronage dividends, etc. Be sure to include any gains or losses from the sale of culled breeding stock, as well as the change in the quantity of raised breeding stock. *Developing an Income Statement* (available from Oklahoma Cooperative Extension Service, see "Resources") details how to calculate breeding stock gains and losses. Next, list all farm business expenses, including purchased livestock, changes in purchased feed inventories, accounts payable, non-current liabilities, and depreciation expenses. Your net farm income is equal to the value of gross farm revenue minus total farm expenses.

Worksheet 2.12 Income Statement

Use this worksheet as a guide for constructing income statements for the past several years. Where possible, include itemized revenue and expense details. Suggested crop and livestock expense categories are listed in worksheets 2.5 and 2.6. You may want to use a computerized package such as FINPACK to collect and process the information needed for your income statement.

For the period beginning 1/1/2000
and ending 12/31/2000

Gross farm income				$ 319,132
Total cash operating expenses			-	271,715
Inventory changes				
Crops and feed (ending – beginning)	+/–	27,427		
Market livestock (ending – beginning)	+/–	12,821		
Accounts receivable (ending – beginning)	+/–	1,181		
Prepaid expenses and supplies (ending – beginning)	+/–	-4,424		
Accounts payable (beginning – ending)	+/–	-69		
Accrued interest (beginning - ending)	+/–	—		
Total inventory change			+/–	36,936
Depreciation			-	19,270
...ations			=	$ 65,083

SOME NUMBERS HAVE BEEN CHANGED TO PROTECT CONFIDENTIALITY.

Figure 23. Example from Cedar Summit Farm—Worksheet 2.12: Income Statement

TASK 2

Balance Sheet. A balance sheet lists all business assets and liabilities, showing what is owned and what is owed. In other words, the balance statement depicts your claim to the business' financial assets or what is called net worth and owner's equity. A series of balance sheets prepared at the same time each year for successive years shows the change in the business' financial position and the progress you have made. A balance sheet can also be used to make accrual adjustments to your income statement.

Assets include items owned by the business, such as land, machinery and breeding livestock, as well as items owed to the business. Liabilities include all claims against the business, such as accounts payable, credit card debt, the current portion of term debt, accrued interest on all farm loans, and taxes.

Balance sheets typically break farm assets and liabilities into at least two categories. The FINPACK balance sheet, reproduced for this Guide in **Worksheet 2.13: Balance Sheet**, breaks farm assets and liabilities into three categories: current, intermediate, and long term. This allows for further analysis of the financial structure of the business.

The example balance sheet provided in Figure 24 (Worksheet 2.13 Example) is based on the Minars' financial analysis for 2000. In this example, the Minars' assets are listed for cost and market values. The difference between the two values is quite dramatic—$382,629 at cost versus $1,276,273 at market. As discussed earlier, if your balance sheets have been

Figure 24. Example from Cedar Summit Farm—Worksheet 2.13: Balance Sheet

TASK 2

Worksheet 2.13 Balance Sheet

Construct your current and historical balance sheets. Where possible, include itemized details under each asset and liability category. You may want to use a computerized package, such as FINPACK (see "Resources"), to collect and process the information needed for your Balance Sheet.

Balance Sheet Date *January 1, 2000*

Assets (in dollars)		Market Value	Cost Value
Current Farm Assets			
Cash and checking balance		$ 2,959	$ 2,959
Prepaid expenses & supplies		25,698	25,698
Growing crops			
Accounts receivable		23,000	23,000
Hedging accounts			
Crops and feed		34,862	34,862
Crops under government loan			
Market livestock		26,786	26,786
Other current assets			
Total Current Assets	(a)	113,305	113,305
Intermediate Farm Assets			
Breeding livestock		189,010	2,987
Machinery and equipment		124,458	50,587
Other intermediate assets			
Total Intermediate Assets	(b)	313,468	53,574
Long-term Farm Assets			
Farm land		617,200	40,129
Buildings and improvements		48,000	43,717
Other long-term assets		1,576	1,576
Total Long-term Assets	(c)	666,776	85,442
Total Farm Assets	(d) = (a + b + c)	1,093,549	252,321
Nonfarm Assets	(e)	182,724	130,308
Total Assets	(f) = (d + e)	1,276,273	382,629

Liabilities (in dollars)		Market Value	Cost Value
Current Farm Liabilities			
Accrued interest		$ 69	$ 69
Accounts payable & accrued expense			
Current farm loans		5,860	5,860
Principal on CCC loans			
Principal due on term loans		25,690	25,690
Total Current Farm Liabilities	(g)	31,619	31,169
Intermediate Farm Liabilities	(h)	126,492	126,492
Long-term Farm Liabilities	(i)	88,908	88,908
Total Farm Liabilities	(j) = (g + h + i)	247,019	247,019
Nonfarm Liabilities	(k)	7,000	7,000
Total Liabilities	(l) = (j + k)	254,019	254,019
Retained Earnings	(m) = (f_2 – l)		128,610
Net Worth	(n) = (f_1 – l)	1,022,254	
Market Valuation Equity	(o) = (n – m)	893,644	

f_1 = Market Value of Total Assets
f_2 = Cost Value of Total Assets

SOME NUMBERS HAVE BEEN CHANGED TO PROTECT CONFIDENTIALITY.

based strictly on market values, realize that not all of your net worth changes may have resulted from business earnings. Moreover, because farms and ranches typically are owner operated, it can be difficult to separate personal and business assets. If your business is a sole proprietorship and you have included nonfarm information on your balance sheet (like Dave and Florence Minar), be aware that net worth changes over time will reflect what was earned on and off the farm minus what was consumed in family living and taxes.

Use Worksheet 2.13 to reconstruct historical balance sheets for your business if possible. Divide your assets and liabilities into *current* (cash and other assets that are easily converted to cash or liabilities due within the current period), *intermediate* and *long-term* categories (items not normally for sale, but rather held for the production of livestock or crops and liabilities due beyond the current period). Then value your assets and liabilities using either the cost or market valuation method. Add assets and liabilities in the space provided and calculate your net worth.

For more information about balance sheets and how to construct them, see *Developing a Balance Sheet* from Oklahoma State University. You may also want to check out the FINPACK or Farm Biz computer software, which can walk you through the balance sheet input and provide the beginnings of computerized analysis for the farm business. See "Resources" for more information.

Once you've prepared historical balance sheets and income statements, your next task is to look at the value of retained earnings generated by the business if one of your goals is to increase owner equity over time. Retained earnings can be estimated using the earned net worth change calculation. The earned net worth change is calculated by adding all nonfarm income to net farm income. Family living expenses, partner withdrawals and taxes are then subtracted to arrive at a value that represents income that either contributed to or depleted the farm's net worth in the given period. This simple calculation is depicted in Figure 25, **Worksheet 2.14: Earned Net Worth Change Analysis**.

Note that for family farms, the earned net worth calculation includes non-farm components since the nonfarm withdrawals for family living purposes are the primary draw on income and because net worth growth can occur by bringing in income from off the farm, cutting living

TASK 2

Figure 25.
Example from Cedar Summit Farm—Worksheet 2.14: Earned Net Worth Change Analysis

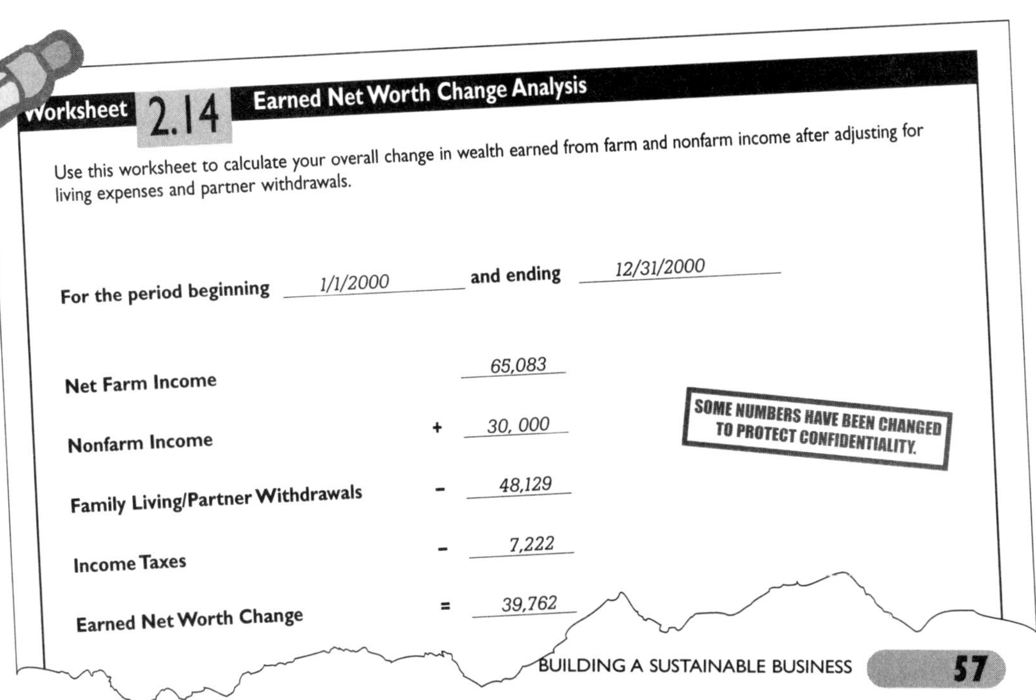
Worksheet 2.14 Earned Net Worth Change Analysis

Use this worksheet to calculate your overall change in wealth earned from farm and nonfarm income after adjusting for living expenses and partner withdrawals.

For the period beginning 1/1/2000 and ending 12/31/2000

Net Farm Income		65,083
Nonfarm Income	+	30, 000
Family Living/Partner Withdrawals	-	48,129
Income Taxes	-	7,222
Earned Net Worth Change	=	39,762

expenses, or improving tax management.

The national Farm Financial Standards Council (FFSC) has identified 16 measures, or "ratios", around the five basic financial performance area measures (liquidity, solvency, profitability, repayment capacity and efficiency). *Ratio analysis* is a tool financial management experts and lenders use to judge the absolute and relative strength of a business. A full description of the FFSC's "sweet sixteen" financial ratios and their calculations are listed in Appendix B. Space is not devoted here to do a complete ratio analysis because it requires very detailed farm records. If your records contain the information needed to calculate each of the financial ratios mentioned, we highly recommend doing so. This will help you pinpoint your business' financial strengths and weaknesses. Using numbers from your Balance and Income Statements (Worksheets 2.12 and 2.13), you can calculate five of the sixteen ratios as illustrated in Figure 26 on **Worksheet 2.15: Financial Ratios Based on the Balance Sheet and Income Statement.**

Worksheet 2.15 Financial Ratios Based on the Balance Sheet and Income Statement

Use information from your balance sheet and income statement to calculate the following ratios that measure liquidity, solvency, profitability, repayment capacity and efficiency.

Current Ratio:
This is a primary measure of liquidity used by most businesses.

Current Assets (Balance Sheet)		$ 113,305
Current Liabilities (Balance Sheet)	÷	31,619
Current Ratio	=	3.58

A current ratio of 2:1, with two dollars of current assets for every dollar of current debt, is usually considered adequate. If your current ratio approaches 1:1, your ability to sustain your business during a financial downturn may be limited.

Debt to Asset Ratio:
This solvency measure is sometimes referred to as your percent in debt.

Total Liabilities (Balance Sheet)		254,019
Total Assets (Balance Sheet)	÷	1,276,273
Debt to Asset Ratio	=	19.9%

When calculated based on the market value of your assets, a debt to asset ratio under 40% is usually considered comfortable; over 60% is usually considered vulnerable.

Rate of Return on Assets:
This profitability measure can be interpreted as the average interest rate being earned on the financial resources invested by you and lenders in your business. Adjust net farm income for the estimated opportunity cost of unpaid family labor to make your figures comparable to those for businesses that hire labor and management

Net Farm Income (Income Statement)		65,083
Interest Expense (Income Statement)	+	23,883
Opportunity Cost for Family Labor and Management (estimated)	–	62,132
Return on Assets	=	26,834
Total Farm Assets (Balance Sheet)	÷	1,093,549
Rate of Return on Assets	=	2.5%

The amount you deduct for labor and management depends on your goals for how much income you feel you need from the farm. Since farming has not historically been a high return business, a rate of return greater than 5% (when assets are valued at market value) is usually considered adequate. Remember, though, if you are earning only 5% and paying interest at 10%, you may be headed for problems. You may be able to maintain this if your debt to asset ratio is low. But if you have substantial debt, you will need to set your profitability goals a bit higher.

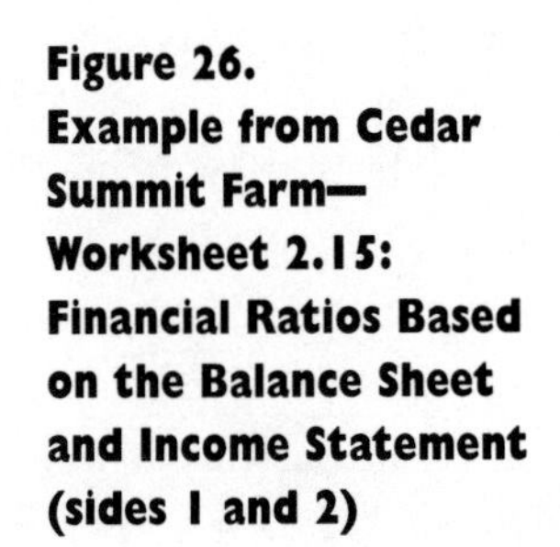
Figure 26. Example from Cedar Summit Farm—Worksheet 2.15: Financial Ratios Based on the Balance Sheet and Income Statement (sides 1 and 2)

There are many other ways to measure financial performance. For small farms that are built around the use of family labor instead of vast amounts of capital, you might want to track labor and management earnings. This measure recognizes that net farm income for a family farm represents returns to unpaid labor, management and equity capital. To estimate labor and management returns, an opportunity cost for owners' equity is subtracted from net farm

TASK 2

Worksheet 2.15 Financial Ratios Based on the Balance Sheet and Income Statement

CONTINUED

Term Debt Coverage Ratio:
This measure of repayment capacity indicates whether your business is generating enough income to make principal and interest payments on intermediate and long term debt.

Gross Farm Income (Income Statement)		319,132
Cash Operating Expenses (Income Statement)	–	237,111
Scheduled Interest Payments on Intermediate and Long-term Debt (Income Statement)	+	23,883
Family Living Expenses and Taxes (from the Earned Net Worth Change Worksheet)	–	55,351
Funds Available for Debt Payments	=	50,553
Intermediate and Long-term Debt Payments	÷	49,199
Term Debt Coverage Ratio	=	103%

A term debt coverage ratio of over 150%, meaning that you are producing $1.50 of income that is available for debt repayment for each $1.00 of scheduled debt repayment, is usually considered adequate.

Operating Expense Ratio:
This measure of overall efficiency indicates the percentage of business revenues that are available for family living expenses, debt repayment and new investments.

Cash Operating Expenses (Income Statement)		237,111
Interest Expense (Income Statement)	–	23,883
Gross Farm Income (Income Statement)	÷	319,132
Operating Expense Ratio	=	66.8%

While thumb rules for the ratios listed above can be used across farm types and across industries, operating expenses will vary substantially from business to business and industry to industry. As a general guideline, most farm business strive to keep operating expenses under 70% of gross revenues. If you are operating a small farm that employs sustainable practices, your financial success probably depends on operating efficiency. In that case, you should probably strive to keep operating expenses below 60% of revenues. If you are involved in a retail business, sales volume might be more important to your bottom line than operating expense levels if cost of goods sold is included. In that case, a much higher operating expense ratio might be expected. So, this ratio is useful for internal tracking of your business, but not very useful for comparisons with other businesses.

income. The remainder is labor and management earnings. Labor and management earnings can be directly compared to your desired amount of family income from the farm.

Worksheet 2.16 Whole Farm Trend Analysis

Use the table below as a guide for doing a trend analysis for important measures of physical resources, operating efficiency, financial position and financial performance.

Year	1998	1999	2000		
Physical Resources					
Number of acres	78	78	78		
Number of cows	122	152	150		
Operating Efficiency					
Hay yield (tons/acre)	5.7	5.2	5.9		
Milk per cow (lbs/year)	13,483	13,260	13,317		
Financial Position					
Ending net worth	$ 578,197	$ 734,911	$ 735,642		
Current ratio	0.76	0.87	3.58		
Debt to asset ratio	48%	40%	42%		
Term debt coverage ratio	99%	153%	103%		
Financial Performance					
Net farm income	$ 78,893	$ 104,953	$ 65,083		
Rate of return on assets	4.6%	5.8%	2.5%		
Labor and management earnings	$ 38,893	$ 50,953	$ 5,083		
Operating expense ratio	73%	71%	66.8%		

SOME NUMBERS HAVE BEEN CHANGED TO PROTECT CONFIDENTIALITY.

Figure 27. Example from Cedar Summit Farm—Worksheet 2.16: Whole Farm Trend Analysis

Regardless of which method you use to evaluate past financial performance, you will find it useful to incorporate all this financial information into a trend analysis. This enables you to put everything together and document a financial history for yourself and for external stakeholders. **Worksheet 2.16: Whole Farm Trend Analysis** can serve as a guide for your own whole farm trend analysis, which should include measures of physical resources, operating efficiency, financial position and financial performance that are most relevant for your farm business. A trend analysis for the Minars' operation is provided as an example.

You've just spent a lot of time and effort accumulating information and calculating ratios or other formulas to describe your business' current financial performance. It's helpful to take a break, and remember where you are in your business planning—that these past few exercises are just a part of the bigger picture of assessing the current performance of your farm or business.

Just to remind you where you are in that assessment:

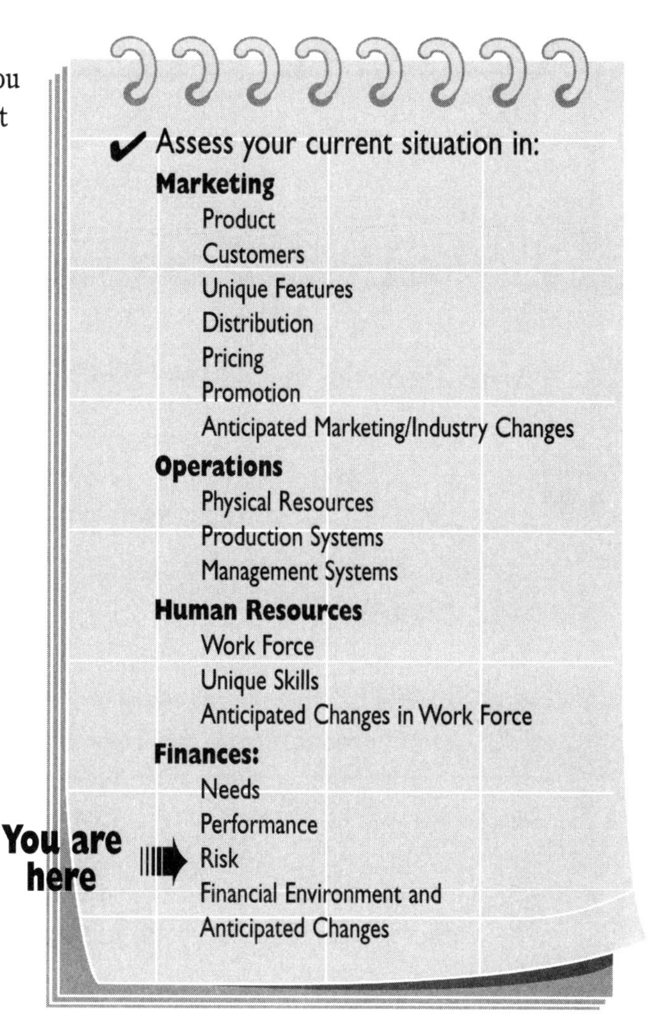

TASK 2

You're now ready to move on to the next area to consider as you continue assessing your financial situation–potential risks.

Risk: To what type of risk is the business exposed?

In today's agricultural industry, risk management has become an important topic, particularly for those producers who have traditionally relied on government intervention to mitigate price and production-related risks. Regardless of whether you produce corn, soybeans, grass-based milk, organic vegetables or specialty fruit trees, risk management will be an important component of your business. Without it, uncontrolled risk and uncertainty reduce the reliability of financial projections and make investment analysis difficult. Unmanaged risk also carries with it a high degree of stress for farm managers and their families.

In this section, you and your planning team will research the potential risks to your business while developing a strategy to minimize and protect against uncertainty. Agricultural risk is typically tied to personal, production and market uncertainties. The Minars' business, for example, was exposed to significant market

Figure 28.

Common Sources of Agricultural Risk[5]

Personal risk is the result of change and uncertainty within the business. Injuries and illness are sources of internal risk that can affect your business' ability to operate. Other sources of personal risk include a change in goals, divorce, death and fire. All of these events can have a significant impact on the long-term performance of your business. You might even consider your own lack of knowledge and experience in a new area a risk, as it may create uncertainty as you transition from one management system to another. The business may be exposed to some internal risk as you learn to control pests and build soil fertility without the use of synthetic chemicals. "This [learning process] may lead to greater production risks and the potential for lower yields," notes organic certification specialist Lisa Gulbranson.

Production and market risks are those risks that result from weather-related events such as drought, excess rainfall, hail, extreme temperatures, insects and disease. External price risks are often tied to below-cost market prices and volatility in commodity and input prices after production commitments have been made. Institutional risk is associated with changes in government policy and regulations that govern market prices, crop insurance, waste management and livestock housing facilities.

Contract risk is associated with the reliability (or lack thereof) of contracting partners. Although the use of production and marketing contracts are cited as risk management tools, you should be aware that the contracts themselves may pose a risk to your operation if the contractor/contractee is unreliable.

Financial risk can occur as a result of fluctuating interest rates on borrowed funds, cash flow difficulties, and erosion of equity or net worth.

5 *Managing Risk in Farming: Concepts, Research and Analysis*, Harwood, et al., 1999.

TASK 2

risk—fluctuating milk prices. Moreover, as a farmer today, you will likely encounter legal and regulatory uncertainty (institutional risk), contract risk, and other forms of financial risk. Each of these sources of risk is described briefly in Figure 28.

Use **Worksheet 2.17: Risk Management** to evaluate your business' exposure to risk. Like the Minars, rank your business' exposure to production, market, financial and personal risk. Then list any tools or strategies that you are using to cope with and manage for that risk.

Financial Environment: What is our current business environment and how is it changing?

This is the last question to consider in assessing your farm's current financial situation. Analysis of financial statements for your operation focuses on internal forces affecting the financial history and current situation of your farm business. Your financial future will also be affected by what is happening externally to your business, within your industry and in the general economy. The following are external forces that are especially important for the financial health of your operation:

- **Interest Rates.** In the late 1970s and early 1980s, high interest rates placed a heavy burden on any business that was using substantial borrowed capital. Could another such situation develop in the future?

- **Employment.** Will dependable, knowledgeable employees be available at a wage (including possible benefits) that you can afford to pay? Quite recently, this was a problem for many small businesses. Wage rates had increased sharply owing to high employment levels and a greater demand for dependable workers.

- **Inflation.** Producers who sell into the commodity markets have long known that inflation tends to increase farm costs much faster than farm prices. Is there potential that we could find ourselves in another inflationary period like that experienced during the 1970s?

- **Government Actions.** If your products are currently supported by government programs, will the current level of

Worksheet 2.17 Risk Management

Briefly rank your business' exposure to production, environmental, market, contract, and personal risk. Then briefly describe how you currently manage for risk.

Market Risk

Exposure to risk: ____ Low ____ Medium __x__ High

Type of risk: *Declining and fluctuating market prices for milk*

Tools for minimizing risk: *Quality premiums to improve prices overall, but nothing to mitigate fluctuations*

Production Risk

Exposure to risk: __x__ Low ____ Medium ____ High

Type of risk: *Hay crop failure, herd disease*

Tools to minimize risk: *Continued placement of herd on pasture*

Contract Risk

Exposure to risk: ____ Low ____ Medium ____ High

Type of risk: *Not applicable*

Tools to minimize risk:

Financial Risk

Exposure to risk: __x__ Low ____ Medium ____ High

Type of risk:

Tools for minimizing risk *Cash reserves or contingencies*

Personal Risk

Exposure to risk: __x__ Low ____ Medium ____ High

Type of risk: *Injury, illness*

Tools for minimizing risk:

TASK 2

Figure 29. Example from Cedar Summit Farm—Worksheet 2.17: Risk Management

support continue as the nation's population becomes more and more urban? Will government policies with regard to wages, environmental regulations, and reporting increase your costs? If your market depends on export demand, is there potential that either domestic political sanctions or foreign governmental actions will disrupt your sales?

As you put together your financial plans, you may want to "shock" your plans to see what would happen with a three percent increase in interest rates, a reduction of government support, or a five percent increase in your costs.

Whole Farm SWOT Analysis

You have now nearly completed a major task of your business plan. Having analyzed the history and current situation of your business with respect to marketing, operations, human resources and finances, you have assembled facts, figures and qualitative impressions about all aspects of your operation. Now you will use that information in an analysis of your *Strengths, Weaknesses, Opportunities and Threats*—a *SWOT analysis*. This can be helpful in defining and clarifying the issues you need to address in the rest of the business planning process.

Remember that in identifying strengths and weaknesses, you will be focusing on factors that are internal to your business. Opportunities and threats refer to the external environment for your business. As noted earlier, the strategy and implementation plan you develop will be shaped by both internal and external factors. Ideally, your business plan should help you build on and further develop your strengths, while minimizing the impacts of your weaknesses, if not eliminating them. At the same time, your plan needs to be responsive to the opportunities and threats your environment offers.

Use **Worksheet 2.18: Whole Farm SWOT Analysis** to summarize the most important strengths, weaknesses, opportunities and threats for your business. In completing their SWOT analysis, the Minar family identified their expertise in grass-based milk production and direct marketing skills, as well as their children's interest in returning to the farm, as major strengths. They considered the increase in urban development and rapidly growing demand for grass-based milk as major opportunities. On the other hand, they considered volatile commodity milk prices and the possibility that someone else would capture the local market for grass-based milk as the most important threats facing their business. The Minars considered the addition of a milk processing enterprise because it would build on their strengths in milk production and direct marketing, and the new enterprise would employ younger family members. It was a response to an attractive opportunity, but a quick response was needed to take advantage of that opportunity.

Worksheet 2.18 Whole Farm SWOT Analysis

Summarize the internal strengths and weaknesses and the external opportunities and threats for your business as it exists today. Consider all aspects of your business—marketing, operations, human resources and finances—as well as the links among these aspects.

	Internal Factors	External Factors
Strengths:	*Family members who want to work on farm*	
	Family has diversity of professional skills	
	Strong financial position	
	Location - close proximity to urban areas	
	Direct marketing experience	
Opportunities:		*Urban development*
		Increasing demand for safe, high-quality food products
		Evidence of local demand for home delivery
Weaknesses:	*Retirement*	
Threats:		*Volatile dairy market prices*
		Policy changes
		Increased regulation

TASK 2

Figure 30.
Example from Cedar Summit Farm—Worksheet 2.18: Whole Farm SWOT Analysis

Prepare the History and Current Situation Section of Your Business Plan

TASK 2

The history and current situation section of your business plan should draw on and summarize material from the Worksheets and exercises associated with this Planning Task. The content and style of this section will be influenced by the purpose of the planning process and by the audience for your plan. A suggested outline could follow that of this chapter as described below. If you decide not to include your value statement in your business plan (Planning Task One), this will be the first section of your business plan.

✔ Preparing the Current Situation Section of Your Business Plan

I. Values Statement (optional)

II. History and Current Situation

A. Brief History of Your Farming Operation

B. Assessing Your Current Situation

i. Marketing

ii. Operations

iii. Human Resources

iv. Finances

C. Whole Farm SWOT Analysis

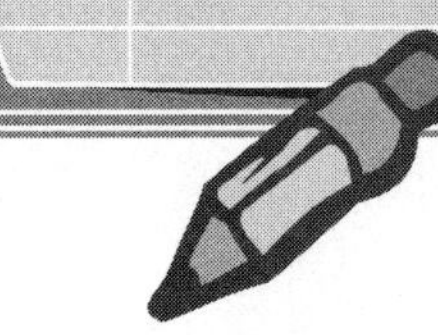

If your business plan is strictly for internal use, your description of the current situation may emphasize documenting key events in the history of your business. You can then assess how well your current business matches up with your personal values and aspirations, and make changes that address problems or take advantage of new opportunities. Recounting your history can help you clarify the issues that you face. It can also remind you, and others in your operation, of the reasons for making changes.

If your business plan will be used primarily as a proposal to lenders or outside investors, the current situation section of your business plan may be quite different. You may choose to use a less personal, more factual business history description in your actual business plan. This might still include a discussion of values, but there is likely to be more emphasis on providing quantitative information on operating efficiency, past financial performance, and the strength of the current financial position. In the Minars' plan, for example, there is a narrative section on history and current situation, but there are also major sections that present detailed data on past performance and the current financial position (see Appendix A).

Regardless of your purpose in developing a business plan and your intended audience, keep in mind that it's almost impossible to know where you are going in the future if you don't know where you are right now. As Ken Thomas says in *Developing a Longer-Range Strategic Farm Business Plan*, "Projecting the future without evaluating the past and present business situation can be difficult and potentially hazardous to the future of an individual farming career." (See "Resources.")

Worksheet 2.1 A Brief History of Our Farm Operation

Write a brief history describing the important events and decisions in your life and operation. Why did you make the choices you did? What have been the most important outcomes resulting from the interaction of your own choices and external circumstances? What key lessons have you learned? Include planning team members in this review. Use whatever time frame (one, five, ten years) best describes why and how you've arrived at your current business situation.

Worksheet 2.2 Current Market Assessment

Complete this worksheet for each of your major products or services. Be as specific as you can and, where relevant, include numeric facts and figures. These will be the basis for projections you'll make later on for the strategies that you consider.

Product/Service: ______________________________

Markets Served: Geographic/Customer Segments
Answer the following questions for each major market segment (geographic and/or customer type) you serve. Use additional sheets if this product has more than three major market segments.

TASK 2

Segment	**1.** ____________	**2.** ____________	**3.** ____________
	____________	____________	____________
Potential Number of Customers	**a.** ________	**a.** ________	**a.** ________
Current Number of Customers	**b.** ________	**b.** ________	**b.** ________
Current Sales Volume	**c.** ________	**c.** ________	**c.** ________
Current Sales per Customer (c / b)	**d.** ________	**d.** ________	**d.** ________
Potential Sales Volume (a x d)	**e.** ________	**e.** ________	**e.** ________

Unique Characteristics
What are the unique features that distinguish this product or service? For which customer segments are they important? How easily can they be imitated by competitors?

Characteristic 1: ______________________________

Appeals to which segments? ______________________________

Easy for competitors to imitate? ____Yes ____ No

Characteristic 2: ______________________________

Appeals to which segments? ______________________________

Easy for competitors to imitate? ____Yes ____ No

Distribution
Describe the current distribution channels for this product.

Logistics: ______________________________

____

____

Market Locations: ______________________________

____

____

Market Intermediaries: ______________________________

____

Marketing Costs (transportation, labor, spoilage, price discounts for intermediaries):

____

____

____

____

CONTINUED

Pricing

What price do you receive for this product or service, and how does it compare to the price of a typical competitor? How much power do you have to set the price for this product or service? How sensitive is demand to price changes?

Typical Price and Price Range:

Price Relative to Competitor:

Our Power to Set Prices: _____ Low _____ Some _____ High

Demand Sensitivity to Price Changes: _____ Low _____ Some _____ High

Promotions

Describe the strategies you use to promote consumer awareness of this product or service. How effective are they in reaching your most important potential customers? How costly are they?

Changing Market Conditions

Describe important trends of the supply and demand side of the market for this product or service. Are there important new competitors or competing products? Is demand expanding?

Worksheet 2.3 Tangible Working Assets

Use this worksheet to describe the non-land physical assets used in your current farm operation. Be as specific as you can be about size, capacity and condition.

	ITEM	SIZE	CAPACITY	CONDITION	VALUE
Buildings/Permanent Structures					
Machinery and Equipment					
Livestock Equipment					
Breeding Livestock					

TASK 2

Worksheet 2.4 Institutional Considerations

Describe institutional factors that currently affect your ability to use and manage physical resources. Include any long-term leasing arrangements, conservation easements, permit requirements, legal restrictions, production or marketing contracts.

Long-term Leasing Arrangements for Real Estate
(specify whether items are leased in for your use or leased out for the use of others)

Long-term Agreements and Easements

Permit and Legal Restrictions
(specify the agency responsible for issuing permits, conditions and compliance factors, fees, and your ability to meet these conditions)

Long-term Production Contracts and Marketing Agreements

TASK 2

Worksheet 2.5 Describing Crop Production Systems

Complete this worksheet for each major crop enterprise. Be as specific and accurate as you can be, since this information will be the basis for projections you'll make later for the strategies that you consider.

Crop Enterprise: ____________________ Current Acreage: ____________

	Machinery Operations				Operating Input				Labor	
Month	Operation	Hrs/ Acre	Machine 1	Machine 2	Item	Quantity/ Acre	Units	Price/ Unit	Hrs/ Acre	Type

Worksheet 2.6 Describing Livestock Production Systems

Complete this worksheet for each major livestock enterprise. Be as specific and accurate as you can be, since this information will be the basis for projections you'll make later for the strategies that you consider. Specify diets on a separate sheet if appropriate.

Livestock/Poultry Production System: ____________________ Current Number of Units: ____________________

Month or Period	Facility Space Req.	Labor		Feed Required	Vet & Medications Items & Amounts	Machinery & Equipment Req.	Other Inputs
		Hours	Type				

TASK 2

Worksheet 2.7 Enterprise/Calendar Matrix

Summarize and combine your crop and livestock production systems in this calendar. Look for bottlenecks or conflicts in timing of operations.

	Hours/Month											
Enterprise and Tasks	**Jan**	**Feb**	**Mar**	**Apr**	**May**	**June**	**July**	**Aug**	**Sep**	**Oct**	**Nov**	**Dec**
Total Hrs/Month												

Worksheet 2.8 Human Resources Matrix

Use this worksheet to identify the people involved in your operations and the roles they play.

Person	Enterprise						

TASK 2

Worksheet 2.9 Assessing Worker Abilities and Needs

Use this worksheet to describe the experience, skills and goals of each member of your workforce. Then estimate your average cost for this person and consider where this person ideally fits into your operation.

Name and Current Position:

1. What is the person's background—experience and education?

2. What particular abilities does this person have?

3. What are this person's strengths and weaknesses?

4. What are the person's interests? What motivates them?

5. What are the person's own personal goals in life?

6. What are we currently paying this person ($/hour)?

7. Conclusion: Where might this person best fit in meeting our human resource needs?

Worksheet 2.10 Likely Changes in Our Human Resources Situation

Use this worksheet to describe likely changes in your human resources situation over the next year, five years or ten years.

Current Workforce: Will anyone who currently works in our operation be leaving for other work or for personal reasons? What activities/enterprises will this affect?

Future Workforce: Will any new people be joining our operation? What new knowledge and skills will they bring? Do we have enough physical and financial resources for them to be fully employed and appropriately paid?

Future Management: Do we foresee a change in the allocation of decision-making and management responsibilities?

Worksheet 2.11 Estimating Family Living Expenses and Income Needs

Use this worksheet as a guide for estimating your annual family living expenses and necessary income contribution from the farm business.

Family Living Expenses ($/year)		
Food and meals		______
Medical care and health insurance		______
Cash donations		______
Household supplies		______
Clothing		______
Personal care		______
Child / dependent care		______
Gifts		______
Education		______
Recreation		______
Utilities (household share)		______
Nonfarm vehicle operating expense		______
Household real estate taxes		______
Dwelling rent		______
Household repairs		______
Nonfarm interest		______
Life insurance payments		______
Other		______
Total cash family living expense		______
Family living from the farm		______
Total family living expenses	**(a)**	______
Other Nonfarm Expenditures		
Income taxes		______
Furnishings & appliances		______
Nonfarm vehicle purchases		______
Nonfarm real estate purchases		______
Other nonfarm capital purchases		______
Nonfarm savings & investments		______
Total other nonfarm expenditures	**(b)**	______
		______
Total cash family living investment & nonfarm capital purchases	**(c) = (a + b)**	______
Nonfarm income	**(d)**	______
Necessary contribution from farm business (net farm income)	**(c) – (d)**	______

TASK 2

Worksheet 2.12 Income Statement

Use this worksheet as a guide for constructing income statements for the past several years. Where possible, include itemized revenue and expense details. Suggested crop and livestock expense categories are listed in worksheets 2.5 and 2.6. You may want to use a computerized package such as FINPACK to collect and process the information needed for your income statement.

For the period beginning ____________________

and ending ______________________________

Gross farm income				________
Total cash operating expenses			–	________
Inventory changes				
Crops and feed (ending – beginning)	+/–	________		
Market livestock (ending – beginning)	+/–	________		
Accounts receivable (ending – beginning)	+/–	________		
Prepaid expenses and supplies (ending – beginning)	+/–	________		
Accounts payable (beginning – ending)	+/–	________		
Accrued interest (beginning - ending)	+/–	________		
Total inventory change			+/–	________
Depreciation			–	________
Net farm income from operations			=	________

TASK 2

Worksheet 2.13 Balance Sheet

Construct your current and historical balance sheets. Where possible, include itemized details under each asset and liability category. You may want to use a computerized package, such as FINPACK (see "Resources"), to collect and process the information needed for your Balance Sheet.

Balance Sheet Date ____________

Assets (in dollars)	Market Value	Cost Value
Current Farm Assets		
Cash and checking balance	______	______
Prepaid expenses & supplies	______	______
Growing crops	______	______
Accounts receivable	______	______
Hedging accounts	______	______
Crops and feed	______	______
Crops under government loan	______	______
Market livestock	______	______
Other current assets	______	______
Total Current Assets (a)	______	______
	______	______
Intermediate Farm Assets	______	______
Breeding livestock	______	______
Machinery and equipment	______	______
Other intermediate assets	______	______
Total Intermediate Assets (b)	______	______
	______	______
Long-term Farm Assets	______	______
Farm land	______	______
Buildings and improvements	______	______
Other long-term assets	______	______
Total Long-term Assets (c)	______	______
	______	______
Total Farm Assets (d) = (a + b + c)	______	______
	______	______
Nonfarm Assets (e)	______	______
	______	______
Total Assets (f) = (d + e)	______	______

Liabilities (in dollars)	Market Value	Cost Value
Current Farm Liabilities		
Accrued interest	______	______
Accounts payable & accrued expense	______	______
Current farm loans	______	______
Principal on CCC loans	______	______
Principal due on term loans	______	______
Total Current Farm Liabilities (g)	______	______
Intermediate Farm Liabilities (h)	______	______
Long-term Farm Liabilities (i)	______	______
Total Farm Liabilities (j) = (g + h + i)	______	______
Nonfarm Liabilities (k)	______	______
Total Liabilities (l) = (j + k)	______	______
Retained Earnings (m) = (f_2 – l)		______
Net Worth (n) = (f_1 – l)	______	
Market Valuation Equity (o) = (n – m)	______	

f_1 = Market Value of Total Assets

f_2 = Cost Value of Total Assets

Worksheet 2.14 Earned Net Worth Change Analysis

Use this worksheet to calculate your overall change in wealth earned from farm and nonfarm income after adjusting for living expenses and partner withdrawals.

For the period beginning ____________________ **and ending** ______________________

Net Farm Income		________
Nonfarm Income	+	________
Family Living/Partner Withdrawals	–	________
Income Taxes	–	________
Earned Net Worth Change	=	________

TASK 2

Worksheet 2.15 Financial Ratios Based on the Balance Sheet and Income Statement

TASK 2

Use information from your balance sheet and income statement to calculate the following ratios that measure liquidity, solvency, profitability, repayment capacity and efficiency.

Current Ratio:
This is a primary measure of liquidity used by most businesses.

Current Assets (Balance Sheet)		________
Current Liabilities (Balance Sheet)	÷	________
Current Ratio	=	________

A current ratio of 2:1, with two dollars of current assets for every dollar of current debt, is usually considered adequate. If your current ratio approaches 1:1, your ability to sustain your business during a financial downturn may be limited.

Debt to Asset Ratio:
This solvency measure is sometimes referred to as your percent in debt.

Total Liabilities (Balance Sheet)		________
Total Assets (Balance Sheet)	÷	________
Debt to Asset Ratio	=	________

When calculated based on the market value of your assets, a debt to asset ratio under 40% is usually considered comfortable; over 60% is usually considered vulnerable.

Rate of Return on Assets:
This profitability measure can be interpreted as the average interest rate being earned on the financial resources invested by you and lenders in your business. Adjust net farm income for the estimated opportunity cost of unpaid family labor to make your figures comparable to those for businesses that hire labor and management

Net Farm Income (Income Statement)		________
Interest Expense (Income Statement)	+	________
Opportunity Cost for Family Labor and Management (estimated)	–	________
Return on Assets	=	________
Total Farm Assets (Balance Sheet)	÷	________
Rate of Return on Assets	=	________

The amount you deduct for labor and management depends on your goals for how much income you feel you need from the farm. Since farming has not historically been a high return business, a rate of return greater than 5% (when assets are valued at market value) is usually considered adequate. Remember, though, if you are earning only 5% and paying interest at 10%, you may be headed for problems. You may be able to maintain this if your debt to asset ratio is low. But if you have substantial debt, you will need to set your profitability goals a bit higher.

Term Debt Coverage Ratio:
This measure of repayment capacity indicates whether your business is generating enough income to make principal and interest payments on intermediate and long term debt.

Gross Farm Income (Income Statement)		________
Cash Operating Expenses (Income Statement)	–	________
Scheduled Interest Payments on Intermediate and Long-term Debt (Income Statement)	+	________
Family Living Expenses and Taxes (from the Earned Net Worth Change Worksheet)	–	________
Funds Available for Debt Payments	=	________
Intermediate and Long-term Debt Payments	÷	________
Term Debt Coverage Ratio	=	________

A term debt coverage ratio of over 150%, meaning that you are producing $1.50 of income that is available for debt repayment for each $1.00 of scheduled debt repayment, is usually considered adequate.

Operating Expense Ratio:
This measure of overall efficiency indicates the percentage of business revenues that are available for family living expenses, debt repayment and new investments.

Cash Operating Expenses (Income Statement)		________
Interest Expense (Income Statement)	–	________
Gross Farm Income (Income Statement)	÷	________
Operating Expense Ratio	=	________

While thumb rules for the ratios listed above can be used across farm types and across industries, operating expenses will vary substantially from business to business and industry to industry. As a general guideline, most farm business strive to keep operating expenses under 70% of gross revenues. If you are operating a small farm that employs sustainable practices, your financial success probably depends on operating efficiency. In that case, you should probably strive to keep operating expenses below 60% of revenues. If you are involved in a retail business, sales volume might be more important to your bottom line than operating expense levels if cost of goods sold is included. In that case, a much higher operating expense ratio might be expected. So, this ratio is useful for internal tracking of your business, but not very useful for comparisons with other businesses.

Worksheet 2.16 Whole Farm Trend Analysis

Use the table below as a guide for doing a trend analysis for important measures of physical resources, operating efficiency, financial position and financial performance.

Year	______	______	______	______	______
Physical Resources					
Number of acres	______	______	______	______	______
Number of cows	______	______	______	______	______
Operating Efficiency					
Hay yield (tons/acre)	______	______	______	______	______
Milk per cow (lbs/year)	______	______	______	______	______
Financial Position					
Ending net worth	______	______	______	______	______
Current ratio	______	______	______	______	______
Debt to asset ratio	______	______	______	______	______
Term debt coverage ratio	______	______	______	______	______
Financial Performance					
Net farm income	______	______	______	______	______
Rate of return on assets	______	______	______	______	______
Labor and management earnings	______	______	______	______	______
Operating expense ratio	______	______	______	______	______

Worksheet 2.17 Risk Management

Briefly rank your business' exposure to production, environmental, market, contract, and personal risk. Then briefly describe how you currently manage for risk.

Market Risk

Exposure to risk: _____ Low _____ Medium _____ High

Type of risk: ________________________________

Tools for minimizing risk: ________________________________

____

____

Production Risk

Exposure to risk: _____ Low _____ Medium _____ High

Type of risk: ________________________________

Tools to minimize risk: ________________________________

____

____

Contract Risk

Exposure to risk: _____ Low _____ Medium _____ High

Type of risk: ________________________________

Tools to minimize risk: ________________________________

____

____

Financial Risk

Exposure to risk: _____ Low _____ Medium _____ High

Type of risk: ________________________________

Tools for minimizing risk ________________________________

____

____

Personal Risk

Exposure to risk: _____ Low _____ Medium _____ High

Type of risk: ________________________________

Tools for minimizing risk: ________________________________

____

____

Worksheet 2.18 Whole Farm SWOT Analysis

TASK 2

Summarize the internal strengths and weaknesses and the external opportunities and threats for your business as it exists today. Consider all aspects of your business—marketing, operations, human resources and finances—as well as the links among these aspects.

Internal Factors	External Factors

Strengths:

Opportunities:

Weaknesses:

Threats:

Vision, Mission and Goals–Where Do You Want to Go?

All of us do it—we dream. Whether from the seat of a tractor, while walking our pastures, or talking with family over coffee, we envision the future. This dreaming or visioning is critical to the business planning process. Visioning will help you identify the mission of your business—why it exists—and goals that will eventually form the basis of your business' strategic plan. These three components—vision, mission and goals—make up Planning Task Three.

This Planning Task should be rewarding. It is a chance to imagine your future and set goals based on any short-and long-term planning ideas that you have for your business. In the next chapter (Planning Task Four), you will research and evaluate your ideas to form a set of realistic business strategies. But for now, recall your values and dream a little as you work through developing a vision, mission statement and goals for your business. If you have participated in Whole Farm Planning, Holistic Management, or other workshops, you may have already gone through the visioning and goal setting process. Utilize any of this work and build on it in the questions and Worksheets that follow.

Planning Task Three

- ✔ Dream a vision for the future.
- ✔ Develop a mission statement.
- ✔ Set and prioritize goals.
- ✔ Prepare the Vision, Mission and Goals section of your Businesss Plan.

See pages 97–101 for a complete set of blank worksheets for Task Three.

To print a complete set of blank worksheets, go to ***www.misa.umn.edu/publications/bizplan.html***

Dream a Future Vision

You've chronicled a history and described your current business situation. Now it's time to sketch a future vision for your family and business. Your vision should paint a clear picture of how your business will function in the future, and incorporate personal values for family, community, the environment and income.

In the IntroductionWorksheet: Why Are You Developing a Business Plan? you identified a critical issue that motivated you to begin the business planning process. If you have ideas about how to address this issue, you should include it in your vision. For example, Dave and Florence Minar conceived of on-farm processing (prior to conducting any brainstorming or strategic planning) as a way to add value and jobs to their existing dairy business. This was their initial vision. It was the first idea that they researched and evaluated in Planning Task Four (Strategic Planning and Evaluation).

TASK 3

Figure 31. Envisioned Northwind Nursery and Orchard Map

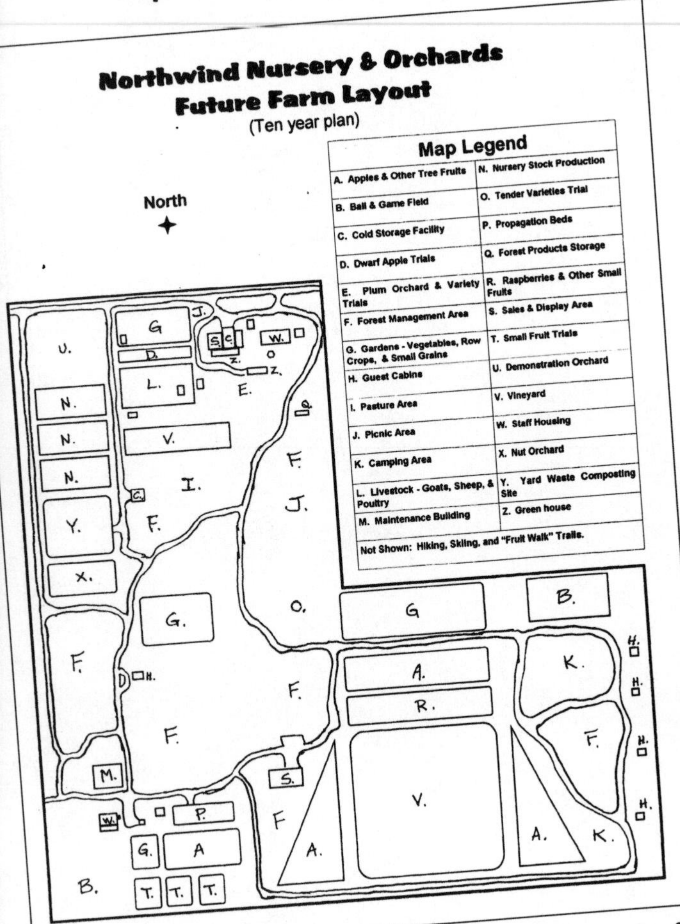

If you have identified a critical planning need but do not have clear ideas about how to address it, begin with a more personal vision for your business. Describe what role you would like to play in the business, what you will be doing. You'll have an opportunity to brainstorm specific marketing, operations, human resources and finance strategies in Planning Task Four.

Begin the visioning process with some brainstorming. Ask what your farm or business will look like in five, ten, or twenty-five years. For example, what product(s) and services will you produce? Will you be working with animals or crops? What will the landscape and community look like? What role will you play in the business? Will you be working alongside family? Will you earn all of your income from the farm? Will there be time for regular vacations?

Include your planning team and even nonteam members in the visioning process. Although Dave and Florence Minar were already considering the idea of on-farm processing, they invited 15 family members and friends from the non-farm community to their home for a visioning session. Family and friends were divided into four groups. Each group was asked to develop *"farm business ideas that will create jobs for the next generation of family members."* After an evening of brainstorming, each group came up with several new ideas ranging from the creation of a bed and breakfast/game farm to the purchase of a local creamery for ice cream production. Ultimately, the Minars rejected ideas that did not fit with their personal and environmental values, but they did incorporate the concept of ice cream production into their initial plan for on-farm dairy product processing.

There are many ways to communicate your future vision: as a story, a short paragraph, a picture or even a map like that created by Northwind Nursery and Orchard owner Frank Foltz. Frank Foltz and his family agreed as part of their vision to continue selling nursery stock and farm-grown fruit in the future, but noted in his plan that *"the most exciting concept we envision implementing is the experience of the farm itself."* The Foltz family drew two maps—one to reflect their current situation and one, like that shown in Figure 31, to reflect the service and tourism components of their envisioned nursery and orchard ten years from now, complete with guest cabins, a picnic area, a ball and game field, a demonstration orchard, and fruit trial areas as well as hiking, skiing and "fruit walk" trails.

Worksheet 3.1 Dreaming a Future Business Vision

Choose a timeframe from one, five to ten years (or more). Revisit your values if necessary. Next, develop a description of your business and personal future using some or all of the questions that follow. Or if you prefer, write a story, draw a map. Dream a little! Don't worry about the development of specific goals or action strategies—you will be setting goals and developing business strategies in the Worksheets and chapters that follow. For now, keep your vision fairly general and, if possible, address your critical planning need in some way. Remember—have each of your planning team members develop their own personal and business vision for the future. Most importantly, ask, What will our farm or business look like in one, five or ten years?

The future looks bright! Cedar Summit Farm is still a diversified livestock enterprise after ten years. We have listened to our customers and have adjusted our product line to suit their needs.

All of our products are sold at our farm store, farmers' markets, CSA's, church drop-off spots, food co-ops or delivered to homes and restaurants within a 25-mile radius of the farm. Included in our product line are a large variety of dairy and meat products.

The customer base at Cedar Summit Farm has grown to the point that we must ally with neighboring sustainable producers. The fact that the farm is almost totally surrounded by homes has played a part in this growth.

TASK 3

Figure 32.
Example from Cedar Summit Farm—Worksheet 3.1: Dreaming a Future Business Vision

Use the questions in **Worksheet 3.1: Dreaming a Future Business Vision** to begin developing a comprehensive future vision for your business. Be sure to involve your planning team members and remain open to new ideas. You may be surprised by what comes out of this process! Next, think about how you would like to share your vision with other family members, customers and potential investors and lenders—through a map, summary statement, story or list. Dave Minar's Worksheet for Cedar Summit Farm is reproduced as Figure 32.

Develop a Mission Statement

A mission statement rolls your values, current situation and vision into a set of guiding principles that describe your business. It serves as a benchmark for you and your partners while communicating how and why your business exists to customers and other community members outside your business. It is, what *Holistic Management* author Allan Savory calls a "statement of purpose."[6]

Your mission statement may include values and beliefs as well as a product, market, management and income description. Moreover, it should draw from your future vision by including an overview of the direction in which your business is headed. It should be general and short, like the mission statement prepared for Riverbend Farm by owner Greg Reynolds:

"The mission of this farming enterprise is to produce organic food that: is sold to local customers at a fair price; will provide us with enough income; will improve the soil, air and water quality on our farm; and is a vehicle to raise community awareness of sustainability and environmental issues."

Consider who will see your mission statement and bear this in mind as you write. For example, will you post your mission statement somewhere visible for customers to read like a label

Figure 33. Example from Cedar Summit Farm—Worksheet 3.2: Creating My Business Mission Statement

TASK 3

Worksheet 3.2 Creating My Business Mission Statement

Use the questions below to begin sketching a brief mission statement that communicates your values, management philosophy, and future vision. Remember to have each one of your planning team members complete this Worksheet. Then share your statements, discuss your similarities and differences, and draft a final mission statement. Going through this process as a team will generate more ideas and will result in a common mission statement that every one of your planning team members support. Try to limit your response to each of the questions so that, once combined, your mission statement does not exceed five to six sentences. Remember, write in the present tense and keep it positive.

I would like our business to be known for the following in the future:

Nutritious, fresh, clean food.

The internal and external purpose of my business is to:

Provide our children with jobs in agribusiness, finance our retirement, and keep agribusiness alive in our community.

Our business mission statement will communicate to:

Our mission statement will be posted at our farm stand and in our processing facility. It will also be printed on our labels and in all of our brochures.

Based on your answers above, write internal and external mission statements that communicate your business' purpose and the qualities for which you would like your business to be known:

Internal mission:

Our mission is to create a successful, fulfilling business that can support our children and ourselves financially while preserving the land and community around us.

External mission:

Our mission is to provide fresh, wholesome meat and dairy products to our growing community; to become the neighborhood farm.

6 *Holistic Management: A New Framework for Decision Making*, 2nd Ed., Savory and Butterfield, 1999.

or brochure? What would you like your business to be known for—a particular quality such as "old-fashioned" taste, environmental stewardship, competitive prices? If the mission will remain within the business, think about how it can be used to inspire and motivate future members of the business.

Draft a preliminary mission statement for your business. You will revisit this mission statement as you research, develop and evaluate business strategies for Planning Task Four. You can then make any necessary changes based on your research and strategic planning decisions. Limit your mission statement to five or six sentences and maintain a positive, active voice when writing. Think about these guidelines as you complete the statements in **Worksheet 3.2: Creating My Business Mission Statement**.

Set and Prioritize Goals

With a vision and mission in mind, you and your planning team are ready to begin the process of goal setting—that critical first step towards the development of a working strategic plan with measurable objectives.

Goal setting is important for all businesses—but it is especially important for family farms because they involve family. Clearly defined goals not only motivate and inspire, but they can also help mitigate conflict for families and help direct limited resources toward value-driven priorities.

Many lenders and other private institutions expect to see clearly identified goals as a part of a business plan. Lisa Gulbranson, author of *Organic Certification of Crop Production in Minnesota*, notes that "some [organic] certification agencies require that producers map out long-term goals and strategies"[7] as a part of their certification application. In this case, goal identification is not only a good idea, but is necessary.

What Are Goals?

Goals describe what you and your family would like to achieve—statements that point in the direction of your future vision for the business. They reflect the "what" and "who" pieces of your vision—what it is you would like to market, what the farm landscape will look like, who will be involved in operations, and what you intend to earn from the business. Goals *do not* describe the "how" components of your business—how you plan to market and price a product, purchase equipment, staff the operation, etc. You will draft and test these "how to" strategy ideas in Planning Task Four.

7 *Organic Certification of Crop Production in Minnesota*, Gulbranson, 2001 (revised).

TASK 3

Author Ron Macher notes that goals come in all shapes and sizes. "There are personal goals, family goals, business goals, community goals and environmental goals. A family goal," he explains, "might be to develop a system of farming that allows you to spend more time with your children. A personal goal might be to have enough farm income to quit your town job and farm full-time. A business goal might be to achieve a 20 percent return on your total investment."[8]

Business goals can be broken down further into marketing, operations, human resources and finance objectives. As an existing business owner, for instance, you may have very specific goals for each functional area of the business—specific sales targets, workload limits, or profit objectives.

While these business goals will be unique to your business and personal values, one goal that is common to most business owners is some level of financial success. Although financial success may not be the most important goal of your farm business, it is usually in the mix. It is often very difficult to reach other personal, environmental, economic and community goals unless you reach a certain level of financial success.

Financial success can have many meanings. For one operator, it might mean making moderate financial progress or just breaking even while meeting other personal, business, and community goals. For someone else, it may not even be necessary to break even if there is another source of income to subsidize the farm. For another, the financial goal may be to make enough money to retire at age 60. There is no right or wrong—your goals should just reflect your personal values and be consistent with your own future vision.

As you sketch goals, think about your family's desired standard of living. Estimate your future family living expenses using your current expenses (Worksheet 2.11: Family Living Expenses) as a starting point. Then factor in any quality of life changes that you foresee in the next two to ten years, such as the need to pay for college tuition, home improvements, retirement or travel as expressed by Dancing Winds Farm Owner Mary Doerr. Alternatively, if you are happy with your current standard of living, one of your goals might be to maintain current spending levels during the start-up phase of a new business enterprise. Be specific about how much income you will withdraw from the business annually to meet family or household living expenses. Will it supply all of your family living needs or only a portion? **Worksheet 3.3: Estimating Our Family's Goal for Profit** will help you estimate your family's future family living expenses and goals for financial success.

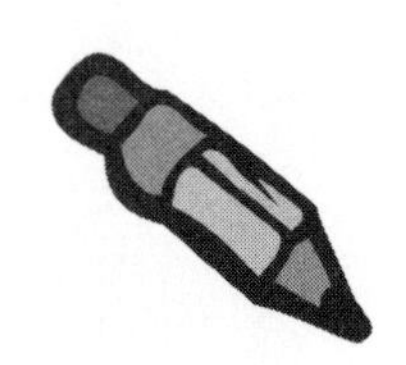

Regardless of what your goals are and how you choose to organize them, planning and goal setting can be made easier by defining a timeframe for each goal. The most common timeframes used for goals are a short-term horizon of one to five years, an intermediate horizon of five to ten years, and a long-term horizon of ten years or more. Look at the Minars' goals (Worksheet 3.4, Figure

8 *Making Your Small Farm Profitable*, Your Goals and Farm Planning, Macher and Kerr Jr., 1999.

34) to get a feel for how these timeframes might be used. They combined personal goals for the community and environment with marketing, human resources and finance goals for the business. All of these goals, however, were broken out into short, intermediate and long-term timeframes.

Worksheet 3.4 Identifying Our Family Business Goals

Have each member of your planning team draft personal goals as well as one or more short-term and long-term goals for each functional management area of your business.

Short-term Goals (1-5 years)

—Process products on the farm.

—Market a wide range of high quality, differentiated dairy and meat products.

—Improve the landscape and local environment.

—Provide at least three full-time jobs for our two sons and daughter.

—Generate enough profit from the business in year one to cover expenses, including all of our children's salaries.

—Support the local community.

Intermediate Goals (5-10 years)

—Reduce year-to-year income fluctuations (reliance on commodity prices).

—Reduce debt.

Long-term Goals (10 Years +)

—Provide employment for any family member who desires to work in the business.

—Transfer the farm business to our children.

—Begin drawing retirement income from the business.

—Create franchise opportunities for other farmers.

Figure 34. Example from Cedar Summit Farm—Worksheet 3.4: Identifying Our Family Business Goals

TASK 3

Long-time business owner, Frank Foltz of Northwind Nursery and Orchards, outlined the following short and long-term goals for his business:

"Our immediate, short-term goal is to make a smooth transition from our current two-pronged (mail order and local) marketing approach to marketing entirely in our local community. While the mail order business has been profitable and offers much more opportunity for expansion, we feel the "local only" sales approach fits more with the values and mission of our business. . . . Therefore, we would like to sell the mail order portion of our business to a like-minded individual or family and begin a process of transition. This will eliminate a portion of our income and a portion of our workload. . . . The lighter workload will enable us to initiate our next goal of a community-oriented nursery fruit farm and sustainable agriculture research facility where customers (community members) come to purchase products, learn how to grow their own fruit, and 'experience' a working farm. A long-term goal is to help other interested families establish their own small-scale, sustainable, agricultural enterprises, thus encouraging the restoration of the family farm and the revitalization of our rural communities."

Frank's task of creating specific goals was made easier by the fact that he has owned and operated his business for seventeen years. However, if you are just starting out or considering an entirely new business venture, your goals may be a little more general and personal in nature like those drafted by organic wheat producer Mabel Brelje:

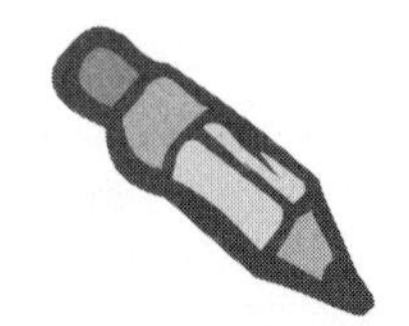

"Prior to 1998, my short-term goal was to convert my farm to organic standard, which has been accomplished. Currently, my short-term goals include sharecropping to overcome ongoing labor and equipment deficiencies while working toward my longer term goal—to sell the farm to a family or organization who will continue to manage it organically and maintain it as a showplace . . . Once the farm sale is complete, I intend to remain active as a consultant and to pursue another lifelong goal: writing."

Figure 35.
Group Goal Setting—Reconciling Different Goals

"A question that arises is how business owners can reconcile their different goals. The individuals that ask this question have already set their own goals and shared them with their family and co-owners. It is at this point in the process that they realize there are differences that need to be resolved. One observation in answering this question is that the goals of family members and co-owners do not need to, and never will, be identical. It is not reasonable to strive to establish one set of goals that fits everyone.

Yet goals cannot be so divergent that there is nothing in common. Instead, group members should strive to find commonalities among their goals and opportunities to work together to accomplish tasks that fulfill goals of several individuals. For example, there may be an activity that fulfills goals for several people even though they are different goals. The key to working out differences among goals appears to be communication and willingness to cooperate." [10]

You may use **Worksheet 3.4: Identifying Our Family Business Goals** to spell out your family's goals.

With these goal-setting ideas in mind, you are ready to:
- Write out individual goals
- Identify common goals
- Prioritize goals

Write Out Goals.

As an experienced business owner or as a far-sighted entrepreneur, you may have very clear goals and objectives for each component of your business. Or, instead you may choose to develop personal, economic, community and environmental goals. It's up to you. The main idea is to get your goals, whatever they may be, down on paper. Written goals will give you "checkpoints" to follow—something to revisit as you evaluate strategic alternatives (Planning Task Four) and monitor your plan following implementation (Planning Task Five).

Identify Common Goals.

Once you and your planning team members have identified goals individually, you should take time to discuss and share them with your planning team. This will enable you to identify common goals, recognize differences, and establish a set of collective priorities for the family and business. "Do not ignore potential conflicts or restrictions that might prevent reaching goals. Identifying possible problems in the planning stage will allow time to resolve conflicts," explains Extension educator Damona Doye. [9]

Figure 35 describes a few guidelines for group goal setting. If you are having trouble reconciling different goals, mediation services are available to facilitate family discussions. Contact the U.S. Department of Agriculture (USDA) Farm Service Agency or your local extension service for more information about certified mediators (www.fsa.usda.gov/pas/publications/facts/html/mediate01.htm).

9 *Goal Setting for Farm and Ranch Families*, Doye, 2001.

10 *Business Planning for Your Farm—Setting Personal and Business Goals*, Saxowsky, et al., 1995.

Prioritize Goals.

Once you are comfortable with the collective business goals identified by you and your planning team, you are ready to begin prioritizing. Few businesses or families have enough resources to reach all of their goals at one time. Prioritized goals "provide clear guidelines for management decisions."[11]

For example, Riverbend Farm owner Greg Reynolds' goal, *"to take a couple of weeks off in the summer,"* may seem modest, but it is one that he and his family identified as a priority. Summer is typically the busiest time of year for Riverbend Farm since it specializes in vegetable production and Greg rarely has time away from the business during this season. Therefore, Greg's business strategy—to hire additional labor—was built around his critical planning need (labor shortages) and one of his top goals (to have time off during the summer).

Worksheet 3.5 Prioritizing Goals

Use the questions below to prioritize goals for your family and business. Remember high priority goals need not receive all of your attention and resources; priorities are not permanent. Simply use this worksheet as a starting point for family discussions and planning in the chapters to come.

(A) Which goals are most important for family well-being and for business success?

Our goals to provide employment, improve the landscape, reduce debt, and control income fluctuations are all important for our family's well-being. Goals to process on the farm, market top-quality dairy products, support the local community, improve the landscape, and mitigate price fluctuations, are all important for the business to succeed.

(B) Which short-term goals, if attained, would help you achieve long-term goals?

If we build the processing plant and are able to secure markets for our products, all of our other goals become possible.

(C) Which short-term goals conflict with or impede your long-term goals?

Our goal of processing on the farm will prevent us from reducing our debt load in the short-run - in fact, we will have to take on more debt to reach this goal. In the long run, however, we hope that by processing on the farm and building markets, we will be able to reduce our overall debt load from current levels while accomplishing other long-term goals that are a priority for our family.

(D) Which goals are so important that they should be attained even if it prevents you from reaching other goals?

Doesn't really apply to us.

(E) List your top five goals by priority.

1. *Provide employment for any family member who wishes to join the operation.*
2. *Reduce income fluctuations and/or reliance on milk commodity prices.*
3. *Process on the farm - add value.*
4. *Market fresh, top-quality meat and dairy products.*
5. *Support the local community.*

Figure 36. Example from Cedar Summit Farm—Worksheet 3.5: Prioritizing Goals

TASK 3

This task of prioritizing your goals won't necessarily be easy since many goals may overlap or conflict. The Minars, for example (Figure 36), envisioned building a processing plant in order to reach their family goals. This idea, however, conflicted with a financial goal to reduce their debt load.

The idea here is to identify which goals are *most* important to your family and for your business—to determine which goals are worth pursuing even if they prevent you from reaching other goals. **Worksheet 3.5: Prioritizing Goals** includes questions to help you with this task.

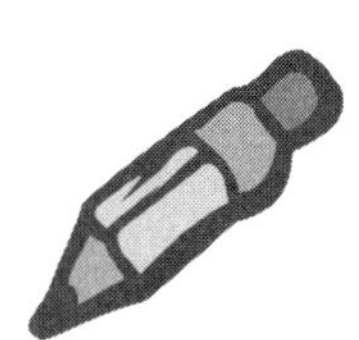

[11] *Goal Setting for Farm and Ranch Families*, Doye, 2001.

Prepare the Vision, Mission and Goals Section of Your Business Plan

Your vision, mission and goals statements are likely to change as you conduct research and develop an overall business strategy in Planning Task Four (Strategic Planning and Evaluation). The Minars, for example, spent weeks on their initial visioning process. However, after analyzing the feasibility of on-farm processing and deciding to implement this strategy, they ultimately chose to include only a short statement about the business component of their vision: *"Our vision is to process and direct market all of our milk and meat products. We would like to help other farmers direct market their own products, possibly by creating a franchise for milk processing plants."*

TASK 3

Your draft business plan might include the elements shown here.

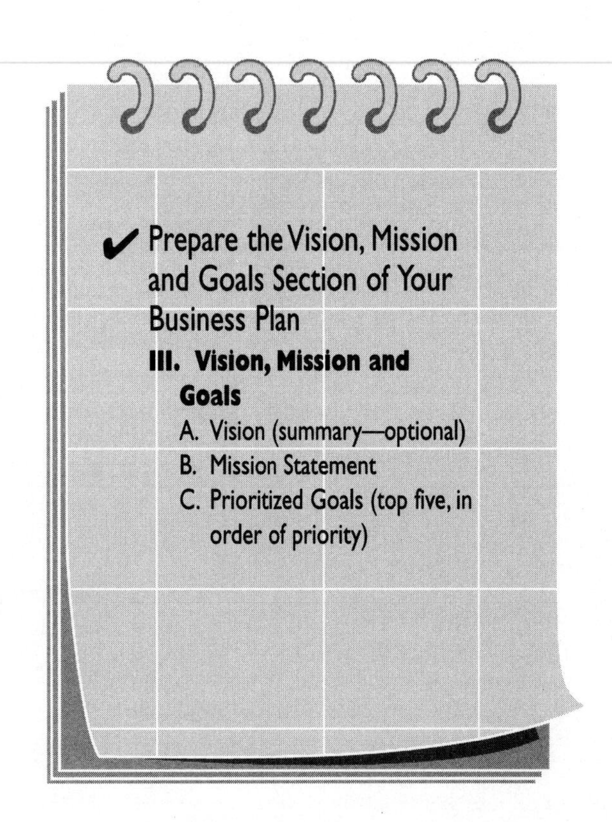

Worksheet 3.1 Dreaming a Future Business Vision

Choose a timeframe from one, five to ten years (or more). Revisit your values if necessary. Next, develop a description of your business and personal future using some or all of the questions that follow. Or if you prefer, write a story, draw a map. Dream a little! Don't worry about the development of specific goals or action strategies—you will be setting goals and developing business strategies in the Worksheets and chapters that follow. For now, keep your vision fairly general and, if possible, address your critical planning need in some way. Remember—have each of your planning team members develop their own personal and business vision for the future. Most importantly, ask, What will our farm or business look like in one, five or ten years?

Worksheet 3.2 Creating My Business Mission Statement

Use the questions below to begin sketching a brief mission statement that communicates your values, management philosophy, and future vision. Remember to have each one of your planning team members complete this Worksheet. Then share your statements, discuss your similarities and differences, and draft a final mission statement. Going through this process as a team will generate more ideas and will result in a common mission statement that every one of your planning team members support. Try to limit your response to each of the questions so that, once combined, your mission statement does not exceed five to six sentences. Remember, write in the present tense and keep it positive.

I would like our business to be known for the following in the future:

TASK 3

The internal and external purpose of my business is to:

Our business mission statement will communicate to:

Based on your answers above, write internal and external mission statements that communicate your business' purpose and the qualities for which you would like your business to be known:

Internal mission:

External mission:

Worksheet 3.3 Estimating Our Family's Goal for Profit

Estimate future family expenses—family living, education, retirement and vacation expenses—to determine your minimum income ("necessary contribution") from the business. It may be easiest to work from your current expenses (Worksheet 2.9) when estimating future expenses.

Family Living Expenses ($/year)		Current	Future
Food and meals		________	________
Medical care and health insurance		________	________
Cash donations		________	________
Household supplies		________	________
Clothing		________	________
Personal care		________	________
Child / dependent care		________	________
Gifts		________	________
Education		________	________
Recreation		________	________
Utilities (household share)		________	________
Nonfarm vehicle operating expense		________	________
Household real estate taxes		________	________
Dwelling rent		________	________
Household repairs		________	________
Nonfarm interest		________	________
Life insurance payments		________	________
Other		________	________
Total cash family living expense		________	________
Family living from the farm		________	________
Total family living expenses	**(a)**	________	________
Other Nonfarm Expenditures			
Income taxes		________	________
Furnishings & appliances		________	________
Nonfarm vehicle purchases		________	________
Nonfarm real estate purchases		________	________
Other nonfarm capital purchases		________	________
Nonfarm savings & investments		________	________
Total other nonfarm expenditures	**(b)**	________	________
		________	________
Total cash family living investment & nonfarm capital purchases	**(c) = (a + b)**	________	________
Nonfarm income	**(d)**	________	________
Necessary contribution from farm business (net farm income)	**(c) – (d)**	________	________

TASK 3

Worksheet 3.4 Identifying Our Family Business Goals

Have each member of your planning team draft personal goals as well as one or more short-term and long-term goals for each functional management area of your business.

Short-term Goals (1-5 years)

Intermediate Goals (5-10 years)

Long-term Goals (10 Years +)

TASK 3

Worksheet 3.5 Prioritizing Goals

Use the questions below to prioritize goals for your family and business. Remember high priority goals need not receive all of your attention and resources; priorities are not permanent. Simply use this worksheet as a starting point for family discussions and planning in the chapters to come.

(A) Which goals are most important for family well-being and for business success?

(B) Which short-term goals, if attained, would help you achieve long-term goals?

(C) Which short-term goals conflict with or impede your long-term goals?

(D) Which goals are so important that they should be attained even if it prevents you from reaching other goals?

(E) List your top five goals by priority.

1.

2.

3.

4.

5.

TASK 3

TASK

3

PLANNING TASK FOUR

Strategic Planning and Evaluation—What Routes Can You Take to Get Where You Want to Go?

Strategy is defined as a "careful plan or method for achieving an end." That's your challenge in this Planning Task. You've envisioned your future, based on your goals and values, so you know what you want the "end" to look like. Now you need to take the time to carefully think through the steps you can take to get there. Think about planning a trip. You know your destination—but what's the best way to get there? You could fly, take a train, or drive. You might sketch out the trip for each possibility, by researching the plane and train schedules and consulting roadmaps. You develop a "careful plan." Then you evaluate. You weigh many factors—the cost of each, your enjoyment using each of those means, possible problems such as road construction, delays at airports, and so forth. Then you choose the best option for you. Essentially, that is what you will be doing in the five steps of this Planning Task. Developing a plan to achieve your envisioned business, weighing it against other options, considering how the situation might change (market, interest rates, labor, etc.), and how that would affect your plan.

Dave and Florence Minar defined very specific personal, family, and business goals for Cedar Summit Farm. Their goals

Planning Task Four

✔ Develop a business strategy:

Marketing Strategy
- Markets
- Product
- Competition
- Distribution and Packaging
- Pricing
- Promotion
- Inventory and Management
- Develop a Strategic Marketing Plan

Operations Strategy
- Production Management
- Regulations and Policy
- Resource Needs
- Resource Gaps
- Size and Capacity
- Develop a Strategic Operations Plan

Human Resources Strategy
- Labor Needs
- Labor Gaps
- Compensation
- Management and Communications
- Develop a Strategic Human Resources Plan

Financial Strategy
- Risk
- Organizational Structure
- Finance
- Develop a Strategic Financial Plan

Whole Farm Strategy

✔ Evaluate Strategic Alternatives:

Long Term Evaluation
- Profitability
- Liquidity
- Solvency
- Risk

Transition Period Evaluation

✔ Choose the best whole farm strategy

✔ Develop contingency plans

✔ Develop the Strategic Planning section of your Business Plan

See pages 186–231 for a complete set of blank worksheets for Task Four.

To print a complete set of blank worksheets, go to ***www.misa.umn.edu/publications/bizplan.html***

are tied to a set of values concerning family, environment and community that have grown through time. Their challenge in this Planning Task was to develop a whole farm strategy that, over a course of five, ten or more years, would live up to their values—a strategy that would move them toward their goals, by taking advantage of current business strengths and perceived market opportunities. The process of developing their strategic plan was not easy or quick. They spent hours identifying alternatives in each of the four management areas (marketing, operations, human resources, finance), evaluating them, and finally, deciding which group of strategies would best move them toward their vision. That, in a nutshell, is the strategic planning process—the fourth and perhaps most important Planning Task.

If you have completed the Worksheets for the preceding Planning Tasks, then you have already laid the foundation for strategic planning. You have chronicled the history of your farm, evaluated your business' current strengths and weaknesses and, most importantly, identified a vision for your family and business as well as specific goals. Your job in Planning Task Four is to begin building a whole farm strategic plan for your future on top of that foundation.

In Planning Task Four you will:

- Develop a business strategy.
- Evaluate strategic alternatives.
- Decide on a whole farm strategic course of action.
- Develop contingency plans.
- Develop the strategic section of your business plan.

Business strategies are realistic actions that communicate how you plan to reach your goals.

Business strategies are realistic actions that communicate how you plan to reach your goals. There are an endless number of potential strategies that can be developed for each functional area of the business or the farm as a whole. Your task will be to narrow the list of possibilities to those marketing, operations, human resources and financial strategies that best address your critical planning needs, and are compatible with your values, vision and goals. A simple rule of thumb to follow when developing strategies is to take advantage of your business' internal strengths. "A farm's strategy ought to be grounded in what it is good at doing (i.e., its strengths and competitive capabilities)."[12]

Where does strategic planning begin? Presumably, you already have a strategy or idea in mind for reaching your goals and addressing the critical planning needs identified in the Introduction Worksheet: Why are You Developing a Business Plan? Perhaps your business idea involves adding a new product or product value, diversifying income, adopting a new management system, or simply shifting workloads within the family. As with all of these examples, your whole farm strategy may be rooted in one functional area (marketing, operations, human resources, finance).

12 *A Strategic Management Primer for Farmers*, Olson, 2001.

Your business situation will be unique. Therefore, it is up to you to decide in what order you want to tackle the functional areas as you develop a business plan, the first step in Planning Task Four. As you work through this section, the need to develop strategies in all four functional areas will become clear. You may begin your strategy development in one area, such as finance, and find it necessary to answer questions about operations before settling on a finance strategy. Work through this section in a way that makes sense for you.

Begin your strategy research and development with the functional area (marketing, operations, human resources, finance) that most clearly addresses your critical planning need.

However, we suggest beginning your strategy research and development with the functional area that most clearly addresses your critical planning need or whole farm strategy idea. Then move on to the other functional areas. Dave and Florence Minar began their strategy research with human resources. They took a look at how on-farm processing might address their critical planning need to provide new jobs and income for family members. They then studied the market to gauge sales potential and competition while simultaneously researching equipment options and processing capacity. The last thing they developed was a financial strategy.

As you research and develop your business strategies, you will consider many of the same marketing, operations, human resources and finance questions that you first considered when you assessed your current situation in Planning Task Two. This time around involves more research. You will answer these same questions, using educated guesses rather than actual experience. You will need to learn more about potential customers, competitor prices, and resource needs while making projections about sales volume, labor and capital needs, input expenses, cash flow, and profitability. Ultimately, your research, projections, and evaluation should point to the most promising whole farm strategy alternative.

Once you have identified a set of feasible strategic alternatives for each functional area of the business through research and evaluation, you will link them together into a system-wide, whole farm business strategy complete with a contingency and implementation plan. When you are done with this Planning Task you should be ready to draft your business plan.

This is a very involved Planning Task—take your time. Most importantly, consult planning team members and get outside help when you need it. Don't expect to be an expert on everything (marketing, operations, people management, legal issues, financial analysis), particularly when researching a new idea. The Minars created a board of advisors, in addition to planning team members, to help them identify and evaluate strategic marketing and operations alternatives. Their advisors included a local banker, farm business management consultant, meat processor, clients, and other farmers. Consult the "Resources"

Gigi DiGiacomo

Dave and Florence Minar seated at the kitchen table with FBM consultant Ira Beckman

section at the end of this Guide for assistance in locating outside help whenever and wherever you need it.

Because each business is unique, every strategic need cannot be addressed in this Guide. Clearly, most of your strategy work will take place in person with your planning team members. Worksheets are provided to help you flesh out and record the details of your business strategy alternatives.

TASK 4

Develop a Business Strategy

This first step in your strategic plan, Develop a Business Strategy, is where you'll spend the majority of your time and effort for this Planning Task. You will consider all four functional areas, and you'll consider many variables within each of those areas. We'll remind you of where you are in the process from time to time. In the sections that follow, you will have the opportunity to identify and research alternative strategies for each functional area of the business—marketing, operations, human resources and finances. Begin by returning to your Whole Farm SWOT Analysis (Worksheet 2.18) to review the internal strengths of your present business and any perceived industry opportunities, as well as the internal weaknesses and external business threats you and your planning team identified. Good business strategies always take advantage of current business strengths and market opportunities. At the same time, a solid business strategy will address current weaknesses and perceived threats. With your SWOT Analysis in hand, you are ready to begin developing specific marketing, operations, human resources and finance strategies for the business.

The Four Key Management Areas:

- **Marketing**
- Operations
- Human Resources
- Finance

Marketing Strategy

The marketing component of your business strategy will determine, in large part, the success of your business. As marketing consultant Barbara Findlay Schenck said: "Without customers, a business is out of business."[13] Your marketing strategy is about defining your customer or target market and

[13] *Small Business Marketing for Dummies*, Schenck, 2001.

ailoring your product, pricing, distribution and promotion strategies to satisfy hat target market. Marketing experts warn that businesses that are product riented—those that try to sell what they can produce without first looking at ustomers' needs—risk developing a product that won't sell. Instead, most uccessful businesses are customer oriented—they design marketing strategies round the needs of their customers.

At the end of this step, you should be able to confidently answer the following questions:

- **Markets:** Who are our target customers and what do they value?
- **Product:** What product will we offer and how is it unique?
- **Competition:** Who are our competitors and how will we position ourselves?
- **Distribution and packaging:** How and when will we move our product to market?
- **Prices:** How will we price our product?
- **Promotion:** How and what will we communicate with buyers or customers?

To complete the Marketing segment of the Develop a Business Strategy step, you will address he issues shown at right.

As you begin your research, track any xpenses associated with the marketing strategies hat you develop. You will be asked to record this nformation in your Marketing Strategy Summary Worksheet 4.9).

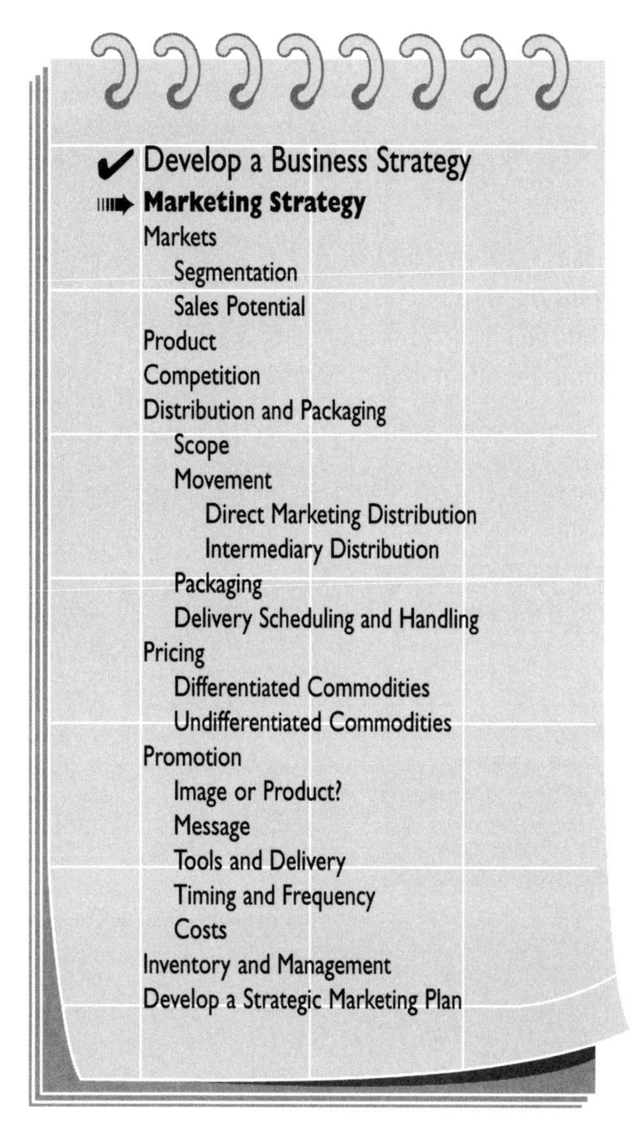

TASK 4

Markets: Who are our target customers and what do they value?

Most marketing plans begin with a description of the business' target market, or its potential customers. Your first task in building a customer strategy is to identify your target market. Target markets are most commonly characterized as either individual households or businesses.

Direct marketing to individual households or customers can be performed on a small scale. This form of marketing tends to be more profitable than business-to-business marketing because of value-added opportunities and the lack of middlemen. Most direct market products are consumer goods or services. Popular direct market opportunities include Community Supported Agriculture (CSA), Pick Your Own (PYO) and farmers' markets.

Business-to-business marketing typically involves sales of a raw commodity or product that will be used as an input. Traditional commodity producers almost always practice business-to-business marketing where customers include grain companies, processors, packers and millers. Today's specialty or differentiated commodity producers, however, are learning to build in more profit by responding directly to market demand for unique products, such as tofu grade soybeans, high oil corn, grass-fed livestock, organic feed, and heirloom vegetables. Don't overlook today's business-to-business opportunities to contract and market specialty commodities.

Figure 37.
Market Segmentation Alternatives [15]

Geographic:
Segmenting customers by regions, counties, states, countries, zip codes and census tracts.

Demographics:
Segmenting customers into groups based on age, sex, race, religion, education, marital status, income and household size.

Psychographics:
Segmenting customers by lifestyle characteristics, behavioral patterns, beliefs and values, attitudes about themselves, their families and society.

TASK 4

That said, if you plan to market a raw commodity directly to an elevator, packer or overseas broker, your marketing strategy will be very different (and presumably less intensive) than that of someone who is looking at direct marketing a differentiated product to a well-defined market of individual customers.

In order to fully define your target market and corresponding customer strategy, you will need to identify your target market segment (who your customers are and what they value) and sales potential (how much they are willing to buy). This research is critical for building your business. Marketing author Michael O'Donnell notes that one of the most common planning mistakes is failure to fully "understand the market makeup and what segment the company will concentrate on." [14]

Segmentation. Dave and Florence Minar identified "individuals" (as opposed to other businesses) as their target market for Cedar Summit Farm dairy products. This target market was very different from their customer, Davisco,

14 *The Marketing Plan: Step-by-Step*, O'Donnell, 1991.

15 *Small Business Marketing for Dummies*, Schenck, 2001.

which acted as a distribution intermediary by purchasing bulk milk for further processing. Consequently, when the Minars began the planning process, they had to conduct substantial research to learn about their new target market size, geographic location, purchasing patterns and preferences.

This process of identifying customers' preferences and dividing the larger target market into submarkets is called market segmentation. By identifying and targeting specific market segments you should be able to develop more effective packaging, price and promotion strategies.[16] Markets can be segmented in a variety of ways. The most common forms of segmentation are by demographic, geographic, psychographic and product-use characteristics.

For instance, a market can be segmented into domestic and international subgroups if you are planning to market organic soybeans like Mabel Brelje; or into on-farm and off-farm buyer groups for gourmet cheese like Dancing Winds Farm owner Mary Doerr. Your market can also be segmented by the frequency of customer purchases, as considered by Riverbend Farm owner Greg Reynolds for weekly versus monthly vegetable customers.

Dave and Florence Minar divided their target market for bottled milk into two major groups by distribution channel, home delivery and retail customers (see Worksheet 4.1). In an effort to learn about their potential home delivery customers, the Minars surveyed 75 New Prague residents about their preferences for flavored milk, weekly milk consumption, and overall interest in home delivery. Based on this research, they developed a customer profile for New Prague home delivery customers.

Like the Minars, begin your target market research by developing a customer profile. Customer profiles can help you determine if a market segment is large enough to be profitable. Break your target market up into segments based on differences in their geographic location, demographic characteristics, social class, personality, buying behavior or

Figure 38.
Cedar Summit Farm Marketing Survey, May, 2001

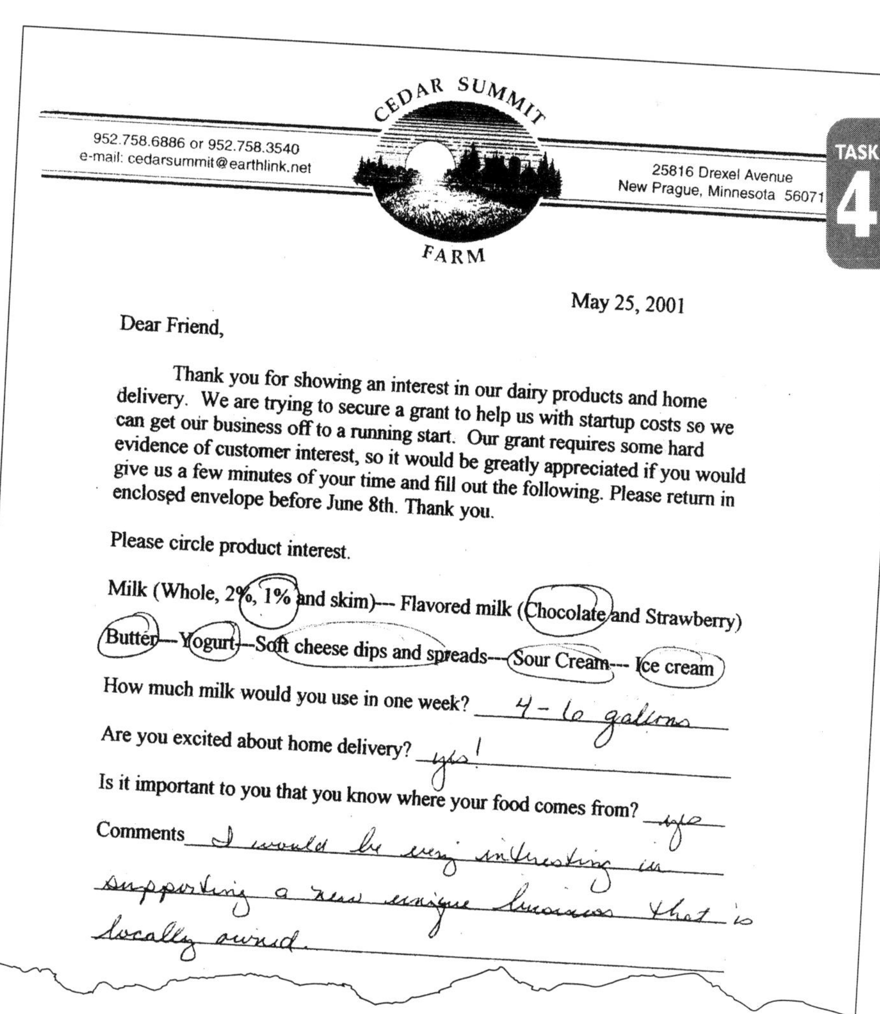

CEDAR SUMMIT FARM

952.758.6886 or 952.758.3540
e-mail: cedarsummit@earthlink.net

25816 Drexel Avenue
New Prague, Minnesota 56071

May 25, 2001

Dear Friend,

Thank you for showing an interest in our dairy products and home delivery. We are trying to secure a grant to help us with startup costs so we can get our business off to a running start. Our grant requires some hard evidence of customer interest, so it would be greatly appreciated if you would give us a few minutes of your time and fill out the following. Please return in enclosed envelope before June 8th. Thank you.

Please circle product interest.

Milk (Whole, 2%, 1% and skim)--- Flavored milk (Chocolate and Strawberry)
Butter---Yogurt---Soft cheese dips and spreads---Sour Cream--- Ice cream

How much milk would you use in one week? 4-6 gallons

Are you excited about home delivery? yes!

Is it important to you that you know where your food comes from? yes

Comments I would be very interesting in supporting a new unique business that is locally owned.

TASK 4

[16] *Finding Customers: Market Segmentation*, Bull and Passewitz, 1994.

Worksheet 4.1 Customer Segmentation

Complete this Worksheet for each major product you plan to produce. Develop a profile of the customer(s) you intend to target by market segment. Note the geographic, demographic, and psychographic characteristics of each segment. Be sure to describe your customers' needs and preferences and what they value. Use additional sheets of paper if this product has more than three major market segments.

Product: *Bottled Milk*

Customer Segment:	1 *Home delivery customers*	2 *Retail customers*	3
Geographic	*New Prague community*	*Twin Cities Metro and New Prague communities*	
Demographic	*Elderly and families with young children*	*Upper, middle class*	
Psychographic	*Health conscious*	*Health conscious*	
Needs/Preferences	*"Old fashioned," safe, healthy products*	*Healthy, high-quality, local products*	

Figure 39. Example from Cedar Summit Farm—Worksheet 4.1: Customer Segmentation

benefits sought. Use **Worksheet 4.1: Customer Segmentation** to help you develop and research customer profiles.

Sales potential. If you plan to produce and market a traditional bulk commodity, you won't have much trouble calculating sales potential. The market for undifferentiated commodities is fluid and can typically absorb all that you produce (albeit at a lower price sometimes). Estimating sales potential becomes more challenging and important when tapping into a specialty commodity market (such as lentils) that may have limited demand, or when your target market is highly sought after and made up of individual households.

As a specialty commodity producer, your customer (usually another business) will make known how much they are willing to buy short-term (one to two years) either through a written contract or verbal agreement. Projecting long-term sales potential may prove more difficult as these markets are usually immature and untested. Similarly, your task of projecting sales potential can be tricky when marketing to individual households. You will need to conduct careful research and be honest with yourself about the market's growth potential. As mentioned earlier, Dave and Florence Minar of Cedar Summit Farm surveyed their local community about milk usage and demand for home delivery services. From this research, they were able to project sales of up to 798 gallons of home delivered bottle milk per week.

Alternatively, if the Minars did not have the luxury of time or funds to survey their target market, they might develop conservative sales estimates based on the number of households/residents within 25-50 miles of their farm.[17] This is how far customers typically travel to purchase something. Cooperative Development Services representative Kevin Edberg says that as a general rule, 75 percent of direct market customers will live within 20 miles of your business.[18]

Using this rule of thumb, Edberg and author Ron Macher suggest a simple way to project direct market sales potential. Begin by locating your farm on a county map and draw 25 and 50 mile radius circles around your farm. Count how many towns or cities fall within the circles. Using this map, add up the number of potential households that live in the nearby cities. These households represent your core potential business customers. Then, with a feel for the number of potential customers, estimate the potential value of sales per household. This is your *sales potential.* Begin by estimating the number of customers in each segment and projecting their weekly, monthly or annual purchases. You can develop sales estimates from household or county purchasing records (available at your public library), from your own surveys, in person interviews, or from secondary sources, such as published purchasing pattern data. Excellent sources for consumer demographic and purchasing pattern data are *CACI Market System Group Sourcebook*, *SRDS Lifestyle Market Analyst*, and New Strategist Publications' *Household Spending: Who Spends How Much on What.* These are available in the reference section of your public library.

Use the space in **Worksheet 4.2: Potential Sales Volume** to begin developing sales estimates for each product that you plan to produce.

Worksheet 4.2 Potential Sales Volume

Complete this Worksheet for each major product you plan to produce. Use your information about average product consumption, geographic location, and customer preferences to develop simple sales projections for each segment of your market. Be sure to specify the timeframe (month, season, year) for each projection. You may want to calculate your potential sales volume for best and worst case scenarios—adjusting the estimated sales volume per customer and the potential number of customers as market conditions may change. If you decide to look at more than three customer segments, more than one sales season, or best and worst case sales projections, use additional paper or Worksheets to calculate and record your business' potential sales volume. Finally, describe any assumptions upon which your sales estimates are based. Be sure to list data sources (such as surveys, market reports, sourcebooks, etc.).

Product: *Bottled Milk*

Time Frame: *2005*

	1	2	3
Customer Segment:	*New Prague home delivery*	*New Prague intermediaries*	*Metro intermediaries*
Potential number of customers: (a)	*5,000 x .05 = 250*	*Five*	*10*
Estimated volume per customer (b)	*3.19 gallons/week*	*25 gallons/week*	*45 gallons/week*
Potential sales volume (a x b) =	*797.5 gallons/week*	*125 gallons/week*	*450 gallons/week*

Market Assumptions/Research Results

Describe your marketing assumptions and research. Include information about general industry conditions, competition, future market potential for your product.

Our research and assumptions are based on a survey that we did of New Prague residents and phone calls made to intermediaries (retail grocery stores). There are 5,000 households in New Prague. Based on positive survey responses, we estimate that by 2005, a minimum of five percent of the New Prague community will be interested in home delivery (250 households). Our consumption or estimated volume estimate is also based on survey responses. We asked each potential customer how much milk they use each week and found that, on average, New Prague households use about 3.19 gallons of milk/week.

The use estimates for intermediaries are based on telephone conversations with dairy buyers and verbal agreements. Linden Hills cooperative, a medium-sized retailer, estimates that it will buy at least 45 gallons (90 half gallons) of milk from us each week.

TASK 4

Figure 40. Example from Cedar Summit Farm—Worksheet 4.2: Potential Sales Volume

17 *Making Your Small Farm Profitable*, Macher and Kerr Jr., 1999.

18 Presentation at University of Minnesota Extension Service Workshop: "Planning for Profit, Land and Family," 2002.

TASK 4

Although much of the market research needed for a business plan can begin with your own impressions and a little footwork at the library, you may reach a point where professional help is needed. Many businesses find it useful to hire a marketing consultant to develop proper surveys, lead focus groups, or to conduct telephone interviews. Representatives from your local Extension service or your state Department of Agriculture may be able to assist you in locating qualitative and quantitative information for a customer profile. The Minnesota Department of Agriculture (MDA), for instance, conducted its own surveys of farmers' market, u-pick, and Christmas tree farm customers about spending patterns. Survey results are available from MDA's Minnesota Grown Program. MDA also offers a comprehensive listing of more than 65 regional businesses that buy or process certified organic grains, oilseeds, fruits, vegetables, herbs and maple syrup.[19]

Financial assistance may also be available to help cover some of the costs associated with your marketing research. You should check with your state Department of Agriculture, your local county Extension service (these phone numbers should be listed in your telephone book), as well as the United States Department of Agriculture (USDA), to see what programs are available in your area. The USDA Service Center locations give you access to the services and programs provided by the Farm Service Agency, Natural Resources Conservation Service, and the Rural Development agencies.[20] You might also contact the Sustainable Agriculture Research and Education (SARE) Program in your region to see if they know of any programs available to fund market research for farmers (www.sare.org/). In Minnesota, the Minnesota Department of Agriculture and the Agricultural Utilization and Research Institute (AURI) both provide some financial assistance for marketing research. AURI provides grants to individual business owners and cooperatives for the development of logos, labels and marketing plans (see "Resources").

Product: What product will we offer and how is it unique?

Although customer research is the single most important component in building a marketing strategy, it is often the product itself that inspires and excites many business owners. Here's your chance to develop a thorough product description. Recall that a "product" is any commodity, final consumer good, or service.

As you think about the products your business will offer, try to describe them in terms of the value they will bring to your customers. What is it that customers are actually buying? Dave and Florence Minar described their bottle milk products as "non-homogenized, cream-top milk from grass-fed cows." In the Minars' case, customers will be buying old-fashioned taste (non-homogenized milk) and perceived health benefits (associated with milk from

19 *Buyers of Organic Products in the Upper Midwest*, Minnesota Department of Agriculture, 2002.

20 To locate the USDA Center nearest you go to: offices.usda.gov/scripts/ndISAPI.dll/oip_public/USA_map.

grass-fed cows). Moreover, New Prague families will also be purchasing a service: home delivery. This service required research and a pricing strategy just like all of the other products offered by Cedar Summit Farm.

Another way to look at your product is in terms of its uniqueness. What makes your product truly unique? Why would customers prefer your product to another farmer's? Are there differences in the production process that make it more wholesome and fresh? Can you appeal to the environmentally conscious? Try to look down the road a bit as you profile your product. Will there be new opportunities to add value through processing, packaging, and customer service? How might your product line or services change over time? Use **Worksheet 4.3: Product and Uniqueness** to describe each of the products that you plan to offer, why they are unique, and how they may change in the future.

Worksheet 4.3 Product and Uniqueness

Complete this Worksheet for each major product you plan to produce. Describe your product and why it will appeal to each market segment. Begin by noting industry trends and general market conditions. Describe supply and demand market trends for this product. Discuss whether they are short-term fads or long-term, emerging trends. Note perceived marketing opportunities that may exist locally, regionally, nationally or internationally. Include evidence that supports your ideas. Then, describe the unique features that distinguish this product within the marketplace. For which customer segments are these unique features important? How easily could competitors imitate these features?

Product: *Bottled Milk*

Industry Trends/Changing Market Conditions:

Dairy market prices have been fluctuating dramatically since 1996 when federal policies were changed. We have seen our prices move around a lot at Davisco - this year's milk price will drop by $2.00/cwt. We believe there are value-added opportunities in the natural foods retail industry as consumer demand for healthy products grows. Every time there is a food scare, for instance, we see our meat sales rise because customers prefer to buy meat from a known source. We think that the same opportunities exist for dairy products.

Characteristic 1 *From grass fed cows*
Appeals to which segments? *Retail and home delivery customers*
Easy for competitors to imitate? Yes/No *No*

Characteristic 2 *Non-homogenized, cream-top*
Appeals to which segments? *Retail and home delivery*
Easy for competitors to imitate? Yes/No *Yes*

Characteristic 3 *Locally produced and processed*
Appeals to which segments? *Retail and home delivery customers*
Easy for competitors to imitate? Yes/No *No*

Summarize the unique characteristics of this product and why it is valuable to your target market:

Our target market is health conscious, upper middle class families with young children and people who remember traditional foods.

Our grass-fed cows produce a different product. Grass-fed cows produce higher amounts of Omega-3 and conjugated linoleic acid in their meat and milk than grain-fed cows. These two fatty acids fight cancer, promote lean muscle mass in humans and have many other health benefits.

Our dairy products will be seen by food retailers as a way to add new products to their stores, thereby adding new customers who are willing to pay more for nutritious products. The cooperative food store managers are excited about adding cream-line milk in returnable glass bottles to their dairy case. Their customers and our home delivery customers will perceive this product as being the ultimate in taste, quality, health and sustainability.

TASK 4

Figure 41.
Example from Cedar Summit Farm—Worksheet 4.3: Product and Uniqueness

Worksheet 4.4 Competition

Complete this Worksheet for each major product you plan to produce. List your competitors in each market segment for this product. Describe competitors' product marketing strategies and the prices they charge for each product. Note any advantages and disadvantages you may have with respect to your competition. Then, develop and describe your strategy for competing or positioning your business in the marketplace.

Product: *Bottled Milk*

	1	2	3
Customer Segment:	*Home Delivery*	*Retail Intermediaries*	
Competitor names	*Meyer Brothers, Schwans*	*MOM's, Organic Valley, Horizon, Kemps*	
Competitor products	*Whole milk, 2%, skim, ice-cream*	*Whole, 2%, and skim milk*	
Major characteristics	*Homogenized milk; wide distribution*	*Organic, homogenized and non-homogenized; paper and plastic cartons; some pasturing of cows; MOM's and Organic Valley produced in Minnesota and Wisconsin*	
Product price range	*$1.99 - $2.10/gallon + delivery charge*	*Range for organic: 1/2 gallons = $ 3.09 - $3.29; Kemps: 1/2 gallon = $1.99*	
Our advantages	*Locally based; just as much local name recognition; superior product*	*Non-homogenized; locally produced; pastured cows*	
Our disadvantages	*Lack of customer and delivery knowledge; logistics*	*Not certified organic; no name recognition*	

Competition strategy:
We will compete by offering a high quality, moderately priced product. It is a common perception that milk in glass bottles stays colder, tastes better, is of higher quality, and has a nostalgic appeal to many customers. We will dominate this market for a number of years in this area by being the first dairy to process on-farm and to use glass bottles for milk from grass-fed cows.

Figure 42.
Example from Cedar Summit Farm—Worksheet 4.4: Competition

TASK 4

Competition: Who are our competitors and how will we position ourselves?

Nearly every business or product has competition of some kind. Find out who your competitors are and what they offer to customers. A trip to the local grocery store, farmers' market, or even a bit of time on the Internet to research how many growers offer organic asparagus or specialty grains may be all that is needed. Is anyone else serving your target market? If so, find out everything you can about their business or their buyers. You might even consider contacting them. Try to find out how they market and price, and, if possible, get a feeling for their cost structure. You need to determine what share of the market you can realistically capture.

Dave and Florence Minar made phone calls to other home delivery services and visited local retailers when beginning their research. They found that *"No farmer in our area is processing and selling his own dairy products. Sources of competition for home-delivered milk into New Prague are Meyer Bros. and Schwans. Meyer Bros. buys milk off the open market and resells it—they do not purchase milk locally or offer non-homogenized products. Schwans will affect us only with ice cream. Some of our competitors in the metro area cooperative groceries are Schroeders, Organic Valley and MOM's."*

Use **Worksheet 4.4: Competition** to analyze the competition that exists for each of the products you plan to offer. List your competitors. Then, consider where you have an advantage over them. Can you produce at a lower cost? Do you have access to markets that they cannot reach? Are you better at working with people—at attracting and keeping customers? Do you have better business skills? In other words, what's your niche? You may want to return to Worksheet 4.3 (Product Uniqueness) where you described your product to ask again, is our product truly unique?

Distribution and Packaging: How and when will we move our product to market?

Now that you have a customer and product in mind, your next task is to identify how to move or distribute products from your farm to the customer's dinner table, store shelves, elevator or barn. Distribution strategies typically describe scope (market reach), movement, packaging and scheduling/handling.

Scope. The first component in your distribution strategy is scope—how widely you plan to distribute your product. Will you pursue an intensive, selective or exclusive distribution strategy?

Intensive product distribution typically involves widespread placement of your product at low prices. Your aim is to saturate the entire market for your goods. This strategy can be expensive and very competitive. Large-scale manufacturers or businesses that market nationwide often employ this method.

Selective product distribution involves selecting a small number of intermediaries, usually retailers, to handle your product. For example, if you plan to produce an upscale product, such as gourmet cheese, you may want to be selective about the stores that stock your product (choosing only those retailers who offer other gourmet, high-quality products). Selective distribution offers the advantages of lower marketing costs and the ability to establish better working relationships with customers and intermediaries.

Exclusive distribution is, in effect, an extreme version of selective distribution. In this case, you grant exclusive stocking rights to a wholesaler or retailer. You agree not to sell to another buyer. In exchange, you might demand that the retailer stock only your farm's salad greens, milk, meat or cheese. You may work closely with a retailer to set market prices, develop promotion strategies, and establish delivery schedules. Exclusive distribution carries promotional advantages, such as the creation of a prestige image for your product, and often involves reduced marketing costs. On the other hand, exclusive distribution may mean that you sacrifice some market share for your product.

Direct Marketing Distribution Alternatives:
- Community Supported Agriculture (CSA)
- Farmers' markets
- Home delivery service
- Internet sales
- Pick-your-own (PYO)
- Mail order
- Roadside stands

Intermediary Distribution Alternatives:
- Retailers
- Wholesalers
- Distributors
- Brokers
- Cooperatives

Figure 43.
Direct Marketing Options

Community Supported Agriculture (CSA)
CSA organizations are similar to a cooperative in that you produce for members. CSA members purchase annual shares of production at the beginning of the year or season. In return, they receive weekly or bi-monthly deliveries of fruits, vegetables, and/or livestock products. CSA projects usually work best close to urban areas. Structures vary and decisions are usually made based on group consensus. You will need good people skills and may have to be creative to keep customers from year to year.

Farmers' Markets
Farmers' markets are a relatively low-cost alternative if there is one already operating in your area. You can plug right into an established market (letting it do the promotion for you) and spend most of your energies on production. Typically a full-year or a per market fee is required to reserve stall space at farmers' markets. The downside is that you will be selling in a very competitive environment and you will not be able to set higher prices.

Mail Order and Internet Sales
Mail order and Internet sales may be a good choice if you are not close to a large urban area and if your product stores and ships well. Perishable and heavy products are not good candidates. These outlets are difficult to get started and work best if you can grow them slowly while relying on other methods for the bulk of your sales. Computerized records or high-quality Web site design are important.

Pick Your Own (PYO)
PYO marketing is a relatively low-cost marketing option. It works best for products in which ripeness is easily recognized. Often you can charge a price that is similar to that for picked produce because the consumer enjoys picking and will pay for the opportunity to do so. Disadvantages include potential damage to the produce, liability concerns, and the fact that a stretch of bad weather can dramatically reduce sales when the product is ripe. Fruit and Christmas trees are traditional examples of PYO enterprises. Fresh flowers are fast becoming a favorite PYO product.

Roadside Stands
Roadside stands require a good location and cheap labor. The most important ingredient to success is attracting repeat customers. Quality, appearance and friendly service are important. Capital requirements can be near nothing if you are in the right location, or they can be substantial if you have to rent space. Check with local authorities for legal requirements and regulations.

Movement. The most common distribution strategies or channels for moving your product to the final customer are direct marketing and intermediary marketing. Examples of each distribution alternative are listed below.

Traditionally, farmers have been positioned at the bottom of the distribution channel—offering a bulk commodity that required further processing or packaging before it could be sold to customers. Distribution intermediaries, such as brokers and cooperatives, were seen as the only option for moving products from their farm to the final customer. However, a growing number of farmers today are doing their own processing, packaging and delivery. This adds value to their raw product and helps them to retain a greater share of the profit. As a result, farmers have expanded their distribution strategies to include direct marketing—selling consumer goods such as goat cheese, bundled fruit trees, or bottled milk directly to the final customer.

In filling out Worksheet 4.5: Distribution and Packaging, the Minars identified two general distribution strategies for their dairy products: direct marketing (via farmers' markets and home delivery), and intermediary sales (via traditional grocers and natural foods cooperatives). As they continued the planning process, the Minars focused their research and evaluation on the two distribution strategies with the most potential for reaching each of their market segments: home delivery to New Prague households and sales to Twin Cities Metro and New Prague retailers.

If you choose to direct market, consider the options listed in Figure 43. Think about the investment required, marketing and labor costs, pricing options, grower liability, and barriers to entry.

Service providers also distribute directly to customers. In this case, it might be from an office, via fax, or on site at the customer's home or business.

While direct sales can be a profitable strategy for the individual grower, they generally make up only a small portion of total sales and can be costly in terms of time. You often take on wholesaler responsibilities such as grading and packing when direct marketing. The majority of consumer goods reach grocery stores or restaurants through some type of intermediary. Intermediaries are businesses that help buy, sell, assemble, store, display and promote your products; they can help you move your product through the distribution channel. Intermediaries include retailers, wholesalers, distributors, brokers and cooperatives. The advantages and disadvantages of distributing through well-known intermediaries are briefly described below.

If your distribution strategy includes sales to retailers or wholesalers, you will need to conduct substantial research. A recent study by the Center for Integrated Agricultural Systems indicated that Minnesota and Wisconsin retailers are very interested in purchasing and stocking local produce. However, they are often unwilling to do so because of inconsistent product quality. "Consistent quality means a predictable product for customers . . . When it comes to quality, many buyers want it all—produce that is shaped and sized consistently and of uniform ripeness and flavor; something they can get from California growers."[22] The study also identified six basic tips for approaching or selling to retail buyers, listed in Figure 45 on the following page.

Similarly, wholesale outlets can be difficult to access. Many of the same retail marketing principles apply to the wholesale market. You will need to

Figure 44.
Intermediary Options

Retailers
Retailers, such as cooperative grocery stores, are an excellent way to reach customers. Retailers can provide some storage, logistical support, and advertising. In exchange, they will expect a larger share of your profit than a wholesaler or broker. Retailers usually are able to dictate quality, packaging and delivery terms.

Wholesalers and Distributors
Wholesalers either buy the products or take possession and act as commission merchants. They can be particularly helpful to businesses that are trying to introduce new products. Wholesalers can use their leverage and expertise in the industry to push your product into a retail outlet. For all of its advantages, the wholesale market is large and typically difficult to access.

Brokers and Handlers
Brokers are agents who represent farmers for a commission but do not take possession or title of your product. They often specify product quality, quantity and price terms in a written contract. If you produce a bulk commodity or plan to ship overseas, a broker is usually needed. The University of Illinois-Urbana Champaign offers a checklist to help you understand and evaluate specialty commodity contracts (see "Resources").

Cooperatives
Cooperatives and other collaborative marketing groups (CMGs) offer their members the opportunity to access otherwise unreachable markets, share risk, and the chance to negotiate favorable prices through increased bargaining power. The Coulee Region Organic Produce Pool (CROPP), which markets under the Organic Valley label, as well as the National Farmers Organization, have been very successful at accessing markets and building profits for member-owners.[21] There are a number of resources available at the national and state government levels to assist with the development of or to help with the decision to join a CMG (see "Resources").

21 *Collaborative Marketing: A Roadmap and Resource Guide for Farmers*, King and DiGiacomo, 2000.

22 *New Markets for Producers: Selling to Retail Stores*, Center for Integrated Agricultural Systems, 1999.

Figure 45.
Recommendations for Approaching Retail Buyers[23]

(1) **Become knowledgeable about the market** by talking with farmers selling to retail stores. Try to find out individual buyers' expectations of volumes and prices to see if they match your situation before approaching the buyer.

(2) **Prepare an availability sheet listing products and prices.** Make it neat and well-organized. Make sure there will be enough produce available to back up what is listed.

(4) **Send the availability sheet to buyers** whose expectations best match what you have to offer. Buyers often prefer to see this sheet before they talk to a producer. You can fax it to the buyer's office.

(5) **Project a professional image** through a growers' manager or representative. This person should be well-informed about production, supply, produce condition, and be confident in the business' ability to meet the buyer's needs.

(6) **Work out the details of the sale** with the buyer, such as volume, size, price, delivery dates and labeling requirements. Some buyers have a set of written requirements for growers.

(7) **Keep in touch with the buyer.** Growers need to keep the buyer informed about potential problems so that buyers can look elsewhere for a product if there is a supply problem.

concentrate as much management on grading and packing as on production. Lastly, and perhaps most importantly, you will need to prove to your buyer that you are a dependable and consistent source of high-quality product.

If one of your distribution alternatives includes the wholesale market, you may want to begin your research by contacting local grocers and restaurants to find out who supplies their produce and other food products. Lakewinds Natural Foods in Minnesota, for instance, purchases approximately 90 percent of its food items from regional wholesale distributors such as the Wedge's Cooperative Partners Warehouse, Roots and Fruits Cooperative Produce, Blooming Prairie Natural Foods, and Metro Produce.[24] Next, contact the wholesaler. Find out their grading, packaging and delivery requirements. If they seem like a good fit—and if the prices they offer are financially acceptable—try selling yourself to them.

There are a number of resources available to help you identify and reach intermediaries. One of the best resources is the Cooperative Grocer On-line. This site offers links to retailers, such as cooperative grocers, as well as other intermediaries, such as manufacturing cooperatives, wholesalers and distributors (see "Resources").

Packaging. Product or service packaging can be both functional and promotional—serving to preserve your product for shipment and, in the case of final consumer goods, to advertise and differentiate your product.

As a producer of bulk commodities, your packaging strategy may seem fairly straightforward since little or no packaging may be involved. However, if you are planning to produce specialty commodities, such as organic grains, be aware that strict industry "packaging" standards may exist.

Packaging final consumer goods for the retail market, on the other hand, can be a daunting yet exciting task. Examples of product packaging include individual product cartons, boxes and containers; bulk shipping containers;

23 *New Markets for Producers: Selling to Retail St* Center for Integrated Agricultural Systems, 19

24 Personal communication, Lakewinds Natural Foods General Manager Kris Nelson, October 2001.

delivery vehicles; and even retail display cases for mass product packaging. Service packaging examples include business cards, invoices, landscaping, building design, signage, brochures and vehicles.

As a producer of consumer products, you may want to begin your research at the supermarket or grocery store. Make note of how similar products are packaged and labeled. There are many rules and regulations governing food packaging and labeling. In general, any product packaged for the retail market must include a description of the common product name, net weight, nutrition facts, ingredients and your business address. All products must meet federal regulations. However, you should also contact your state's food inspection department for more details, since state guidelines may be stricter than federal guidelines. [In Minnesota, see the MDA's *Food Labeling Fact Sheet*. The Agricultural Utilization Research Institute (AURI) also provides technical assistance for the development of nutrition labels (see "Resources")].

Finally, as a service provider, think about what your customers will see, hear and smell when visiting your farm or communicating with you and your staff. Northwind Nursery and Orchard owner Frank Foltz laid out the following plan for "packaging" the service component of his business:

"The sales room for nursery stock and fruit will be decorated with a country theme and include locally crafted items useful for gardening, orcharding and homesteading purposes. We will avoid all but the very highest quality products. Staff will be friendly and knowledgeable in all aspects of fruit growing and orcharding. The property will be developed in a free-flowing, park-like fashion with an interspersion of fruit trees and edible landscaping plants that will elevate our customers from the simple act of buying fruit or nursery stock to that of experiencing our natural environment at its best. This arboretum-type setting will provide customers with the opportunity to take a 'fruit walk' to sample many different fruit cultivars in season and subsequently purchase more fruit, or the nursery stock to grow their own."

As you think about what type of packaging is best suited to your product, don't overlook customer needs, such as convenience, and intermediary requirements. Restaurant owners and cooperative grocery managers will likely have minimal packaging requirements that affect how you clean, bundle and grade your product. Lakewinds Natural Foods General Manager Kris Nelson says produce farmers, in particular, must compete with major distributors and therefore deliver a professionally packaged product. "Kale and other greens come to us from farmers already cleaned and bundled," Nelson says. "They are dropped off at the store in packaging that is similar to what we see from commercial distributors."[25] If you plan to market to retailers and other intermediaries, research their packaging requirements and think realistically about your ability to meet industry standards.

25 Personal communication, Lakewinds Natural Foods General Manager Kris Nelson, October 2001.

Worksheet 4.5 Distribution and Packaging

Complete this Worksheet for each major product you plan to produce. Describe how you intend to move and package this product for each target market segment. Note where and how the product will be shipped (location and scope) and what type of distribution channel you will utilize (movement). Next, based on each distribution plan, research and describe one or more packaging strategies for this product. Consider what type of packaging might be valued by customers (e.g. convenience) or even required by intermediaries and distributors. Describe a delivery and handling schedule by period (month, season, year). Then, summarize your distribution and packaging strategies for this product.

Product: *Bottled milk* **Period:** *Weekly*

Customer Segment: *1—Households*

Location: *New Prague—within 25 miles of farm.*

Scope: *Intensive in New Prague. We have polled our local community, for the past two years, at our local Expo, regarding their interest in home delivery. So far we have 75 names on this growing list. These will be the nucleus of our home delivery service. They are all located within 10 miles of one another.*

Movement (distribution channel): *Direct via home delivery.*

Industry packaging requirements: *Need to research.*

Packaging ideas: *We will explore promotional packaging with a logo design for all products. Bottled milk may be packaged in returnable glass or plastic containers.*
Home delivery coolers will be available to each customer.

Delivery schedule & handling: *We plan to make weekly home deliveries to New Prague residents. Our home delivery schedule will be broken up into daily routes. We will travel approximately 25 miles/day for each home delivery route. Each delivery route is estimated to take eight hours.*

CONTINUED

Figure 46. Example from Cedar Summit Farm—Worksheet 4.5: Distribution and Packaging

TASK 4

Your values and goals, as well as target market preferences, will also affect packaging choices. The Minars, for instance, envisioned marketing to customers "who value old-fashioned taste." As a result, one of their distribution strategies was to package their milk in old-fashioned, returnable, glass bottles. *"It is a common perception that milk in glass bottles stays colder, tastes better, is of higher quality, and has a nostalgic appeal to many customers,"* they say in their business plan. By packaging in glass bottles, the Minars were also able to satisfy one of their environmental values—namely, to minimize their impact on the land through reuseable packaging.

Delivery scheduling and handling. Your distribution strategy should also take into account how often you will need to make deliveries, either to satisfy customer demand or to fill intermediary requirements. What type of delivery schedule will be necessary? If you offer a perishable product, delivery schedules will be critical. The Minars spoke with retailers to research delivery conditions, such as the handling of returnable bottles, and a delivery schedule. Moreover, if you are marketing through an intermediary, your ability to meet delivery commitments may determine their continued business. "Retail buyers rely on delivery at the promised time so they know how much may need to be supplemented to meet demand and so they can schedule workers to handle delivery and display."[26] As you develop a delivery schedule, be aware of peak production periods (if your business is seasonal) as well as industry handling requirements. Organic producers are required, in most cases, to verify that organic grains were

26 *New Markets for Producers: Selling to Retail Stores*, Center for Integrated Agricultural Systems, 1999.

Worksheet 4.5 Distribution and Packaging

CONTINUED

Complete this Worksheet for each major product you plan to produce. Describe how you intend to move and package this product for each target market segment. Note where and how the product will be shipped (location and scope) and what type of distribution channel you will utilize (movement). Next, based on each distribution plan, research and describe one or more packaging strategies for this product. Consider what type of packaging might be valued by customers (e.g., convenience) or even required by intermediaries and distributors. Describe a delivery and handling schedule by period (month, season, year). Then, summarize your distribution and packaging strategies for this product.

Product: *Bottled milk* **Period:** *Weekly*

Customer Segment: *2—Retail customers*

Location: *Scott County and Twin Cities Metro Area*

Scope: *Fairly extensive in Scott county and the Twin Cities Metro area*

Movement (distribution channel): *Intermediaries*

We have spoken with dairy managers from each of the following retail stores - all have verbally agreed to stock our milk: County Market—Northfield, MN; County Market—Prior Lake, MN; Cub Foods—Shakopee, MN; Econo Foods—Northfield, MN; Hampton Park Co-op—St. Paul, MN; Lakewinds Natural Foods—Minnetonka, MN; Linden Hills Co-op—Minneapolis, MN; Lorentz Meats and Deli—Cannon Falls, MN; Mississippi Market—St. Paul, MN; North County Co-op—Minneapolis, MN; Rademacher Super Value—Jordan, MN; River Market—Stillwater, MN; Seward Co-op & Deli—Minneapolis, MN; Valley Natural Foods—Burnsville, MN; Wedge Community Food Co-op—Minneapolis, MN

Industry packaging requirements: *Need to research.*

Packaging ideas: *We will explore promotional packaging with a logo design for all products. Bottled milk may be packaged in recyclable or re-useable glass or plastic containers. The manager of the Hampton Park Co-op in St. Paul originally told us she didn't have enough room for our products in her dairy case. When we told her the milk would be non-homogenized, creamline milk in glass bottles, she changed her mind. She posted her own survey on the dairy case, asking her customers if they wanted "Milk in Glass." Twenty-four of the 26 respondents responded positively. This kind of reaction among retail customers and co-op managers has been very typical.*

Delivery schedule & handling: *We plan to make weekly deliveries to retailers. A specific delivery schedule will be worked out with each manager when milk is available.*

Figure 46. Example from Cedar Summit Farm—Worksheet 4.5: Distribution and Packaging (side 2)

handled (cleaned, stored and transported) in accordance with organic standards.[27]

Use **Worksheet 4.5: Distribution and Packaging** to develop and describe your overall distribution strategy or strategies. The decisions you make here will affect your future workload and consequently, your human resources strategy.

TASK 4

Pricing: How will we price our product?

Farmers are all too familiar with the challenges of pricing bulk commodities for profit. As price takers, low market prices are often the number one reason traditional commodity producers find themselves sitting down to develop a business plan. Today's producers, whether they are adding value or marketing a specialty commodity, have a greater ability to influence price in these highly defined markets. Depending on your goals, vision, target market, and product strategy, you may want to consider one or more pricing strategies for undifferentiated (traditional) commodities and differentiated (value-added, specialty) products.

In general, pricing strategies are based on two factors: prevailing market prices and your costs. In the long run, your price has to cover your full costs—

27 *Organic Certification of Crop Production in Minnesota*, Gulbranson, 2001 (revised).

WHOLESALE PRODUCE PRICING
For Current Blooming Prairie Customers as of 11/26/01*
*prices & availability subject to change

ITEM #	PRODUCT	ORDER UNIT	PRICE	PRICE/#
78136	RED POTATOES/BAGGED	1/5# BAG	2.33	0.47
78137	RUSSET POTATOES/BAGGED	1/5# BAG	2.42	0.48
78138	YUKON GLD/YELLOW POTATOES/BAGGED	1/5# BAG	5.27	1.05
78142	YELLOW ONIONS/BAGGED	1/3# BAG	1.64	0.56
78145	CARROTS/BAGGED	1/5# BAG	3.38	0.68
78146	JUICING CARROTS/BULK	1/25# BAG	17.92	0.72
78148	RED DELICIOUS APPLES/BAGGED	12/3# BAG	2.48	0.83
78149	GOLDEN DELICIOUS APPLES/BAGGED	1/3# BAG	2.48	0.83
78151	ORANGES/BAGGED (VALENCIA)	1/4# BAG	4.41	1.10
78007	ORANGES/BULK (VALENCIA)	1/36# BOX	50.86	1.41
78009	TABLE CARROTS/BULK	1/25# BAG	21.36	0.85
78021	SPECIALTY APPLE (GALA)	1/3# BAG	2.59	0.87
78159	GINGER	1/1# BAG	5.89	5.89
78160	BABY PEELED CARROTS	1/1# BAG	1.46	1.46
78161	GARLIC	1/1#BAG	4.16	4.16
78158	LEMONS	1/2#BAG	2.36	1.18
78164	GRANNY SMITH APPLE	1/3#BAG	2.60	0.87
78162	PEARS	1/3#BAG	2.30	0.77
78166	RED GRAPEFRUIT/BAGGED	1/5#BAG	3.46	0.87

Figure 47. Blooming Prairie Wholesale Produce Pricing List

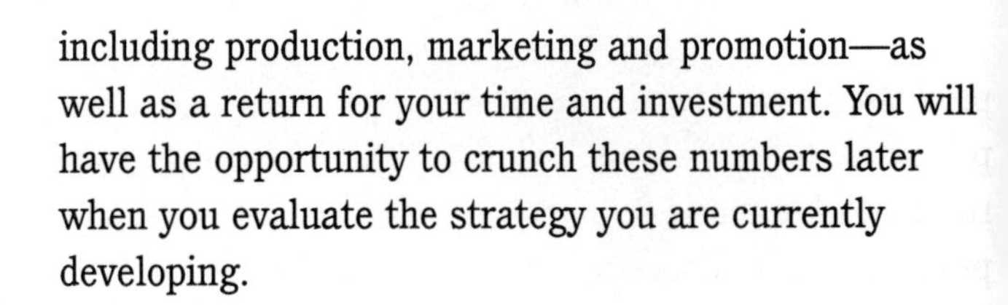

including production, marketing and promotion—as well as a return for your time and investment. You will have the opportunity to crunch these numbers later when you evaluate the strategy you are currently developing.

For now, begin developing a pricing strategy around prevailing market prices. Learn about what customers are willing to pay and what prices your competitors charge. Begin your research by listing competitor prices for similar products—note any seasonal pricing changes, premiums and discounts offered by intermediaries (brokers, grain companies, processors, retail groceries, etc.). Check with your state Department of Agriculture, or your University Extension Service for a list of current market prices for traditional commodities, such as livestock and forages. Specialty commodity prices may be difficult to locate or only available for a fairly substantial fee. Markets for organics, non-GMOs, and other specialty commodities, such as lentils, are relatively immature and little information is available. Therefore, you will have to do a little digging when searching for historic, current, and projected market prices. In general, a good source for alternative product prices, including organics, is the Internet. Food cooperatives, like Blooming Prairie, list weekly wholesale prices for produce. Retail prices for a range of processed dairy and grain products, fresh produce, flowers, herbs and spices often are available on individual company Web sites. Moreover, the Appropriate Technology Transfer for Rural Areas (ATTRA) has compiled a listing of relatively low-cost organic market price and industry research called *Resources for Organic Marketing* (see "Resources"). If you have Internet access or are willing to make a few phone calls, your market price research needn't take long.

Once you are familiar with prevailing market prices and your costs of production, you are ready to begin developing a pricing strategy. There are a variety of strategies to consider depending on your ability to set prices. Common pricing strategies for differentiated (value-added or specialty) commodities including consumer goods and services (with relatively high price setting ability) are discussed in Figure 48.

If you are a small or mid-sized producer selling in a local market, be careful not to place too much emphasis on price competition. You will likely have better results competing based on quality, value added and communications. Still, you need to think about how to price your commodity or product.

One common product pricing approach, skim pricing, is to establish a relatively high market entry price to recover costs before lowering the price to expand the customer base. This practice, however, can attract more competition if your prices remain too high for too long. The alternative is penetration pricing. Similar to promotional pricing, you initially set a product price below your intended long-term price to secure market acceptance of your product. The advantage of penetration pricing is that it will not attract competition. When selecting a pricing strategy for differentiated commodities, products or services, take a peek at the options listed in Figure 48.

Figure 48.
Differentiated Product Pricing Strategies[28]

Competitive pricing. Competitive pricing strategies are common among large manufacturers and are aimed at undermining competition. Predatory pricing, where a company sets its price below cost to force its competitors out of the market, is a typical competitive pricing strategy. Although these strategies may work well for large commercial companies, they are not recommended for small-scale, independent businesses. Price wars are not easily won. That said, the food industry is considered a "mature" marketplace and your ability to compete on the basis of price may be very important.[29] There are several well-capitalized players, even in the organic market, offering similar services.

Cost-oriented pricing. The cost-oriented pricing strategy is probably the most straightforward. Based on your production costs, you and your planning team make a subjective decision about whether to price your product at 10 percent, 50 percent, or 100 percent above current costs. Of course, you will need to conduct marketing research to determine whether or not your customers are willing to pay the cost-plus price that you have established.

Flexible or variable pricing. Flexible pricing strategies involve setting a range of prices for your product. Flexible pricing is common when individual bargaining takes place. The prices that you set may vary according to the individual buyer, time of year, or time of day. For instance, farmers who sell perishable fruits, vegetables and herbs at farmers' markets often establish one price for their products in early morning and by day-end are willing to lower their prices to move any excess product.

Penetration or promotional pricing. A penetration pricing strategy involves initially setting your product price below your intended long-term price to help penetrate the market. The advantage of penetration pricing is that it will not attract competition. Before pursuing a penetration pricing strategy, you should thoroughly research prevailing market prices and crunch some numbers to determine just how long you can sustain a below-cost penetration price. Penetration or promotional pricing usually takes place at the retail level when marketing direct to your product's final consumers.

Product line pricing. If you plan to market a line of products, you might consider a product line pricing strategy where a limited range of prices is established for all of the products that you will offer. For instance, if you envision marketing to low-income customers, then your price line or price range must be based on "affordability." In this case, you might establish an upper limit or ceiling for prices so that your price line is bounded by your production costs on one end and an affordable ceiling on the other end.

Relative pricing. Relative pricing strategies involve setting your price above, below or at the prevailing market price. Clearly, this strategy requires that you research the prevailing market price for your product.

Skimming or skim pricing. The price skimming strategy is based on the idea that you can set a high market entry price to recover costs quickly (to "skim the cream off the top") before lowering your price to what you intend as the long-term price. This pricing strategy is possible only when you have few or no competitors. The primary disadvantage of the skimming strategy is that it attracts competition. Once competitors enter the market, you may be forced to match their lower prices.

Contract pricing for specialty commodities. Contracts for specialty commodities vary dramatically in terms of the price paid, payment conditions, grower responsibilities, storage and shipping arrangements. The advantage of pricing on contract is that you know in advance what price will be paid for the commodity. Be aware, however, that when producing a specialty variety crop or when employing a new production management system, your yield and output risk increases as does your exposure to quality discounts. Use a contract checklist if you are considering this method of pricing for specialty crops or livestock.[30]

TASK 4

28 *Marketing,* Kurtz and Boone, 1981.

29 *Cooperative Grocer,* Natural/Organic Industry Outlook, Southworth, September-October 2001.

30 *Contract Evaluation,* University of Illinois, 2001 (reviewed).

Common pricing strategies for undifferentiated (raw) commodities (with low price setting ability) are discussed in Figure 49.

Traditional commodity pricing strategies also have their advantages and disadvantages as described in Figure 49. When considering each of the commodity pricing strategies, remember that there are many factors that can affect your overall market price strategy, such as storage capacity, cash flow and taxes.[31]

Whatever type of pricing strategy you choose, think through your rationale. Are you trying to undermine the competition by offering a lower price? Set a high price that reflects your quality image or market demand as is the present case with organic products? Are you simply looking to cover costs and reduce volatility?

Figure 49.
Undifferentiated Commodity Pricing Strategies[32]

Advance pricing prior to harvest. The advantage of pricing your commodity prior to harvest is the ability to lock in a price that ideally returns your cost of production plus a profit. The primary disadvantage of forward pricing or futures contract pricing has to do with harvested yield and market prices. You will need to be careful when making commitments so that you are not obligated to deliver more than you can safely produce. Extension Educator Erlin Weness suggests forward pricing your crop in staggered amounts to protect against crop failure and other disasters. There are several tools available to price your grain forward, including futures and options and hedge-to-arrive contracts.

Cash pricing at harvest. This strategy is quite simple—it involves selling your crop directly from the field at harvest. This puts you at the most financial risk, by forcing you to sell your commodity at the time of harvest when prices are likely to be low.

Delayed pricing after harvest. This strategy involves delivering your commodity after harvest or storing it and then pricing. The most common post-harvest pricing tools include basis contracts, hedge-to-arrive contracts, forward contracts, delayed pricing, and the government loan program.

The Minars identified two pricing strategies for bottled milk (relative and cost-based pricing) to help place their product in retail and wholesale markets. By introducing new customers to Cedar Summit Creamery's "old fashioned" bottled milk at a price well below that of organic milk, the Minars hoped to encourage quality and health-conscious shoppers to try their product. The Minars' break-even analysis in the evaluation step of this Planning Task helped them determine whether or not a relative or cost-oriented pricing strategy would be financially feasible.

Use **Worksheet 4.6: Pricing** to develop your pricing strategy for each product. Begin by recording research about competitor's prices.

31 *Marketing Strategies for Agricultural Commodities*, Weness, 2001 (reviewed).

32 Ibid.

Worksheet 4.6 Pricing

Complete this Worksheet for each major product you plan to produce. List the price range for similar products offered by competitors (Worksheet 4.4) or industry buyers. Next, think about how you might price this product. Consider how much power you have to set the price for this product and how sensitive the demand for this product is to price changes. Then describe your pricing strategies for this product and list your low, expected, and high product price under each pricing strategy alternative. Finally, summarize your pricing strategy in the space provided.

Product: *Bottled milk*

Competitor/Industry Price Range: *$1.99 (conventional, retail)*
$3.29 (organic, retail)

Our Power to Set Prices: ___Low X Some ___High

Demand Sensitivity to Price Changes: ___Low X Some ___High

Pricing Strategies / Price Range:	Low	Expected	High
Strategy #1: *Relative pricing*			
—Home delivery			
		$2.20/half gallon	*$2.45/half gallon*
		(plus delivery fee)	*(no delivery fee)*
—Retailers			
		$1.65/half gallon	
Strategy #2:			

Pricing Strategy:

We plan to price our milk between organic and conventional super market prices - around $2.20/half gallon for home delivered milk (plus a delivery fee) and about $1.65/half gallon at the wholesale level for retail intermediaries. We will have to further negotiate wholesale prices with buyers and do more research on our own cost of production to make sure that this is covered.

Figure 50. Example from Cedar Summit Farm—Worksheet 4.6: Pricing

Figure 51. Common Pricing Strategy Mistakes[33]

Marketing author Michael O'Donnell outlines the following common "mistakes" to be aware of when building a market price strategy.

1. Pricing too high relative to customers' existing value perceptions; prices not in line with target market needs, desires or ability to pay.
2. Failing to adjust prices from one area to another based upon fluctuating costs and the customer's willingness and ability to pay from one market to another.
3. Attempting to compete on price alone.
4. Failing to test different price levels on customers, from one area or market to another.

33 *The Marketing Plan: Step-by-Step*, O'Donnell, 1991.

TASK 4

Promotion: How and what will we communicate to our buyers or customers?

Promotion is a must if you are going to gain product recognition among customers. Promotional strategies often are built around a "message." The message that you deliver about your product or business is just as important as the product itself. Equally important is how and when you deliver that message through the use of advertising tools and media.

Image or product. Before beginning detailed promotions research, think about an overall strategy approach. Will you concentrate promotions on your business image, the product, or both (total approach)?

Businesses use brand or image advertising to build awareness and interest in their products. A brand is represented by a name, term, sign, symbol, design or some combination. A brand or logo is used to identify the products of your business and to distinguish them from other competitors.[34] Although the establishment of a brand can be expensive, particularly for small businesses, many of today's alternative farm businesses are concentrating their promotional efforts on image advertising—promoting the concept of "healthy" or "locally produced" or "eco-friendly" products.

TASK 4

Promotion Strategy

Your promotion strategy should include a promotional method, specific promotional tools, and your ideas for actual promotion or delivery.

Message: What do I want my customer to know about my product?

Tools and Delivery: What will I use to communicate my message?

Timing and Frequency: How often will I contact my customers via advertising and communications?

Costs: How much will my advertising and communication cost?

The Minars plan to promote Cedar Summit Farm products through the use of a new label and logo design that will appear on all products and in their brochure. They hired a family artist to develop a variety of logos that would communicate their overriding values and new business mission statement.

Product advertising aims to create immediate sales through some type of special product offer, such as seasonal discounts, frequent buyer clubs, and in-store samples. For instance, Northwind Nursery and Orchard owner Frank Foltz developed a three-pronged product strategy to: *"(1) Make use of excess products by distributing them as advertising samples—we will give it to customers who can use it. They will repay us many times over in 'word of mouth' advertising; (2) Give our customer discounts for bringing in other customers or distributing our literature, etc. . . . Give those who organize group orders a bonus; and (3) Reward loyal customers with extra services that will help them succeed."*

[34] *Marketing*, Kurtz and Boone, 1981.

Product promotion aims to increase sales directly and immediately for an advertised product. Here are several low-cost product promotion alternatives.

- Coupons and rebates
- Tasting and cooking demonstrations
- Frequent buyer clubs
- Publicity
- Samples
- Recipes

While most small businesses opt for product advertising because it offers more immediate returns, marketing consultant Barbara Findlay Schenck recommends combining both image and product promotion strategies. She calls this promotional strategy total approach advertising.[35] Total approach advertising offers direct farm marketers a chance to build a long-term image of their business and its values while encouraging timely product purchases.

Dancing Winds Farm owner Mary Doerr, for example, promotes the image of her business with flyers that read "Dancing Winds Farm is a small farm enterprise using sustainable agriculture practices" as well as her business' product by offering free cheese samples and recipes at the St. Paul Farmers' market every other weekend.

Use **Worksheet 4.7: Promotion** to describe your general promotions strategy. Next, with a broad strategy approach in mind, begin sketching out the particulars of your advertising message, tools, delivery and schedule.

Figure 52. Cedar Summit draft logo designs

TASK 4

[35] *Small Business Marketing for Dummies*, Schenck, 2001.

Worksheet 4.7	**Promotion**		
Complete this Worksheet for each major product you plan to produce. Choose an advertising approach (product, image, total) for each customer segment. Then use your information about customer needs and preferences (Worksheet 4.1) to develop a promotional message for this product. Next, think about what advertising tools and delivery methods you can use to communicate your message. Describe how often you intend to promote your product and communicate with customers (timing and frequency). It may be helpful to use a calendar or blank sheet of paper to map out an advertising plan that corresponds with slow demand periods or peak product availability. Finally, summarize your promotion strategy for this product.			
Product:	*Bottled Milk*		
Customer Segment:	1 *Home Delivery*	2 *Retail Intermediaries*	3
Approach (product, image, total):	*Total approach*	*Total approach and product advertising*	
Message:	*"The way milk used to taste"*	*Same as home delivery*	
Tools:	*Newspaper ads, flyers, press releases*	*Tasting/samples, ads in co-op MIX magazine, MN Grown Directory*	
Delivery:	*Food shows, local radio, word-of-mouth*	*In supermarket, cooperatives, and Internet*	
Timing/frequency:	*Press release at ground breaking, plant opening and prior to open-house. Holiday flyers will be sent out at Christmas.*	*Samples will be offered quarterly. Ad costs will determine the timing and frequency of placement.*	

Promotion strategy:
We will continue to promote our products via word-of-mouth, newspapers, brochures, MN Grown Directory, radio and sampling- these have all been successful outlets for us in the past with our meat products. In addition to these standard advertising practices, we expect to gain considerable recognition through press releases for new products since we will be the first on-farm milk processor in our area and an asset to the community. Our business and products will also be recognized and promoted by our Chamber of Commerce.

Figure 53. Example from Cedar Summit Farm—Worksheet 4.7: Promotion

Message. Advertising messages can be fun, serious, or factual. They can describe business values, the product itself, production practices, prices, or the volume available for sale.

If you intend to use a product promotion strategy, your message can describe the unique characteristics of your product or a special offer. On the other hand, if your strategy is centered on image promotion, your message should paint a clear picture of what you want your business to be known for among customers. Return to your Business Mission Statement (Worksheet 3.2), in which you first answered this question; it is a good place to start formulating your promotional message. Either way, if you plan to produce a retail product, try to keep your messages short so that it can be incorporated into product packaging.

Take a look at the following image and product-related messages advertised by several well-known Midwest retail food suppliers:

"Our organic products are not only good for the earth, but for you and your family too! Together we can change the world—one organic acre at a time"
—Horizon Organic

"Bob's Red Mill is dedicated to the manufacturing of natural foods in the natural way . . . We stone grind all common and most uncommon grains into flours and meals on our one-hundred-year-old mills . . . Our product line of natural whole grain foods [is]the most complete in the industry"
—Bob's Red Mill

"Applegate Farms is working to improve the meat Americans eat . . . All of our products are gluten-free, contain low or no carbohydrates, are lower in fat than other major brands and free of all taste or texture enhancers"
—Applegate Farms

Research other business messages on-line, in advertisements, or at the grocery store.

Tools and delivery. Frank Foltz, owner of Northwind Nursery and Orchards, promotes his business' products using a range of promotional tools, including fact sheets that are distributed at farmers' markets and educational on-farm displays. *"Quality products and knowledgeable, personal service along with a series of informative fact sheets on fruit growing culture and problems are an integral part of our catalog sales strategy,"* says Frank. *"Those, along with on-farm learning opportunities, community activities and cultural events are the back-bone of our local promotions efforts."*

The Foltzes' experience suggests that educational fact sheets are one of the best ways to reach their target market customer—individuals interested in learning more about backyard orcharding and edible landscaping.

Page 35

Homesteading Workshops & Family Fun Day

Saturday, August 29, 1998 - 8:00 AM to ??

A biannual event designed for the entire family that encourages networking and sharing of personal skills and experiences. Join us and learn from a wide selection of basic homesteading skills that can help you live more simply and sensibly in an increasingly chaotic world. Family participation is encouraged and children are welcome under the care and guidance of their parents.

Each participant will have the opportunity to take up to four classes on subjects such as: **Root Cellaring, Wind & Solar Power, Seed Saving & Starting, Square Foot and Raised Bed Gardening, Food Preservation, Bread Making, Solar Cookers, Growing & using Herbs, Backyard Orcharding, Trapping & Tanning, Straw Bale and Log Home Construction, Pruning & Grafting Fruit Trees, Wild Edibles, Homeschooling, Homebirthing, Meatless Cooking, Homemade Lumber, Commercial Fruit Growing, Home Building, Soil Nutrition, Weed Management, etc.**

PLUS:

- ★ ***Activities for the Children:*** The more the merrier!
- ★ ***Homesteading Skills:*** Workshops, Displays, and Demonstrations.
- ★ ***Farmer's Market:*** Bring your produce-no setup fee for registered participants
- ★ ***Swap & Sell Meet:*** Bring your homesteading items to swap or sell-no setup fee for registered participants.
- ★ ***Appropriate Vendors:*** Community minded vendors welcome. Call about fees.
- ★ ***Barn Dance!*** We conclude the day with an old fashioned, traditional barn dance. All dances are taught. Pay at door. $5.00 / person or 10.00 / family.

Write or call to get on the mailing list for the particulars of this event when things are finalized later in the spring.

This is your event, too! If you have something to demonstrate, display, or teach in keeping with the theme of the day, let us Know! Workshop instructors are not paid but can take the other workshops free with their families.

REGISTRATION INFORMATION

To help us prepare for this event, **please register as soon as possible.** If something happens that you can't come **we will refund your money on request.** Registrations at the door are welcome if you can't plan in advance, but all participants who ***pre-register*** will receive a registration packet at the door containing all handouts that are available from **all** the classes, not just the ones you attend. Make checks payable to Northwind Nursery. Barn dance not included in fees below (please pay at door the night of dance).

FEES: Families - $25.00 for entire day
$15.00 for morning or afternoon
Individuals - $15.00 for day or $5.00 per class.

More Info? Call Frank at 612/389-4920

Figure 54. 1998 Educational Classes from Northwind Nursery Catalogue

Promotion or advertising tools typically include display ads, billboards, yellow pages, mailings, flyers and catalogues. Your state Department of Agriculture likely has a program promoting locally grown products. The *Minnesota Grown Directory* is an excellent advertising resource for farmers in Minnesota and Wisconsin who have seasonal and year-round products to sell. Minnesota Grown program participants, like the Minars, are listed in an annual directory and receive permission to use the trademarked Minnesota Grown logo (see "Resources").

Every advertising tool has its advantages and disadvantages. Think about which tools will help you best reach your target market. Once you've developed a list of potential advertising tools, think about where you will deliver or distribute your promotional message.

Gigi DiGiacomo

Figure 55. Cedar Summit Farm price list with Minnesota Grown logo posted at their farm stand

Holiday Gift Boxes

With fall fast approaching, the holiday season is just around the corner. We at Cedar Summit Farm can help you with holiday gifts.

We are having cheese made from the milk from our dairy herd. All our animals enjoy the healthful benefits of being in an outside environment; as a result, no antibiotics are needed to keep them healthy. We have never used rGBH (bovine growth hormone). Our customers feel that the taste of cheese made from milk from grass fed cows is definitely a superior product.

We are offering a selection of gifts in two, three and four-pound boxes:

The two-pound box contains four ½ lb wedges of Cheddar, Gouda, Herb & Spice Gouda and Tomato Basil Gouda.

The three-pound Gouda box contains one pound each of plain Gouda, Herb & Spice Gouda and Tomato Basil Gouda.

The four-pound box contains one-pound each of the same cheeses as the two-pound box.

We also offer gift boxes with sausage made from our own steers. These will be in the same configurations as above, but will include a 12 oz. tube of each-summer sausage and cotto salami.

Remember, the best products are wholesome products from your neighborhood family farm. We know you will be happy with our products as we are a family operation and will settle for nothing but the best.

Orders may be mailed to the above address or you can call (952) 758-6886 or E-mail at cedarsummit@earthlink.net. **Quantities are limited.**

Detach along dotted line for mail orders

Name__________ Telephone__________

Preferred Pick-Up Date__________ (not before December 1, 2001)

Item	Price/Box	Quantity	Total Price
2 lb Gourmet Cheese Gift Box	$25.00		
3 lb Gourmet Cheese Gift Box	$35.00		
4 lb Gourmet Cheese Gift Box	$45.00		
2 lb Gourmet Cheese Gift Box with Sausage	$32.50		
3 lb Gourmet Cheese Gift Box with Sausage	$42.50		
4 lb Gourmet Cheese Gift Box with Sausage	$52.50		

Figure 56.
Cedar Summit Farm holiday flyer/advertisement for cheese and meat boxes

Trade shows, farmers' markets, county fairs, radio, television, and the Internet are just a few promotional delivery options. Be sure to brainstorm with your planning team. Identify creative, low-cost, effective ways to get the word out. You might consider a word-of-mouth campaign or a strategic alliance with another farmer.

Mary Doerr of Dancing Winds Farm linked up with a nearby Community Supported Agriculture (CSA) business owner to offer "cheese shares" in its CSA brochure. The Minars negotiated a verbal agreement with a meat producer in West Central Minnesota to market Cedar Summit Farm milk products to that producer's existing direct market customers. That agreement would allow the Minars to promote their milk products beyond South Central Minnesota and gradually increase the size of their target market.

Timing and frequency. Promotional strategies should include a plan for timed delivery or an advertising schedule that describes how often you will communicate with customers to follow-up on a sale, inform them of holiday specials (see Figure 56), or let them know about new products and prices. Regular communication is a way to build and preserve your market.

Frank Foltz of Northwind Nursery and Orchards maintains regular contact with customers by informing them about new orchard research and varieties. How will you advertise and maintain contact with your customers? Through regular personal contact, periodic promotional mailings, or a holiday mailer? It may be helpful to develop a calendar for promotional "events" to help time promotions with seasonal demand or peak production periods. This will also help you plan for advertising expense outlays when developing your cash flow plan as you evaluate your proposed strategy later in this Planning Task.

A series of interviews with Minnesota and Wisconsin retail buyers found that farmers who communicated regularly with buyers regarding deliveries and product availability were more successful at maintaining these customers.[36] When communicating with intermediaries, it is a good idea to appoint a single representative to deal with the buyers so that a personal relationship can be built. This person should be knowledgeable about your business' products and able to negotiate with buyers.

36 *New Markets for Producers: Selling to Retail Stores*, Center for Integrated Agricultural Systems, 1999.

Your communication strategy might also incorporate feedback elements to obtain information from customers. Frank Foltz describes this strategy approach best in his business plan: *"We will treat our customers as an extension of our research and development departments. Their problems and complaints about our products can help us eliminate future production problems and their suggestions may be as helpful as any hired consultant. We will listen attentively to their concerns, dealing with problems immediately and always give the customer the benefit of the doubt."*

Regardless of the promotional strategy you pursue, you and your planning team will need to be creative to catch the attention of your customers and stretch your advertising dollars. Promotion, though seemingly overwhelming, should be fun.

Return to **Worksheet 4.7: Promotion** to sketch a promotional strategy and advertising plan for each of your products. Think about your values and goals as well as your target market, product and potential competition. Like the Minars, be sure to detail your overall promotional strategy, message, advertising tools, delivery ideas and communication plans.

TASK 4

Inventory and Storage Management: How will we store inventory and maintain product quality?

Storage and inventory management are integral and important parts any business strategy, affecting product quality, marketing opportunities, and the business' legal standing. While this may seem to be more of an operations issue, many marketing strategies may depend on whether or how long you can store your product.

What role will inventory and storage management play in your business? Like traditional grain producers who use storage as a way to mitigate seasonal price declines, Riverbend Farm owner Greg Reynolds devoted a substantial portion of his operations research toward the development of a low-cost storage system for organic vegetables. He sought to preserve his produce and prolong his marketing season.

You might shape your storage strategy around marketing or to satisfy regulatory considerations. Certified organic producers, for example, must maintain detailed storage and harvest records in order to market their crops. Similarly, in accordance with the USDA Pasteurized Milk Ordinance and the Minnesota Department of Agriculture Food Handlers License/Processing Plant Permit, the Minars are required to test all milk transported to Cedar Summit Creamery for traces of antibiotics, bacteria and proper pasteurization once it has undergone this process. According to Worksheet 4.8, Cedar Summit Creamery will house a testing lab and storage cooler on-site to assure the quality of milk and preserve bottled milk, cheese, sour cream, butter and ice-cream products.

Think about your storage and inventory management objectives, then research your options and use **Worksheet 4.8: Storage and Inventory** to describe this piece of your marketing strategy.

TASK 4

Worksheet 4.8 Inventory and Storage Management

Using the space below, describe how you will store and manage inventories for each product. Consider any regulations or industry standards that might apply to your business (Worksheet 4.11). Note how you will comply with any standards for product quality.

Product: *Bottled Milk*

Industry regulations/standards:

We will need to comply with the USDA Pasteurized Milk Ordinance and the Minnesota Department of Agriculture Food Handlers License/Processing Plant Permit requirements.

Product storage:

We will acquire a walk-in cooler and freezer to preserve all processed products. Bottled milk and all other products, with the exception of ice-cream, will be stored at 39 degrees - a temperature recommended by Pladot and the food industry.

Inventory management:

Quality control:

We will test all milk transported to the Creamery for traces of antibiotics, bacteria, and for proper pasteurization (as required by USDA Pasteurized Milk Ordinance and the Minnesota Department of Agriculture Food Handlers License/Processing Plant Permit). The Creamery will house a testing lab to test product quality.

Figure 57.
Example from Cedar Summit Farm—Worksheet 4.8: Inventory and Storage Management

Develop a Strategic Marketing Plan.

Think about how all of your individual product marketing ideas (product, distribution, pricing and promotion) can fit together into one or more general marketing strategies for the whole farm. Use **Worksheet 4.9: Marketing Strategy Summary** to summarize your marketing research and strategies for each product and to note how these strategies and external conditions (such as competition) may change throughout your transition or start-up period. Then think about how individual product strategies fit together into one, whole-farm marketing plan. This is the time to refine your initial product strategies if necessary to incorporate new information.

Business Plan Input—Marketing Strategy Summary:

Our primary marketing strategy is to target health-conscious, upper middle class families with young children and people who remember traditional foods. The consumer will perceive our products as being very different from the regular dairy products in the grocery stores. Our grass-fed cows produce higher amounts of Omega-3 and conjugated linoleic acid in their milk than grain-fed cows. These two fatty acids fight cancer, promote lean muscle mass in humans, and have many other health benefits. Milk from our grass-fed cows will also be processed and marketed as non-homogenized or cream-top milk.

We plan to package our milk in returnable bottles, either glass or plastic depending on costs. It is a common perception that milk in glass bottles stays colder, tastes better, is of higher quality, and has a nostalgic appeal to many customers. We are considering several distributional alternatives in the New Prague and Twin Cities areas: (1) Home delivery; (2) retail; (3) on-farm; (4) farmer's markets and (5) alliances. We expect that the first two distribution options will account for the bulk of our sales. By marketing locally, we hope to build name recognition, a loyal customer base, and dependable sales. Costs may clearly be a disadvantage with home delivery-both in terms of packaging and the need for additional marketing staff to make regular deliveries and communicate with individual customers. We will dominate the market in the New Prague and Twin City areas for a number of years by being the first dairy to bottle milk from grass-fed cows in returnable containers.

Figure 58. Excerpt from Cedar Summit Farm's Worksheet 4.9: Marketing Strategy Summary (side 2)

TASK 4

The Minars completed the Marketing Strategy Summary Worksheet 4.9 for each product in their proposed cream-top product line. An excerpt from their Worksheet for bottled milk—in which they identified several pricing, distribution and packaging strategy alternatives—is shown above. Note that they still had a lot of details to work out, such as expenses associated with glass versus plastic milk cartons and the economic feasibility of on-farm sales and collaborative marketing efforts. But the beginnings of a very strong marketing plan were in place.

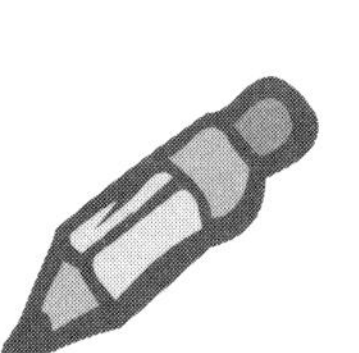

If you haven't already done so, take time now to complete Worksheets 4.1—4.8 for each product that you plan to market. Refine your target market, if necessary, based on your research. Do this together with your planning team. Next, using **Worksheet 4.9: Marketing Strategy Summary**, briefly describe your distribution, packaging, pricing, and promotion strategies for each product and begin gathering expense estimates. Then summarize your product strategies into a whole farm strategic plan. Note any strengths, weaknesses, opportunities and threats (SWOT) associated with each general marketing plan, listing supporting evidence from your research.

The Four Key Management Areas:
- Marketing
- **Operations**
- Human Resources
- Finance

Operations Strategy

With a clear idea of who will buy your product and why, the next planning question you must answer is: How will we produce it? A detailed operations strategy—one that is clear to all involved in the operation—is necessary for sound management and is sometimes an institutional necessity. Organic producers, for example, are required to submit a detailed farm management plan when seeking certification each year. According to certification guidelines, the plan must describe all resource management strategies directed at improving soil fertility; controlling weeds, pests and disease; managing manure; and limiting erosion.[37]

In this section you will have the chance to develop a production management and operations strategy by answering questions about:

- Production Management: What production/management alternatives will we consider? How will we produce?
- Regulation and Policy: What institutional requirements exist?
- Resource Needs: What are our future physical resource needs?
- Gaps: How will we fill physical resource gaps?
- Size and capacity: How much can we produce?
- Storage and Inventory Management: How will we store inventory and maintain product quality?

TASK 4

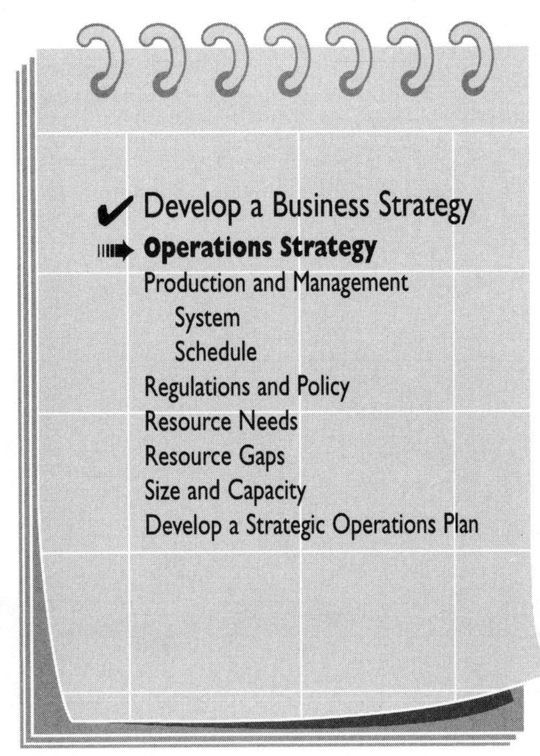

To complete the Operations section of Developing a Business Strategy, you'll consider the issues shown at left.

The operations section of your business plan should address your long-range, strategic approach for production. How will you produce commodities, goods and services? Satisfy legal and regulatory requirements? Use physical resources? Maintain output?

Production and Management: How will we produce?

All operations strategies begin with a detailed description of the business' production (management) system and a production schedule. As a current producer, you may have very clear ideas about how you would like to produce, what management system to use and resource requirements. If so, this portion of the planning process may be a welcome break from the research that was necessary to learn about your customers and competition in the previous section. If you are a beginning farmer, however, you may find that this component of the planning process is just as research-intensive. Take your time, and, most importantly, talk with other experienced farmers when fleshing out the details of your production system and production schedule.

[37] *Organic Certification of Crop Production in Minnesota*, Gulbranson, 2001 (revised).

Production system. Before making their decision to process, the Minars traveled thousands of miles to Maryland, Virginia and West Virginia to visit four other farmer-owned milk processing plants. Each of the plants was similar in size to the Minars' proposed operation. They processed with "Mini-Dairy" equipment from an Israeli-based company called Pladot. By visiting the plants, observing production, and talking first-hand with plant owners, Dave and Florence feel they gained invaluable insights that helped them with decisions about plant construction, equipment purchases and marketing.

Worksheet 4.10 Production System and Schedule

Use the space below to describe the production management system(s) that you use for each enterprise. You may have more than one enterprise for each product that you plan to produce. Be sure to detail your management plans for all enterprises. If you plan to gradually transition into a new management system, complete this Worksheet for each year or season during the transition period. You might find it helpful to use a map or calendar to describe any seasonal or transition-related management plans.

Enterprise ______________________

Year ______________

System

At Cedar Summit Farm we will continue to graze our dairy herd and use all milk from the herd for on-farm processing by 2005. Milk will be hauled to the Creamery with a bulk tank trailer and pumped into a raw milk storage tank. The milk will then move to a pasteurizer and be pasteurized. Next it will be separated into skim milk and cream, and then some cream will be added back to make the assorted milk products. The rest of the cream will be made into ice cream, butter, and other products.

Each batch of milk brought from the dairy barn to the plant will be tested at an on-site lab for traces of antibiotics and butterfat content. Once milk is pasteurized, each batch will be further tested for proper pasteurization. The Minnesota Department of Agriculture will periodically test the milk for bacteria. Finally, all bottled milk and products (except ice cream) will be moved to a 39-degree cooler for storage.

Figure 59. Excerpt from Cedar Summit Farm's Worksheet 4.10: Production System and Schedule

Your choice of production system will be heavily influenced by your social, environmental and community values. This might be a good time to revisit your values and goals, and to recall your objectives for the whole farm. Each production system carries with it different resource requirements, production outcomes, labor demands and natural resource implications.

As you define one or more production system strategies, try to be specific about how the system will work on your farm. If your vision includes a major change in production, think about the resource requirements and the trade-offs between labor, productivity, conservation and profitability that may be associated with different production management systems. Use the space in **Worksheet 4.10: Production System and Schedule** to describe your production system strategies for each farm enterprise. If you plan to produce crops or livestock, for instance, detail your plans for:

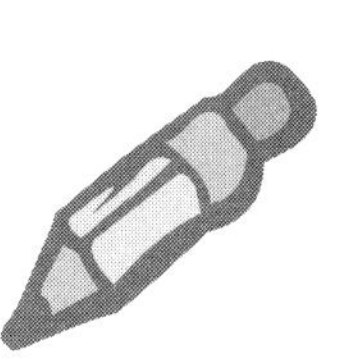

- Weed, pest and disease control
- Soil fertility
- Rotation
- Tillage
- Irrigation
- Water quality
- Seed selection
- Breed selection
- Fencing
- Feed
- Housing
- Stocking
- Waste and quality control

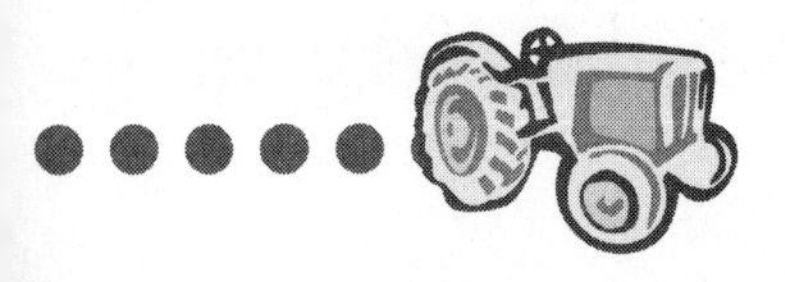

Similarly, if you plan to process or offer a service, the systems component of your plan might address your business' strategy for workshops or on-farm consultations. Northwind Nursery and Orchard owner Frank Foltz, for instance, took time to describe his operation management plans for farm tours and pruning demonstrations.

There are many resources that describe traditional and, increasingly, alternative production systems. Most universities have published research studies on reduced input, organic and livestock grazing systems. Two excellent publications are the *Grazing Systems Planning Guide* and *Making the Transition to Sustainable Farming* (see "Resources"). Most importantly, talk with other farmers—learn from their mistakes and their successes.

Production schedule. Once you have identified one or more production system strategies, think about how management within each system may change over time (e.g., from season to season or from year to year). For instance, how might your livestock management change as you transition from a system of confined farrowing to pasture farrowing for hogs, or from summer grazing to winter feeding for cattle if you plan to seasonally graze? Similarly, think about your annual crop rotation schedule, weekly vegetable harvesting schedule, or daily farm tour schedule. This type of detailed operations planning is critical for any business—it can help you estimate physical and labor resource needs and production potential, as well as cash flow projections. And in many cases, detailed production schedules may be necessary for institutional compliance. Crop producer Mabel Brelje, for example, is required to submit a crop rotation plan annually in order to obtain organic certification. For this reason, she included a rotation map in her final business plan (Figure 60).

Figure 60. Mabel Brelje's Five-Year Crop Rotation Plan

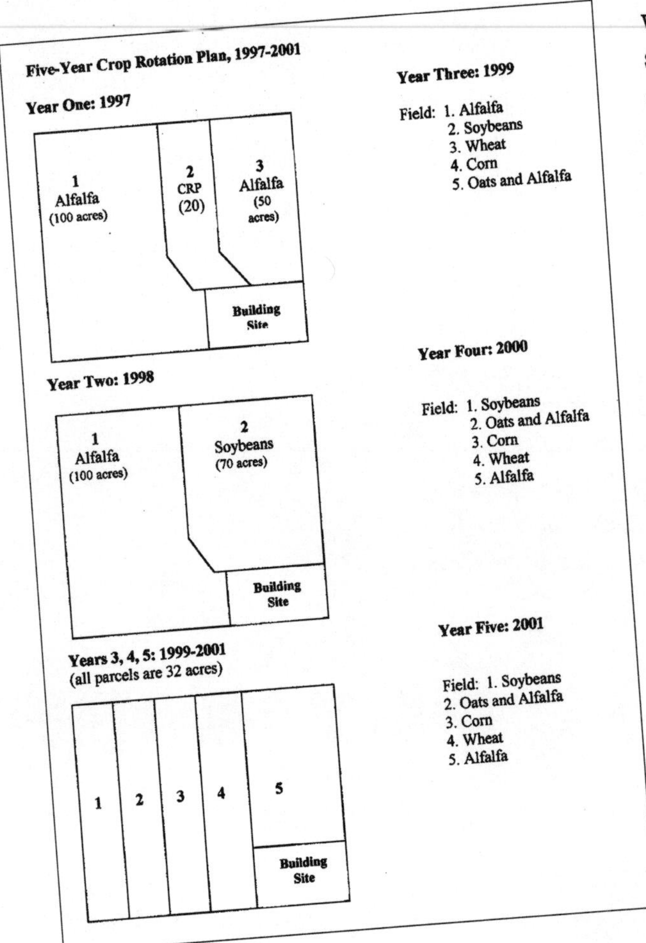

Similarly, Dave and Florence Minar included a proposed processing schedule in their final business plan to communicate financial needs and performance to their lender:

"We plan to process and sell 30 percent of the milk produced on our farm the first year. Processing will then be increased by five percent each month until May 2004 when all of our milk will be processed." The Minars also developed a detailed product processing

schedule for each batch of bottled milk, yogurt, sour cream, butter and ice cream that was not included in their business plan. It served as an internal guide for operations.

Use **Worksheet 4.10: Production System and Schedule** to describe your operations schedule. If you plan to make a gradual transition over time, either from one system to another or through the addition of new enterprises, use Worksheet 4.10 to map out a short-term production plan and descriptions for each phase of the transition. Use a map, a calendar or the space provided. Discuss your schedule with experienced farmers, planning team members, and consultants to determine if your production system and overall schedule are realistic.

Figure 61.
Permits Required by Cedar Summit Farm to Build Plant and Process

1. Conditional Use Permit from Scott County Planning and Zoning
2. Septic Tank Permit from Scott County Environmental Health
3. Health and Safety Plan Approval from the Minnesota Department of Health
4. Building Permit and Inspection from the Scott County Building and Inspections Division
5. Environmental Operating Permit from the Minnesota Pollution Control Agency
6. Food Handlers' License from the Minnesota Department of Agriculture
7. Dairy Plant License from the Minnesota Department of Agriculture

TASK 4

Regulations and Policy: What institutional requirements exist?

Like it or not, if you are going to operate a retail business, process on your farm, or greatly expand livestock production, you will run into local zoning, permitting, licensing and regulatory issues. Regulations can have a major impact on your production and operations plans as well as on start-up costs. Dave and Florence Minar, for example, had to obtain seven permits to build a plant and process their own milk (Figure 61).

The type of permits or licenses required for your business will depend on where you are in the business life-cycle (whether you are just starting up or growing your business), where you live, what type of product you offer, and the overall size of your operation. Therefore, before going too far with your operations research, it's a good idea to check with your state's Small Business Association as well as your local or county regulators to learn about environmental, construction, finance, bonding and product safety regulations. In Minnesota, *A Guide to Starting a Business in Minnesota*[38] lists all necessary state permits and licenses as well as informational contacts. Some examples of the agriculture-related licenses and permits required by the State of Minnesota are listed in Figure 62.

Figure 62.
Some Agricultural Licenses and Permits Required by the State of Minnesota

- Aquaculture License
- Apiary Certificate of Inspection
- Farmstead Cheese Permit
- Dairy Plant License
- Grade A Milk Production Permit
- Feedlot Permit
- Retail and Wholesale Food Handler License
- Livestock Meat Processing and Packing License

38 *A Guide to Starting a Business in Minnesota,* Minnesota Small Business Assistance Office, updated annually.

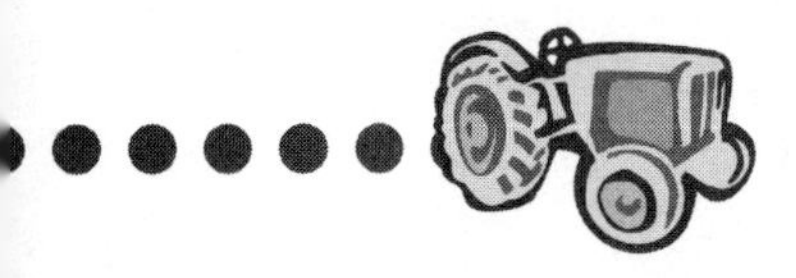

Moreover, if you plan to produce, process or market organic crops, you will need to conduct thorough research about national and international certification requirements. You should contact your state Department of Agriculture for information about the new federal organic certification program.

Use **Worksheet 4.11: Regulations and Policies** to begin your research, listing required permits and licenses, filing requirements, and fees. Next, determine whether or not you will be able to meet legal requirements. Discuss your ideas with planning team members and outside consultants, such as an attorney, when appropriate.

Resource Needs: What are our physical resource needs?

Traditional resource management plans address land, labor and capital. Here you will identify needs in all of these areas, but limit your strategy development to land, buildings, breeding livestock, equipment and variable inputs or supplies. Labor-related strategies are discussed separately in the Human Resources Strategy section.

Take stock of your operation's future resource needs for each enterprise and ultimately, the whole farm. Think about how much land you will need, what type of equipment you will use, and any other physical inputs necessary to produce your product. The choices that you make regarding resource use, acquisition and ownership can have a big impact on the overall profitability of your business. The costs of owning and operating farm machinery in Minnesota, for example, account for 20 to 30 percent of the annual per acre production costs for corn and soybeans.[39]

If you are new to the business or industry and uncertain about resource requirements, try talking with experienced producers or your local Extension educator to begin brainstorming a realistic list of land, livestock, machinery, equipment, labor and other input needs. If you plan to produce a specialty commodity or use an alternative management system, accurate production input records may not be readily available. In this case, your research may take you to the Internet or some of the alternative experiment stations located at universities across the country. Your regional SARE office (see "Resources") may be able to help you locate information sources in your area.

Dave and Florence Minar developed a list of processing resource needs by visiting other on-farm dairy processing plants and from business plans shared by these same business operators. Using this information, the Minars were able to generate a fairly detailed list of needed machinery, equipment and start-up inputs (Figure 63).

39 *Sharing Farm Machinery*, Weness, 2001.

Referring to your completed Worksheets 2.5 and 2.6, use **Worksheet 4.12: Describing Potential Crop Production Systems** and **Worksheet 4.13: Describing Potential Livestock Production Systems** to record future resource needs for crop and livestock enterprises, respectively. Think about how your operating schedule and corresponding resource needs will change as you transition into a new management system over a period of seasons or years.

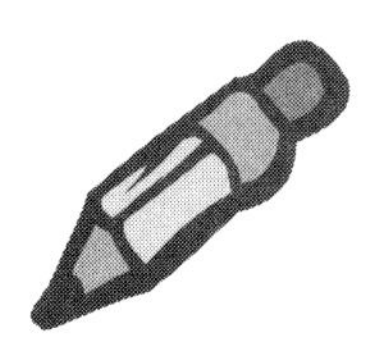

Resource Gaps: How will we fill physical resource gaps?

Another critical component of your operations strategy involves your plan for filling resource gaps. Return to your crop and livestock production schedules (Worksheets 2.5 and 2.6) from Planning Task Two in which you described current crop and livestock input needs and equipment use. Compare these lists to those that you completed for future operations (Worksheets 4.12 and 4.13). Are there any gaps? Or perhaps you now have underutilized resources?

Consider some of your strategy alternatives for filling or eliminating gaps between current land, building, machinery and equipment availability and future physical resource needs. Will you:

- Make better use of existing machinery and equipment?
- Acquire additional (new or used) resources?
- Gain access to additional resources through business arrangements (formal and informal)?

Making changes in your current resource use may mean making "better" use of underutilized resources. Based on your evaluation of current resource availability and future needs, are there any resources that are underutilized or that will become underutilized as you move toward your future vision? If so, one of your resource management strategies might be to "make better use of underutilized resources." How you define "better" will depend on your values and goals. For example, it may mean sharing or renting out equipment with another family member or neighbor.

If the gap between current resource availability and future resource needs is significant, you may need to look at acquiring additional physical resources. This can be a financially risky alternative. You will need to carefully evaluate cash flow in the next section before implementing your plans. For now, however, consider the following acquisition options if you think additional capital will be needed to meet future operating needs.

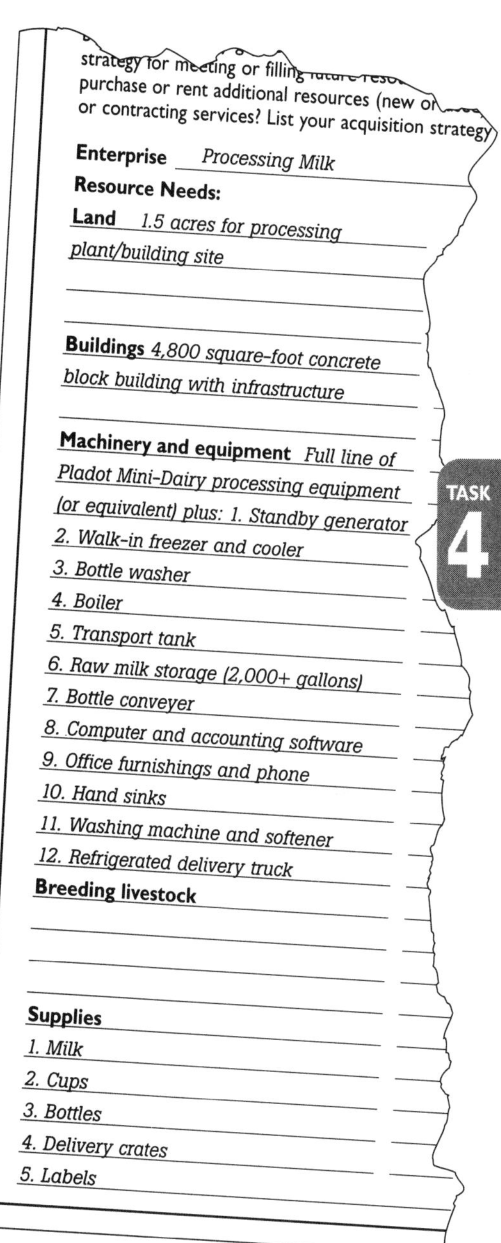

strategy for meeting or filling ... purchase or rent additional resources (new or ... or contracting services? List your acquisition strategy

Enterprise *Processing Milk*

Resource Needs:

Land *1.5 acres for processing plant/building site*

Buildings *4,800 square-foot concrete block building with infrastructure*

Machinery and equipment *Full line of Pladot Mini-Dairy processing equipment (or equivalent) plus: 1. Standby generator*
2. Walk-in freezer and cooler
3. Bottle washer
4. Boiler
5. Transport tank
6. Raw milk storage (2,000+ gallons)
7. Bottle conveyer
8. Computer and accounting software
9. Office furnishings and phone
10. Hand sinks
11. Washing machine and softener
12. Refrigerated delivery truck

Breeding livestock

Supplies
1. Milk
2. Cups
3. Bottles
4. Delivery crates
5. Labels

Figure 63. Excerpt from Cedar Summit Farm's Worksheet 4.14: Resource Needs and Acquisition

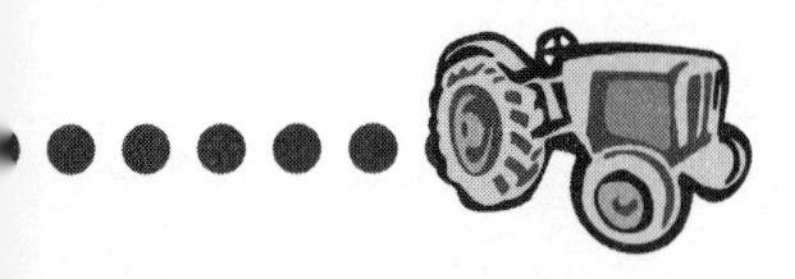

Land and buildings. Land and buildings can be purchased, rented or leased (Figure 64). Each of these acquisition options has financial advantages and disadvantages, which will be discussed further later, when you address finance strategies. For now, though, you should realize that land acquisition options should be weighed carefully. Land purchase decisions can make or break your business. They often require a large amount of capital and a long-term commitment. In a video presentation, Gayle Willett says "Purchasing real estate is one of the most important decisions a business may make . . . It is important not to let emotion overrule sound business judgment . . . .Consider both what the land is worth to the business and what you can pay for the land and still have cash flow."[40] If purchasing land is a part of your operations strategy, you'll evaluate the feasibility of that strategy carefully in the finance sections. You'll need to discuss cash flow, tax and equity implications with an accountant.

Machinery and equipment. If additional machinery and equipment will be needed—either to replace old equipment or to meet new resource requirements—you have several acquisition options, such as purchasing, renting, leasing, custom hiring, or exchanging labor for access to equipment (Figure 64).

TASK 4

If you plan to purchase additional equipment, you should also consider the advantages of buying new versus used equipment. The financial, labor, and production-related advantages and disadvantages of new versus used equipment are outlined in Figure 65. Think about these issues as well as your ability or willingness to perform equipment repairs and to finance large capital purchases.

As you brainstorm machinery and equipment acquisition options, it's a good idea to talk with other farmers, equipment dealers and competitors about their experiences. The Minars conducted research about equipment alternatives by visiting with other farmers in person and on the phone. They traveled around the state of Minnesota and as far as West Virginia to visit other on-farm dairy processing operations.

Based on their conversations with other on-farm processors, the Minars decided to pursue the use of new equipment from Pladot, an equipment manufacturer located in Israel. The Pladot Mini-Dairy system can be sized according to the Minar's milk production capacity. Moreover, Pladot provides training, technical support and product recipes as part of the Mini-Dairy equipment package. They felt that by purchasing the turn-key processing system from Pladot, they would be able to produce a range of quality products from their first batch of processed milk. They were concerned that their other alternative, purchasing used equipment, would risk difficulties in locating and fitting equipment, in getting the system up and running efficiently, and in developing their own recipes.

40 *Analyzing Land Investments, Business Management in Agriculture* videotape series, Willett, 1988.

Figure 64.

Machinery Acquisition Options[41]

Full ownership. Ownership is the most common method of acquiring long-term control of farm machinery. Ownership advantages include control over the machine's use and scheduling. The disadvantages of full ownership include responsibility for machine operation, repairs, maintenance, liquidation and obsolescence, and capital investments.

Joint ownership. Joint ownership is becoming more and more common as a way to distribute responsibility for investment costs, repairs, and labor among two or more businesses. However, cooperation is essential. Equipment use must be coordinated and capital payments made in a timely manner. Problems can arise when the parties involved do not share a similar work and finance ethic. Written agreements are highly recommended.

Exchange work. Machinery exchange among neighbors is one of the oldest forms of farm machinery acquisition on a short-term basis. Two or more farmers working together to share labor and equipment can reduce their individual investments in machinery while giving each access to a complete system. Exchange work is still a common method of machinery acquisition among young or beginning farmers who need machinery and an older neighbor who requires labor. As with joint ownership, a working agreement is very important to determine whose farm is serviced first and who pays for repair costs.

Custom hire. Under traditional custom hire arrangements, the farm operator or landowner hires a custom operator to do one or more field operations. The custom operator provides the machinery, labor and fuel and agrees to perform specified duties at predetermined costs. Today, however, custom farming (the landowner hires a custom operator to perform most or all field operations) is gaining more interest. Under this arrangement, the landowner usually pays all cash costs, including seed and fertilizer. If you are considering a custom farming arrangement, you will need to specify the following in a written agreement: location and acreage involved, custom services required, landowner obligations, provisions for default, and a schedule of custom rates and a payment plan.

Rental. Rental usually takes place for a short, specified period. In this case, the farm owner rents a particular piece of machinery and performs all required work. The renter is responsible for daily maintenance of the machinery. Generally, there are two rental options—pure rental and rental purchase. If you are considering a rental arrangement, be sure to review the terms of each option.

Leasing. Unlike rental, leasing allows the farm business owner to gain access to machinery over a long period of time, such as 5-7 years. The advantage of the lease arrangement, from a cash flow perspective, is that payments are typically less than payments on borrowed money to own the machine. Leasing also carries its disadvantages. Often the lease payment schedule extends beyond a debt payment schedule and therefore the total amount paid for the machine usually exceeds the full ownership cost. Moreover, by leasing, it is often more difficult to enforce warranty claims against the lessor or dealer.

Figure 65.

New Versus Used Machinery and Equipment[42]

Used machinery and equipment. Purchasing used equipment requires relatively low up-front investment costs. However, used equipment is generally less dependable than new equipment, hence labor, repair, lubrication and fuel costs are usually higher than for new machinery and equipment. Ultimately, this means that buying used equipment results in higher variable costs for the business.

New machinery and equipment. New equipment is typically more efficient and convenient and may include training or technical assistance. As a trade-off, however, new equipment can be more expensive up front, requiring larger capital investments, insurance, interest costs and depreciation.

41 *Acquiring and Managing Resources for the Farm Business*, Thomas, 2001.

42 Ibid.

Dave Minar

Figure 66.
Pladot bottle filler used by Valley Fresh Dairy, West Virginia

TASK 4

"Without recipes we would have to experiment one product at a time in order to develop quality milk, cheese, sour cream and yogurt," explains Florence Minar. *"With the Pladot recipes, we wouldn't waste any time or money developing our product line, which means that we could begin marketing a wide range of products almost immediately."*

Return to Worksheets 2.5 and 2.6 where you described current crop and livestock resource use. Combine this information with the list of current tangible working assets (Worksheet 2.3) to identify any gaps between current and future resource needs. Look at the status of current buildings and equipment to realistically determine what can be used. Ask yourself whether there will be any overlapping demand for building space, equipment and machinery or whether replacements may be needed.

Then return to **Worksheet 4.14: Resource Needs and Acquisition** to begin brainstorming resource acquisition options. Be creative as you think about how to fill your machinery and equipment needs. Mabel Brelje, for example, settled on a resource management strategy that included both crop sharing and cash rental agreements. *"Under these agreements,"* Mabel writes in her business plan, *"much needed labor and equipment is contributed by the contracting parties. I am continuing to conduct portions of the fieldwork for which I have equipment, as well as most of the planning, decision making and soil analysis."* Look for opportunities to meet your land, labor and equipment needs through strategic alliances, formal partnerships, or crop sharing arrangements.

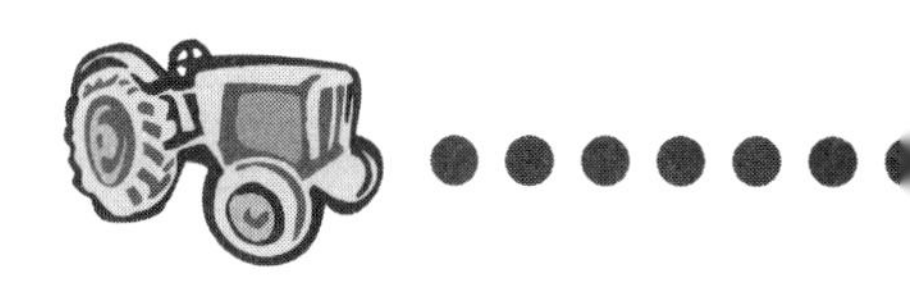

Size and Capacity: How much can we produce?

Your goals for growing or contracting the business as well as upper and lower limits on size will affect your choice of business organization (discussed next in the Finance Operation Strategy section) and your operations schedule. Farm size refers to the amount of land in production (number of acres), the number of animals you raise, and the value of gross income from the business. Someone who is planning to convert from a traditional cattle finishing operation to management-intensive grazing, for instance, may be limited in size during the transition period while pastures are developed and management techniques fine-tuned.

How will you size the business and plan for any growth? Begin your research with a little number crunching to determine realistic production estimates for each future enterprise and production schedule. Use information about the future carrying capacity of your land, the processing capacity of your equipment, boarding capacity of your Bed and Breakfast, or harvesting capacity of your family and staff to develop output projections. Use **Worksheet 4.15: Institutional Considerations** to help you think through any legal or regulatory agreements or policies that will affect the use and management of physical resources under your new operations strategies.

Historical information about yield performance and productivity are available for traditional enterprises from a number of resources. Check with your local Extension office or your state Department of Agriculture. In the Upper Midwest, check out FINBIN[43] and Farm Business Management's Annual Report.[44] Again, alternative production system information might be a little harder to find, but your local Extension office or state Department of Agriculture should be able to give you some ideas of who to contact in your area if they don't have that information. Check also with sustainable agriculture organizations in your area or your regional SARE office. One of your most useful resources may be other farmers—those who are on the cutting edge—using a new production system or technology.

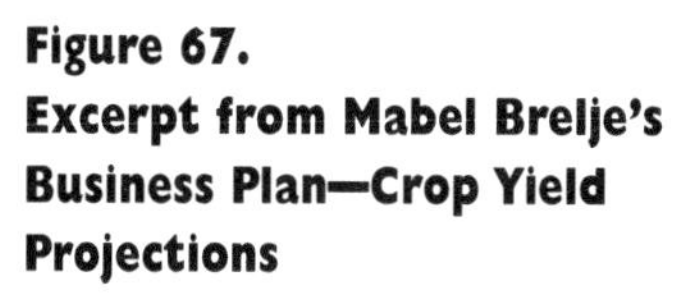

Figure 67. Excerpt from Mabel Brelje's Business Plan—Crop Yield Projections

Crop Yield Projections

Crop	Yield/Acre	
	High	Low
Alfalfa	Six Tons	Three Tons
Soybeans	55 bushels	30 bushels
Wheat	50 bushels	30 bushels
Corn	150 bushels	100 bushels

As you develop output/production estimates, particularly for alternative enterprises with little recorded performance history, you may want to estimate "best" and "worst" case production scenarios, or high and low output projections. Organic crop producer, Mabel Brelje chose to develop high and low yield projections for her oilseed and grain crops as shown in Figure 67. She used these projections in her financial analysis to evaluate profitability and risk.

Dave and Florence Minar developed an upper limit for bottled milk production based on pasture acreage, herd productivity, and equipment capacity. At current productivity levels and herd size, the Minars' cows produce 166,913 pounds of

43 FINBIN database (online), Center for Farm Financial Management, 2002.

44 *Farm Business Management Annual Reports*, Crop Information, 2002.

Worksheet 4.16 Estimating Output and Capacity

Complete this Worksheet for each major product you plan to produce. Compile your market research (Worksheets 4.1–4.7) for each year in your transition period and for your long run or expected market outlook, as appropriate. Begin with a description of your target market (by segment). Then summarize product characteristics and competition, as well as your plans for distribution, pricing and promotion. Next, use the space below to estimate gross sales revenue and to record marketing expense estimates. You will use this expense information when evaluating the business' projected financial performance in the Evaluation section of Planning Task Four. Finally, summarize your marketing strategies for this product or the whole farm. Be sure to include a SWOT (strengths, weaknesses, opportunities, threats) analysis. This will be the start of your marketing strategy section for the written business plan.

Enterprise: *Bottled milk*

	Long Run (Expected)	**Transition Period** Year 1	Year 2	Year 3
Typical output				
Expected output	*166,916 pounds milk/month (34,993 half-gallon bottles)*	*50,075 pounds milk/month*	*110,000 pounds milk/month*	*166,916 pounds milk/month*
High output				
Low output				
Production capacity	*207,666 pounds milk/month (43,536 half-gallon bottles)*			

Using Pladot equipment, our maximum production capacity would be 207,666 pounds of milk/month or 43,536 half-gallon bottles/month. The carrying capacity of all of land in pasture is 250 cows, which would yield 278,188 pounds of milk/month. Our Creamery output will therefore be limited by the processing capacity of our equipment, unless we eventually decide to contract out a portion of our processing or sell some of our milk on the open market.

At the whole-farm level, we plan to (grow/maintain/contract) our business:

We will not grow the herd beyond the maximum carrying capacity of our current land holdings. We will grow the processing portion of our business gradually from 50,075 pounds of milk/month in November 2001 to 166,916 pounds per month by May 2004. Approximately 40 percent of all raw milk will be processed as skim, two-percent, and whole bottled milk (flavored and unflavored).

Figure 68. Example from Cedar Summit Farm—Worksheet 4.16: Estimating Output and Capacity

milk per month. The Pladot Mini-Dairy equipment can process between 148,333—207,667 pounds of milk per month. Should market demand increase for their products, the Minars could increase their herd (and output) to 187 cows and process at the plant's full capacity. They have the acreage to support more cows. However, this would necessitate converting some of their hay fields to pasture or acquiring access to additional land resources. These are issues that the Minars will need to evaluate in their contingency plan should future opportunities arise.

Use **Worksheet 4.16: Estimating Output and Capacity** to estimate production/output potential and begin shaping a size-related strategy for the business. If appropriate, describe your growth or contraction strategy for the whole farm and for each future enterprise.

Develop a Strategic Operations Plan

You're ready to develop a whole farm operations plan! Use **Worksheet 4.17: Operations Strategy Summary** to briefly describe the management system you intend to implement for each enterprise. Detail crop rotations, pasture layout and rotation, milking schedules, etc. Think about how these might change throughout your start-up or transition period. Next, list new resource needs and your strategy for acquiring them. Then record all operating expenses associated with each enterprise or the whole farm (if appropriate). Finally, you're ready to pull your enterprise-specific operations strategies together into one, whole-farm production and operations strategy.

The Minars summarized their operations strategy on Worksheet 4.17, as shown in Figure 69.

Total expenses

Business Plan Input - Operations Strategy Summary:

Our operations strategy is to eventually process all of our milk on the farm. We will begin by processing 30 percent of our milk in November 2001 and increase production by five percent each month until all milk from our current-size dairy herd is processed into milk, butter, and other cream-top products.

We will need to build a processing plant on the farm and will most likely acquire processing equipment new from Pladot. There are several advantages of going with the new Pladot Mini-Dairy system:
1. Their equipment can be sized to our operation;
2. Pladot will supply all technical training and product recipes so that we can process a full line of dairy products right away instead of experimenting on our own, one product at a time; and
3. We will have a turn-key system up and running almost immediately.

The only disadvantage of going with the new equipment is cost - we will have to explore financing alternatives and cash flow.

Figure 69. Excerpt from Cedar Summit Farm's Worksheet 4.17: Operations Strategy Summary

As you draft a whole-farm operations summary, be sure to include supporting research and note the strengths, weaknesses, opportunities and threats (SWOT) associated with each strategy alternative. You will use this information in the next section to evaluate the feasibility of each strategy alternative and to settle on a final course of action for the business. It's also a good idea to have each planning team member summarize a whole farm operations strategy and work through a SWOT analysis on their own. Then you can compare notes and brainstorm about internal and external threats, and make sure everyone agrees on which overall operations plan you will pursue.

Human Resources Strategy

The Four Key Management Areas:
- Marketing
- Operations
- **Human Resources**
- Finance

Labor and management are important to the success of any business—particularly family farm businesses. Working together, managing each other, making key decisions collectively all can be challenging when you not only work together but live together. These challenges grow when a major change in business strategy is involved—when the roles of managers, family members, and employees can shift from production management to marketing management for instance.

In this section, you and your planning team will begin to build a human resources strategy to address your changing management and work force needs. This strategy should embrace your family goals while meeting new business needs.

You will begin your strategic planning by answering questions about:

- Labor needs: What are our future workforce needs?
- Skills: What skills will be required to fill workforce needs?
- Gaps: How will we fill workforce gaps?
- Compensation: How will we pay family and members of our workforce?
- Management and communication: Who will manage the business and how?

You'll work through this Human Resources section of Developing a Business Strategy by working through the following aspects of Human Resources in the order shown below.

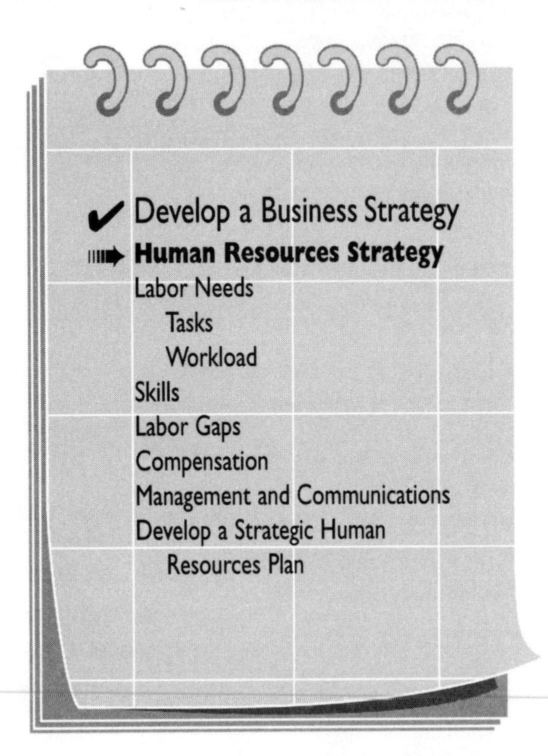

You will begin your research by determining projected labor needs for each enterprise (product). Next, you will compare your projected labor needs against current labor resources to identify any gaps, as you did in the operations section for physical resources. You and your planning team will then need to consider how to fill those gaps and to identify one or more strategies for doing so. Finally, you will develop a strategy for managing labor and the business. This is perhaps one of the most critical components of your business strategy. Without an effective management plan or business manager, even the best of business plans can fall apart. Take your time developing a human resources management strategy—it will be one of your keys to success.

Labor Needs: What are our future workforce needs?

Begin building your human resources strategy with some critical thinking about the type of work and accompanying workloads that will be necessary to reach your future vision and to carry out the marketing-, operations- and finance-related work within the business.

Tasks. What new marketing-, operations- and finance-related tasks will be required to produce and market a new product or to implement and manage a new production system? Be realistic about your labor needs and consider the not-so-obvious elements of business ownership and management, such as time required to communicate with staff, make equipment repairs, and handle administrative needs. For example, if you are considering organic production, be sure to plan ample time for record keeping. The paperwork necessary to track inputs, harvest and storage in an organic system can be tedious and time consuming.

"Many organic producers consider the organic premium to be primarily a payment for the extra administrative efforts required by credible certification agencies," notes certification specialist Lisa Gulbranson. "The audit trail for a certified organic product must be maintained with great detail."[45]

45 *Organic Certification of Crop Production in Minnesota*, Gulbranson, 2001 (revised).

Workload. Once you and your planning team have brainstormed a list of new tasks, try to estimate how much time each task will require and note any seasonal bottlenecks. This will help you to visualize the peaks and valleys of work demands, which in turn will help determine how to fill workforce needs or reduce workloads. Be sure to include work involved in producing and marketing products, maintaining equipment and facilities, and in managing the business when calculating your labor needs. If you are uncertain about how much time will be needed for each task, talk with other farmers, like the Minars did, or consult Appendix E for a list of traditional enterprise-related labor requirements. If you haven't already done so, return to Worksheets 2.8 and 2.9, in which you described the labor requirements for current tasks. You could also begin this research by tracking your own current hours (if you are already in business) to get a sense of just how much time is involved in seemingly routine tasks. You may be surprised by the results. Then use these actual recorded hours as a basis for developing realistic projections for your future labor and staff needs.

Worksheet 4.18 Tasks and Workload

Use the space below to describe the marketing, operations, human resources and finance tasks associated with each new enterprise. Refer to Worksheets 4.11–4.12 (Describing Potential Crop and Livestock Systems) for operations workload estimates. Then estimate the workload (hours) associated with each task. If your business tends to be seasonal, distribute the total hours for each activity by periods of the year. Use a separate sheet of paper if more space is needed or make copies of this Worksheet to detail workload changes for each year in your transition period, as appropriate.

Enterprise *Processed dairy products* **Timeframe** *January–June 2002*

Tasks	Hours/Month											
	Jan	Feb	Mar	Apr	May	June	July	Aug	Sep	Oct	Nov	Dec
Marketing:												
Customer service (orders)	56	56	56	56	56	56						
Deliveries, loading	120	120	120	120	120	120						
Promotion	20	20	20	20	20	20						
Operations												
Order supplies	20	20	20	20	20	20						
Transport milk, test	40	40	40	40	40	40						
Pasteurize, process and package milk	320	320	320	320	320	320						
Management:												
Oversee plant operations	40	40	40	40	40	40						
Manage staff	20	20	20	20	20	20						
Oversee training, meet with Pladot representative	40	40	40	40	40	40						
Finances:												
Bookkeeping	10	10	10	10	10	10						
Payroll	4	4	4	4	4	4						
Tax preparation	1	1	1	5	5	1						
Financial analysis	10	4	2	2	2	2						
Total Hrs/Month	701	695	693	697	697	693						

TASK 4

Figure 70.
Example from Cedar Summit Farm—Worksheet 4.18: Tasks and Workload

In Worksheet 4.18, shown in Figure 70, the Minars summarized their labor needs for processed products. Dave and Florence anticipated some seasonal bursts of marketing activity during winter and spring holidays. Preceding each

Figure 71. Florence Minar (left) working on the Minnesota Organic Milk (MOM's) processing line.

holiday season, the Minars budgeted extra staff time to handle on-farm customer sales. Similarly, their financial staff needs are expected to increase at year-end and prior to tax reporting. Product promotion and delivery workloads are expected to remain fairly constant throughout the year, as will time needed to process products. Staff needs may increase as the Minars reach full processing capacity in 2004. Labor estimates for plant staff are based on conversations with other on-farm processors and a Pladot equipment representative. Look at the Minars' completed **Worksheet 4.18: Tasks and Workload** for Cedar Summit Creamery's processing enterprise and begin to develop your own labor and staff estimates.

TASK 4

Skills: What skills will be required to fill workforce needs?

Before you begin to develop a strategy for filling workforce needs, you should get a good feel for the type of skills required for each new task or position. This information, combined with workload estimates, should help you better decide how to fill your human resources needs.

Begin your research by learning more about any new work that you and others will be required to do. Ohio State University economist Chris Zoller recommends developing "well thought-out job descriptions" that are compatible with the business' mission and goals for each new position that will be created.[46] Job descriptions—even for those positions that will be filled internally with family labor—can help make your human resources strategy a positive one by clearly identifying desired skills, expectations, responsibilities and compensation. A sample job description form is included in Appendix C to help you with this task.

As part of their "skills" research, Dave and Florence Minar pitched in at Minnesota Organic Milk (MOM's)—an on-farm processing plant located in Gibbon, Minnesota (Figure 71). They worked on the MOM's processing line one afternoon to help with butter production and packaging. Based on this experience and their visits to other on-farm dairy processing plants around the country, the Minars developed a good feel for future workloads and tasks. Consequently, they felt confident developing a realistic strategy for meeting some of their future labor needs. Explore similar opportunities as you begin identifying tasks. Try to get a feel for skills that may be required for each task.

Use **Worksheet 4.19: Filling Workforce Needs** to begin describing the skills that are required for each new task or position.

46 *Filling a Position in the Farm Business*, Zoller, 1997.

Gaps: How will we fill workforce gaps?

Next, think about how you will fill current and future workforce gaps. In other words, begin building your human resources strategy. You could:

- Redefine tasks for the current workforce.
- Add new labor to the workforce.
- Access additional labor through work-trade, contracting, or new business arrangements.
- Substitute capital for labor.

Will you shift responsibilities or reassign tasks among your current workforce? Will you hire family or community members to fill new jobs? Will you reorganize the business to reduce your own workload? Any one of these strategies may be appropriate for your business depending on the values and goals identified by your planning team, your financial picture, and the skills of your current workforce.

The labor strategy that you choose will depend on how much of a gap exists between your current workforce and your projected workforce needs. For instance, if most of your projected labor needs can be met through your current workforce, you may decide to hire part-time workers or custom operators to meet seasonal bottlenecks or remaining needs. On the other hand, if you anticipate major gaps between current and future labor needs, you may want to consider hiring additional permanent or temporary staff, substituting capital for labor, or reorganizing the business into a partnership so that labor (and equipment) can be shared.

Figure 72.
Filling Workforce Needs[48]

Contract service providers. Contract workers may be self-employed or an employee of the contract provider. Crop harvesting is one of the most common contract services provided. If you plan to contract for services, be sure to consult your tax accountant regarding tax withholding and employer liabilities.

Custom operators. Custom operators are usually the cheapest source of temporary labor. Custom operators often are well trained and supply their own equipment. They require no tax withholding or benefit packages. The primary advantage of custom operators is that they free up family labor and employees for other specialized tasks.

Employees. Hiring full- and part-time employees requires time (searching, hiring, training, managing) and raises new issues to deal with, including compensation, benefits packages, discipline and sometimes firing. They can make a business more profitable only if they are truly needed and are a good match.

Family labor. Farm operators and other "unpaid" family members account for two-thirds of the production workforce in agriculture. They offer the advantage of knowing your business well, but can also carry family conflict into the business.

Seasonal hired labor. Hired labor is typically used to fill seasonal workforce shortages when operators and family members are unable to supply the necessary labor. Hired labor is usually paid less than other workers or employees. There are many laws and regulations that govern seasonal or migrant labor.

If you've decided to reassign current tasks or jobs, refer to the skills assessment that you developed in Planning Task Two (Worksheet 2.7), along with each team member's personal workload goals (Worksheet 3.3) to determine who will fill projected work force needs. Be realistic! On the other hand, if you plan to add labor, consider the range of acquisition options such as contract labor, custom operators, employees, family labor, interns and volunteers. The advantages and disadvantages of some of these alternatives are described in Figure 72. Some of these strategy alternatives may have significant tax, equity and cash flow implications.[47] You will have an opportunity to evaluate workforce plans from a financial perspective later, before finalizing the labor

47 *Labor Laws and Regulations*, Miller, 1997.

48 *Economic and Business Principles in Farm Planning and Production*, James and Eberle, 2000.

component of your whole farm business strategy.

According to their workforce strategy in Worksheet 4.17, the Minars could fill nearly all of their workforce needs through the creation of permanent jobs for several family members. Their daughter, Laura Ganske, would become the business' new distribution manager. She would coordinate and staff home deliveries and on-farm sales. Mike Minar and his wife, Merrisue, would also both join the business as permanent employees. Mike would become the processing plant manager. He would oversee production, testing, and packaging. Merrisue would work part-time as the business' office manager. She would handle bookkeeping and payroll. The Minars' youngest child, Dan Minar, also will join the business full-time as a marketing manager once he has completed his university degree. Dave, Florence, and their current partner, Paul Kajer, would be reassigned to new tasks. Dave and Florence would work full-time in the plant while Paul would take over Dave's current work as livestock manager, performing all pasture and dairy production-related management tasks. This shift would create a new gap—the need for a full-time milker—that the Minars planed to fill with external hired labor.

TASK 4

Worksheet 4.19 Filling Workforce Needs

Use the space below to flesh out new position titles and task descriptions for each new enterprise or existing enterprise that is short on labor. Next, if adding labor, describe the type of position that will be created—full-time or part-time, temporary or permanent, seasonal or year-round—as well as the skills desired for each position. Lastly, describe your strategy for addressing workforce gaps and acquiring and training labor. Workforce strategies may include: reassigning current labor; adding new labor (family, employees, volunteers, interns); hiring out work to custom operators or consultants; or developing work trade arrangements with neighbors or relatives. You might also consider reducing some of your labor needs through the use of additional equipment and machinery or through new business arrangements.

Position/Task (title)	Type of Position (full time/part time, temporary/permanent)	Skills/Experience Desired	Acquisition Strategy
Office Manager (bookkeeping, payroll, tax preparation)	*One part-time, permanent*	*Accounting background; good with numbers; accurate*	*Fill internally with family labor: Merrisue Minar*
Marketing Manager (communicate with customers, wholesale buyers, take orders, promote products)	*One full-time, permanent position*	*Marketing experience; personable; articulate; creative; excellent knowledge of products and grazing philosophy*	*Fill internally with family labor: Dan Minar*
Distribution Manager (load, unload truck, deliver products)	*One full-time permanent position*	*Driver's license; personable; physically able to haul products*	*Fill internally with family labor: Laura Ganske*
Processing Plant Manager (oversee processing, monitor quality, fine-tune processing schedule, haul milk to plant, back-up plant staff)	*One full-time, permanent position*	*Management experience; mechanical skills; good communication skills*	*Fill internally with family labor: Mike Minar*
Processing Plant Staff (operate equipment, test milk and products)	*Two full-time, permanent positions*	*Willingness to operate equipment; mechanical skills; friendly, cleanliness*	*Fill internally with family: Reassign Dave and Florence Minar from current farm management and marketing roles*
Computer Technician (set up computers, software programs, maintenance, staff training)	*One part-time, permanent position*	*Software and hardware training and experience*	*Fill internally with family labor: Eric Ganske*
Farm manager (manage hay crop production, pastures, livestock production, monitor herd health, relief milker)	*One full-time, permanent position*	*Knowledge of forages, pasture rotation; field work/equipment operating experience; comfortable around animals; milking experience*	*Fill internally: Reassign current CSF partner, Paul Kajer, from milking staff position to management position*

CONTINUED

Figure 73. Example from Cedar Summit Farm—Worksheet 4.19: Filling Workforce Needs (both sides)

Worksheet 4.19 Filling Workforce Needs

CONTINUED

Position/Task (title)	Type of Position (full time/part time, temporary/permanent)	Skills/Experience Desired	Acquisition Strategy
Farm staff (new milker)	*One full-time, permanent position*	*Milking experience; comfortable around animals; reliable*	*Fill externally: hire CSF employee*
Designer/Artist (New logo)	*One part-time, temporary position*	*Experience with logo design; graphic art skills; creativity*	*Fill internally with family labor: Bob White*

1. Describe training that may be required for new positions or new members of the workforce:

All processing plant staff will need to be trained in equipment use, product safety/quality testing, and packaging procedures. Our current partner, Paul, will need to be trained in pasture management. Our other workforce members bring the necessary skills to the operation so there should not be very much training.

2. How will training be accomplished?

Pladot [equipment manufacturer] will provide all training on-site at our plant once it is built - they will help us learn how to operate equipment, select recipes, and package our products. They provide several weeks of initial training and additional technical support as needed. Dave [Minar] will be responsible for working with Paul Kajer on pasture management.

Ultimately, your labor strategy—your decision to hire workers, purchase equipment or reorganize the business—will depend on your financial goals and personal values. For instance, there is clearly more than one way for the Minars to staff their processing plant and to fill distribution and production positions. In addition to family labor, they could have considered hired labor and employees for processing and crop production. However, because their values and planning purpose are rooted in the idea of creating jobs and income for family members, they limited their strategy options to hiring family members and redefining family member roles as a way to fill most new jobs/tasks. As you develop a workforce strategy, revisit your values and goals for human resources. Think about your willingness to perform fieldwork, communicate with customers, work with livestock, or maintain financial records, among other things.

Use **Worksheet 4.19: Filling Workforce Needs** to describe your strategy for addressing workforce gaps or acquiring and training labor.

Compensation: How will we pay family and members of our workforce?

Wages and other benefits that you offer family, employees, hired labor, interns and contracted labor will vary with industry rates and standards as well as the type of work involved and, of course, your values. You and your planning team will need to consider all of these factors when developing a labor compensation package as part of your overall human resources strategy.

A good place to begin developing your benefits strategy is by looking at industry standards. Find out what salary and other benefits are typical for your business (check with your state Department of Agriculture or talk to other farmers) and adjust them according to your own values and goals. The Minars, for instance, decided to pay their son a salary that was comparable to what he earned as a production supervisor at a high-tech medical supply manufacturer. Although this salary may be well above dairy industry standards, Dave and Florence agreed to offer their son a comparable salary because of his commitment to the business, family needs, and their own vision of a "fair" wage. Of course, the Minars' plan to pay an above-average salary must be balanced against their financial objectives for cash flow, profitability, and net equity growth—something they had to consider when evaluating their strategic plan.

In addition to a cash wage or salary, common forms of labor compensation include housing (room and board), products (milk, meat, nursery stock, cheese), automobile, insurance (health, accident), stocks or shares of the business, and retirement investments, such as a Simplified Employeed Pension (SEP) Plan or 401K.[49] You may want to review business organization alternative strategies (addressed as you develop a Finance Strategy in the next section) to explore tax and other institutional requirements before settling on a labor compensation strategy. An accountant or attorney will be able to help you work out the details of human resources compensation.

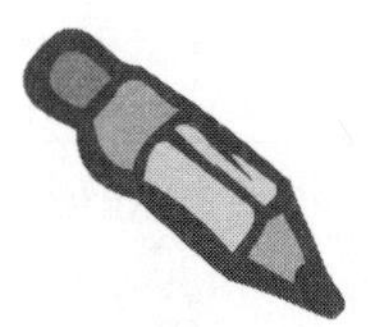

Use **Worksheet 4.20: Compensation** to research and draft a compensation plan for each new position or worker. Then use this information to develop monthly and hourly labor input expense estimates for each position in **Worksheet 4.21: Human Resources Expense Estimates**. These will be used as you evaluate the profitability and cash flow of your alternative strategies.

Management and Communication: Who will manage the business and how?

Good management and communication are pivotal and often intangible qualities of a successful business. No matter how well a business strategy has been researched and evaluated, it will not help accomplish your goals unless there is an effective manager behind it— one who knows how to communicate.

49 *Acquiring and Managing Resources for the Farm Business*, Thomas, 2001.

Therefore, spend a little time fleshing out a management and communication plan for the business.

Management. Farm business managers, like most independent small business owners, are responsible for a range of tasks that include planning, organization, decision-making and control of resources.[50] They are responsible for the long-term development and success of the business—implementing the business plan, monitoring performance, and facilitating change.

Based on your skills assessment in Planning Task Two (Worksheet 2.9), think about your ability and desire to manage the farm business—to plan, organize, make decisions and communicate with your workforce. Taking on management responsibilities yourself is only one of several strategic options. You might consider other strategic alternatives such as:

- Hiring out management.
- Partnering with someone else to share management duties.
- Transferring the management duties to someone else within the business.

Dave and Florence Minar planned to retain overall management responsibility for Cedar Summit Farm and their new business Cedar Summit Creamery. However, they planned to share specific marketing, operations, and finance-related management duties with their children and current business partner, Paul Kajer. This management strategy required constant communication and a clear understanding of the business' objectives by all members of the Minar's management team. Dave and Florence explained that they feel well prepared to manage as a team. They have been planning and visioning together with their children on a regular basis for more than ten years.

Figure 74.
Barriers to Effective Communication[53]

- **Muddled Messages**—be clear when communicating ideas or details.
- **Stereotyping**—don't assume that you know how the other person feels.
- **Wrong channel**—use appropriate forms of communication (written communication for transactions, work agreements, etc. versus verbal agreements).
- **Language**—make sure that you speak the same "language," that terminology is clear to those involved.
- **Lack of feedback**—prompt detailed feedback by checking in regularly.
- **Poor listening skills**—always be prepared to listen; tune out other thoughts. Search for the meaning in what is being said.
- **Interruptions**—try to anticipate and limit interruptions or other distractions.
- **Physical distractions**—make sure there are no physical distractions (noise, extreme temperatures) when communicating.

Communication. Regardless of whether you plan to manage as a team, with a partner, or on your own, effective communication will be important. As Ohio State University specialist Bernard Erven notes, "Although communication does not guarantee success of a farm business, its absence usually assures problems. A communication problem may soon become a crisis or it may linger on for years."[51] See Figure 74 for tips on how to become an effective communicator—particularly if you plan to play any role in managing the business. *Making It Work*[52], a one-hour video on family communication and conflict resolution for business planning is an excellent communication resource.

Use **Worksheet 4.22: Management Strategy** to identify your management strategy for the business. Think hard about your willingness to perform the duties of an effective communicator. Your management strategy

50 *Economic and Business Planning Principles in Farm Planning and Production*, James and Eberle, 2000.

51 *Overcoming Barriers to Communication*, Erven, 2001 (reviewed).

52 *Making It Work*, Passing on the Farm Center, 1999.

53 *Overcoming Barriers to Communication*, Erven, 2001 (reviewed).

Business Plan Input - Human Resources Strategy Summary:

Our business strategy includes the creation of seven new jobs to market and process our milk: two full-time processing plant staff positions, one full-time plant manager position, one full-time marketing management position, one full-time delivery management/staff position, one part-time book keeping position, and one quarter-time technician staff position. Salaries and wages will be competitive with industry standards. Eventually, we plan to offer health care and vacation benefits for full-time staff.

We have children with many abilities and envision this business as a future for them and their families. We plan to fill most of our labor needs - including management positions - internally with family labor. We feel that the use of family labor is a great strength - our kids know the business well and are familiar with one another's skills and work style. Our children have participated in all of our visioning sessions and have a long-term, vested interest in seeing the processing business succeed. Of course, one disadvantage of hiring family members is that family or personal conflicts have the potential affect the business.

Each family member will be trained in at least two positions so that we have backup for vacation or illness and injury. We will communicate daily as needed and through quarterly meetings with our Board of Advisors.

Figure 75. Excerpt from Cedar Summit Farm's Worksheet 4.23: Human Resources Strategy Summary

should include a short- and long-term back-up plan to arrange for management in the case of an emergency due to illness or shift in goals on the part of management team members. A written management plan can be particularly useful, and may become a final part of your business plan if you decide to manage as a team. Management teams and boards often use written management plans to clearly specify management responsibilities, check-in meeting dates, and a description of grievance procedures.

TASK 4

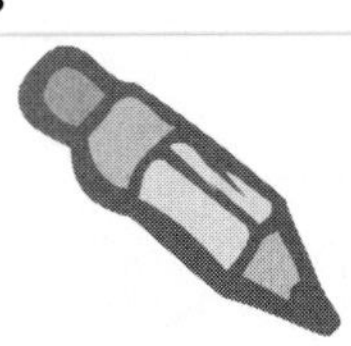

Develop a Strategic Human Resources Plan

Briefly summarize your human resources strategy for each enterprise or the whole farm (if appropriate) using the space in **Worksheet 4.23: Human Resources Strategy Summary**. Carefully review your research, and describe workforce needs and plans for filling them. Note the strengths, weaknesses, opportunities and threats (SWOT) associated with each strategy. This also is a good time to list human resources expense estimates for each enterprise. You will use this information when you evaluate the feasibility of each strategy alternative.

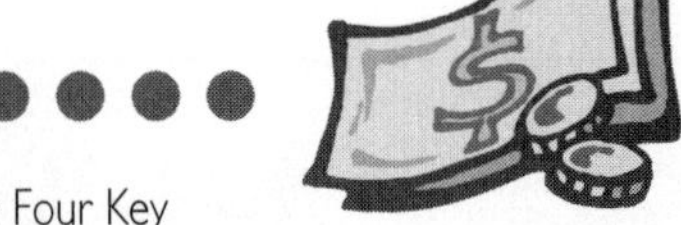

The Four Key Management Areas:
- Marketing
- Operations
- Human Resources
- **Finance**

Financial Strategy

Financially successful businesses are usually built around strategies that incorporate risk management, tax-efficient organization, and careful use of financing.

In this section you will build a financial strategy by looking at:

- Risk: What does our future business environment look like and how will we manage for risk?
- Organization: How will we legally organize and structure the business?
- Financing: How will we finance capital requirements?

When you evaluate your strategic plan, you will have the opportunity to evaluate enterprise and whole farm strategies from a financial perspective by looking at projected profitability, liquidity and solvency. For now, however, concentrate on the development of risk management, organization and finance strategies.

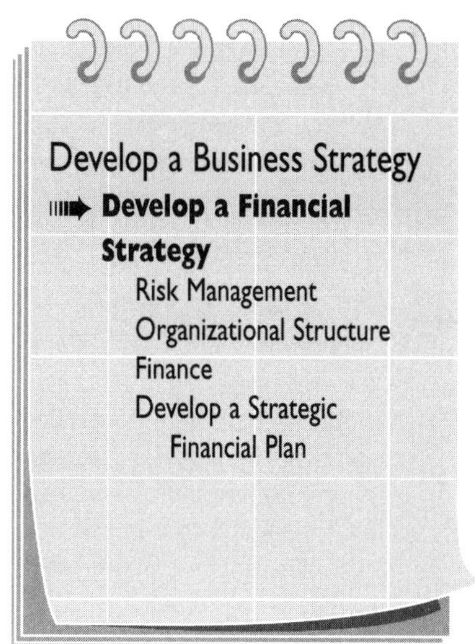

As you do so, recall your financial values and goals. What is important to you? Paying down debt? Putting money away for the future? Being able to save for "down times"? Reducing overall financial risk? Generating most or all of your income from the farm business? Use your values and goals along with your SWOT assessment to guide the development of one or more whole farm financial strategies.

Risk management: How will we manage risk?

In today's farm economy, risk management has become an important topic, particularly for those producers who have traditionally relied on government intervention to mitigate price and production-related uncertainties. Regardless of whether you produce corn, soybeans, grass-based milk, organic vegetables or specialty fruit trees, risk management will be an important component of your business plan. Without it, uncontrolled risk and uncertainty reduce the reliability of financial projections and make investment analysis difficult. Unmanaged risk and uncertainty also carry with them a high degree of stress for farm managers and their families. In this section, you and your planning team will first research the potential business risks that stem from new marketing, operations and human resources strategies. Then you will be ready to develop a whole farm risk management strategy (or combination of strategies) to minimize and protect against future uncertainty.

As described in Planning Task Two, farm businesses, particularly family farm businesses, often are exposed to many forms of risk: personal risk, production risk, market risk, institutional risk and financial risk.[54] What type of risk will your business be exposed to in the future as you look at new products, farm management systems, and labor strategies? How will you manage this new risk? Common risk management strategies are to: minimize production- and market-related risk; transfer risk outside of the business; and build internal capacity to bear risk financially.

Production- and market-related risk management alternatives include enterprise diversification, cultural production practices (irrigation, short season crop varieties), hedging with futures and options, and storage.

Risk transfer outside the business can be done by purchasing insurance (crop, property, health, home, liability), signing production or sales contracts, and participating in government programs.

TASK 4

54 *Managing Risk in Farming: Concepts, Research and Analysis*, Harwood, et al., 1999.

Figure 76.
Risk Management Alternatives[55]

Cash and credit reserves. Holding your own cash reserves or building credit reserves with your lender are common risk management strategies for improving liquidity. Credit reserves take the form of carry-over debt, refinancing and emergency credit. Use of credit reserves typically requires that you have a good, established relationship with a lender as well as a strategy for managing production and market-related risk.

Insurance. Insurance is often used by crop producers to reduce yield-related income risk. The Federal Crop Insurance Corporation (FCIC) and private crop insurance vendors offer insurance programs to help producers control crop production risk at a reasonable cost. Insurance provides a financial safety net in case of severe production losses or low crop prices. It provides two important benefits: a reliable level of cash flow and more flexibility in marketing plans.[56] Other forms of insurance include property, health, liability and export insurance.

Enterprise diversification. Farms that produce one product are vulnerable to changes in market trends. Enterprise diversification provides some financial protection in fluctuating markets and against production catastrophe should one product fail. Enterprise diversification also allows the business owner to average profit and loss over different products and to combine two products (such as cheese and herbs) for value-added profit.[57] One of the disadvantages of enterprise diversification can be the loss of production and management efficiency that is present with specialized operations.

Government programs. Historically, government programs have helped farmers mitigate short-term, price-related market risks. Under the Farm Security and Rural Investment Act 2002 direct payments, counter-cyclical market price supports and marketing loans were instituted for program crops and qualifying acreage. Moreover, provisions were made in the 2002 bill to defer some of the costs associated with organic conversion and compliance, among other things. For a full description of current farm bill provisions, contact the USDA or visit their website: www.usda.gov/farmbill/.

Hedging with futures. Hedging involves the sale of a futures contract at harvest time with the expectation of market price increases. You earn the difference between the price at which you initially sold the futures contract and the price at which you buy it back weeks or months later. Of course, if the price falls between the time that you hedged your crop or livestock and repurchased the futures contract, you will incur a loss. Futures are not available for all crops and livestock. When using futures, you must determine whether or not you can realistically meet product quantity and delivery dates.

Income diversification. Supplementing farm income with cash from other sources, such as off-farm employment, can help balance negative fluctuations in cash farm income and, in some cases, provide a reliable or steady stream of income for your household. According to a 1996 nationwide survey by USDA, 82 percent of all farm households generated off-farm income that exceeded their farm income.[58]

Investment diversification. Diversifying investments among farm and nonfarm assets is a relatively new risk management strategy among farmers. Research has shown that farm and nonfarm asset values fluctuate inversely. In other words, when farm asset values are declining, the value of stocks, treasury bills, certificates of deposit and bonds are typically on the rise.[59]

Leasing. Leasing land, machinery, equipment or livestock is one way to minimize financial risk and create flexibility. Leasing allows you, the producer, to gain access to equipment and land without making long-term payment commitments. This frees up cash and investment funds for other uses. The primary disadvantage to leasing is that you do not have the opportunity to build equity or loan collateral.

Production and marketing contracts. *Production contracts* typically give the contractor considerable control over the production process. Under the contract, the contractor specifies varieties, breeds and production timing to ensure final-product quality. Inputs are usually supplied by the contractor. In exchange for their loss of management control, producers are usually compensated with financial incentives. Production contracts have become common in the livestock sector and are increasingly available in the specialty commodity sector. Brokers, handlers, seed companies, grain processors and other intermediaries regularly contract for specialty commodities such as food-grade corn, tofu-grade soybeans and organic feed grains. *Marketing contracts* are either verbal or written agreements between the buyer (contractor) and producer (contractee). Typically, responsibility for breed or variety selection is retained by the producer. A price is usually determined in advance of harvest and delivery terms are specified. Premiums and discounts may be established for grain that does not match quality specifications under both production and marketing contracts. Flat price contracts, where the buyer agrees to pay a fixed price per unit, are the most common form of marketing contracts.

Storage. On-farm storage such as grain bins, containers and freezers allow grain producers to spread out sales over a 12-month period, much like livestock producers, and extend the marketing season (in the case of fresh vegetables, grain and meat cuts). One disadvantage of storage as a risk management tool is expense, although the use of containers for small lots of identity-preserved grain is a fairly low cost option.

Building internal capacity to bear financial risk can be accomplished by adjusting household consumption, diversifying income sources within and outside the business and investments (farm and nonfarm), increasing liquidity (holding cash, establishing credit reserves), leasing short- and long-term assets, and spreading out asset sales and purchases.

You may already be familiar with many of these risk management alternatives. Each alternative has its own advantages, disadvantages and resource requirements. Some of these risk management alternatives are described in Figure 76. The appropriate alternatives and overall risk management strategy for your business will depend, in large part, on your willingness to adjust production practices, spend time on the phone or in front of the computer, and to take on more management responsibilities.

Worksheet 4.24 Risk Management

Complete this Worksheet for each enterprise or the whole farm as appropriate. Briefly rank your business' exposure to market, production, environmental and personal risk. Talk over risk management ideas with members of your planning team, a financial consultant, or an accountant. List tools that you might use to reduce future risk. Then, summarize your strategy for managing and minimizing your business' risk exposure.

Enterprise: ______

Production Risk

Exposure to production risk: _X_ **Low** ___ **Medium** ___ **High**

Type of production risk: *Hay crop failure, herd disease, bacterial contamination of milk.*

Tools to minimize production risk: *Cash reserve, continued placement of herd on pasture, bio-security monitoring, and stockpiling of one-day's worth of milk for processing.*

Market Risk

Exposure to market risk: ___ **Low** _X_ **Medium** ___ **High**

Type of market risk: *Predatory pricing by competitors.*

Tools to minimize market risk: *Build customer confidence; loyalty.*

Financial Risk

Exposure to financial risk: _X_ **Low** ___ **Medium** ___ **High**

Type of financial risk: *Lack of sales*

Tools to minimize financial risk: *Legal organization as LLC, good marketing, conservative cash flow plan, financial reserves or contingencies.*

Personal Risk

Exposure to personal risk: _X_ **Low** ___ **Medium** ___ **High**

Type of personal risk: *Injury, illness, change in family goals.*

Tools to minimize personal risk: *Two people trained in each job/position so that we have back-up; risk of injury in plant is low.*

Our risk management strategy can be summarized as follows:

We will continue to research the market, establish excellent customer communication and promotion, and maintain financial buffers.

TASK 4

Figure 77. Example from Cedar Summit Farm—Worksheet 4.24: Risk Management

Use **Worksheet 4.24: Risk Management** to develop a risk management strategy for your business and identify future sources of risk. Begin by returning to Worksheet 2.17 (Risk Management) where you identified current sources of risk. Ask yourself how these will change in the future as you pursue new marketing, operations and human resources strategies. Then identify a plan for coping with and managing this future risk. Your lender and financial planner are excellent resources for analyzing risk potential.

55 *Managing Risk in Farming: Concepts, Research and Analysis*, Harwood, et al., 1999.
56 *Managing Production and Marketing Systems*, Thomas, 2000.
57 *Sustainable Agriculture*, Mason, 1997.
58 *Managing Risk in Farming: Concepts, Research and Analysis*, Harwood, et al., 1999.
59 *Financial Management in Agriculture*, Risk Management, 7th Ed., Barry et al., 2002.

Organizational Structure: How will we legally organize and structure our business?

The legal organization that you choose for your business will have risk, finance, tax and estate planning ramifications. Legal organization is typically one of the first decisions made when structuring a new business.[60]

As a current business owner you might consider re-evaluating your organization strategy here to determine if one of the alternatives provide legal or financial benefits. As a new or potential business owner who is at the beginning of the business life-cycle, however, you have a range of organizational strategy alternatives to consider.

Traditionally, most farm businesses have legally organized as sole proprietorships or partnerships. This is still a common legal structure, but a growing number of today's farms are incorporating as Limited Liability Corporations (LLCs) or Cooperatives. These structures offer some financial protection, tax advantages, and other benefits. The Minars, for instance, considered three organizational alternatives: LLC, S-Corporation (a corporation in which the owner holds 100% of the shares), and Partnership. After researching each alternative and weighing the advantages and disadvantages of each, they decided to organize the processing business as an LLC. This structure enables them to gradually pass shares and ownership of the business on to their children in advance of retirement. *"We also hope that by making our children shareholders, they will have more of a long-term, vested interest in the business,"* explains Florence Minar.

Figure 78.
Legal Organization Options[61,62]

Sole proprietorship. In a sole proprietorship, the business is owned and controlled by one person. This means that if a husband and wife or father and son plan to operate the business together, only one of them can hold legal title to the business. The primary advantage of sole proprietorship organization is that you are independent and free to make all business decisions without an obligation to partners or shareholders. The disadvantage of a sole proprietorship is that you are personally liable for any debt, taxes, or other financial and regulatory charges.

Partnership. Partnerships may be formed between two or more family members or third parties. Each partner is liable for all partnership obligations. One of the primary advantages of a partnership may be the infusion of business capital and other assets by one or more partners. Each partner pays taxes individually based on his or her share of income, capital gains and losses. There are two types of partnership: general partnerships and limited partnerships. In a general partnership, one or more partners are jointly responsible or liable for the debts of the partnership.

Corporation. Corporations are owned by one or more shareholders and are managed by elected directors. A corporation must be established in compliance with statutory requirements of the state of incorporation. In Minnesota, articles of incorporation and by-laws are legally required. The corporation, not its shareholders, are responsible for corporate debts and other obligations. One disadvantage of corporate organization is that its owners and family members are considered employees of the business and are therefore subject to labor laws and taxes.

Limited Liability Company (LLC). This organizational form offers owners limited liability like a corporation—investors are liable only for their investment in the business—but it may be classified as a partnership for tax purposes. Two or more business partners may form an LLC.

Land trust. A land trust is a legal entity that allows a land owner to transfer property to a trustee. While the trustee is the legal owner of the property, the beneficiaries are given possession and management of the land. This type of legal organization can be beneficial for estate planning purposes as it allows the beneficiaries to avoid probate upon death of the owner.

Cooperative. A cooperative is a legally incorporated business entity capitalized by its member patrons or owners. Dividends are paid out to its patrons. A cooperative is taxed on income at corporate rates, but patronage refunds are often tax-deductible to the cooperative. Many farmers are now using cooperative organization to acquire and provide machinery, livestock breeding and equipment maintenance, as well as marketing and advisory services.

TASK 4

60 *Planning the Financial/Organizational Structure of Farm and Agribusiness Firms: What Are the Options?*, Boehlje and Lins, 1998 (revised).

61 Ibid.

62 *A Guide to Starting a Business in Minnesota*, Minnesota Small Business Assistance Office, updated annually.

Worksheet 4.25 Business Organization

Use the space below to record information about the organizational alternatives that you are considering for the business. Your state's Small Business Association is an excellent place to begin your research. If you are planning a major reorganization of the business, be sure to consult a lawyer regarding necessary documentation and tax ramifications. Be sure to note advantages and disadvantages of each alternative as it pertains to your current situation, business vision and personal goals.

Organizational Alternative 1 *Limited Liability Corporation*

Ownership: *Shareholders*

Tax rates: *Can be taxed as partnership or corporation.*

Filing requirements: *Articles of Incorporation filed with Secretary of State + filing fee; annual registration with Secretary of State; tax payments to IRS and MN Department of Revenue.*

Advantages: *We can pass shares of the business on to our children; no personal financial liability on part of partners; easy to dissolve.*

Disadvantages:

Organizational Alternative 2 *S-Corporation*

Ownership: *Shareholders*

Tax rates: *Individual shareholder income tax rates.*

Filing requirements: *Annual "Business Activities" report and registration; tax return to IRS and MN Department of Revenue.*

Advantages: *Can pass on shares.*

Disadvantages: *Difficult to dissolve.*

Organizational Alternative 3 *Partnership*

Ownership: *Partners*

Tax rates: *Individual partners' income tax rates.*

Filing requirements: *Annual federal and state "information" returns; sales tax return to IRS and MN Department of Revenue.*

Advantages:

Disadvantages: *Personal liability.*

Figure 79. Example from Cedar Summit Farm—Worksheet 4.25: Business Organization

TASK 4

The advantages and disadvantages of sole proprietorship, partnerships, LLCs and other legal business arrangements are described in Figure 78.

Use **Worksheet 4.25: Business Organization** to list the organizational alternatives that you would like to consider for your business. Next, use the space provided to research ownership authority, tax rates and filing requirements for each alternative as well as the advantages and disadvantages of each for your business. When doing so, remember that the legal and business arrangement that you choose must be compatible with your overall financial values and goals.

Figure 80.

Finance Alternatives

Capital leases. A capital lease can be categorized as a property "rental agreement" when ownership rights are not transferred and as a "purchase" when the lease gains you ownership of an asset at a reduced purchase price at the end of the agreement. Capital lease purchase agreements can provide effective control and may reduce costs while building equity. Whether it reduces cost or risk in the long term will depend on the fine print of the agreement. It is always advisable to have a lawyer look over the details of any agreement that will have such a major impact on your financial future. For more information about how to calculate lease values and returns, see *Capital Leases* by Haefner and Doye in "Resources".

Contributed capital. Most business owners have to invest some of their own equity in the business to get it up and running. This may be a basic requirement to getting your business started. Initial capital contributions may not be the end of your use of contributed capital to finance the business. Many farmers continue to inject money into the operation from off-farm income. This "subsidization" of the farm from off-farm sources is often looked at as a negative, and it can be if it is eaten up by farm losses. However, it can also be looked at as an alternative place to invest off-farm earnings. If your farm is profitable and your alternatives for financing replacement/improvements are between debt capital and contributions from nonfarm sources, you may decide that capital contributions are a sound investment.

Debt. Debt financing (for land acquisition, intermediate, and operating loans) is the traditional source of external financing for most farm operations. As long as you are earning a higher return with borrowed funds than the interest rate, it is profitable to grow your business using someone else's money. Commercial banks, insurance companies, Farm Credit Services, and the Farm Service Agency offer debt financing. Your long-range vision and goals probably say something about how much debt capi you are comfortable with. The major plus to using debt financing is control. When structured correctly, debt can be an effective way to eventually build equity as the debt reduced. However, just because you are paying down del particularly intermediate term debt, you may not be increasing equity as assets may need to be replaced as fa as the debt is being paid off. Depreciation is a real cost. The more debt capital you use, the more your financial alternatives will be reduced.

Operating leases. Operating leases, such as traditional land rental arrangements, give you less control, and usua (but not always) come at a lower cost than ownership. They can be flexible and reduce risk. Don't be afraid to to negotiate some flexibility into an operating lease arrangement. Sometimes, the owner may hold all the car and will not see the need to take on any of the risk face by the operator. In other situations, you may be able to pass on some of the risk in return for higher lease payments during high-income times. Also, don't forget to cultivate personal relationships with your landlords. Remember them at holiday times and provide them with information that shows you are doing a good job. Most successful operating leases rely on the fact that the own is more comfortable with you managing his property tha alternative renters, and therefore, is willing to give you a break in rental rates or terms.

TASK 4

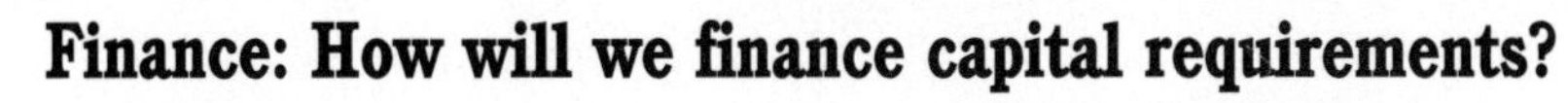

Finance: How will we finance capital requirements?

The financial strategy you develop will depend on your choice of business organization and your values as they relate to risk, control, costs and maturity.

Historically, farm businesses have financed themselves internally through family equity—relying on debt only when internal equity was not adequate to finance growth of the business.[63] Today, however, external financing through debt, leasing, and outside equity is common.

If you anticipate the need for financing to pay for start-up, annual operating, or long-term capital expenses, you have several options to consider. Some commor internal and external financing alternatives are described in Figure 80. Additional information is available in *Financing the Farm Operation* by Kunkel and Larison (see "Resources"). Pay particular attention to real estate financing. Land and

63 *Planning the Financial/Organizational Structure of Farm and Agribusiness Firms: What Are the Options?*, Boehlje and Lins, 1998 (revised).

Outside equity. Most agricultural corporations are still family farms today. Using external equity capital has traditionally been a very unusual method of financing agricultural activities. More recently, however, there have been a number of creative approaches to attracting external capital. Often these business structures have been similar to networking, with a group of producers creating a business structure, such as a cooperative, to give them some sort of competitive advantage. Equity contributions from outside of agriculture are usually somewhat limited by corporate farming laws. Some states now allow the formation of agricultural Limited Liability Companies (LLCs) that offer some of the benefits of outside equity contributions while limiting the liability of the investor for the legal obligations of the business. If you are interested in these options, do some further research.

Retained earnings. Another way to finance your business that you are probably already using is retained earnings. You may not be consciously thinking about it, but most small businesses continually inject their earnings back into the operation. Of course this requires that there be earnings remaining after all costs and owner withdrawals. Using equity capital, either from farm or nonfarm earnings, to finance your business will gain you ownership with a great degree of control. The cost of equity capital is the return it could have earned in an alternative investment. The risk of using equity capital is that you could lose your equity if the business fails. So you might want to consider a balanced strategy that invests at least some of your earnings outside of the farm business.

Shared ownership. Experts will usually tell you that there is too much capital invested in production agriculture. One way to reduce your ownership cost may be to share ownership of expensive equipment that is only used for short portions of a year with a neighbor or someone else. Shared ownership gives you reduced control, but at half or less of the cost. Timing concerns usually limit the use of this option. One of the more creative solutions that is being used to some degree today is to share ownership with someone who farms in another part of the country where the cropping season is different. Again, you may be able to think outside the box and come up with a creative shared ownership strategy. Whenever shared ownership is used, you should put the agreement in writing to avoid future disputes.

Strategic alliances/networking. This may be a way of gaining control of some needs of your operation without having to own them. You may be able to gain access to a specific input into your production process by either investing in someone else's operation or by contracting with that operator. While the most visible use of networking in agriculture has been in large pork production operations, you may be able to think of ways to network with other operators or suppliers that are not as grand. Businesses have long relied on alliances and joint ventures to reduce individual costs or to guarantee access to inputs or markets. Such reliance on relationships may be vital to the sustainability of both parties.

TASK 4

building investments typically account for the largest farm expense and have the potential to make or break your business. If your business' operations strategy necessitates land and building acquisition, be sure to thoroughly review your financing options with a lender, accountant, or attorney. If you decide to invest in land, you need to consider market price, the value of the land to you, financial feasibility, and the risk to cash flow. Complete **Worksheet 4.26: Farmland Affordability** to determine the maximum financially feasible price you should pay for land. You can view *Analyzing Land Investments* by Gayle S. Willett for additional suggestions and information (see "Resources").

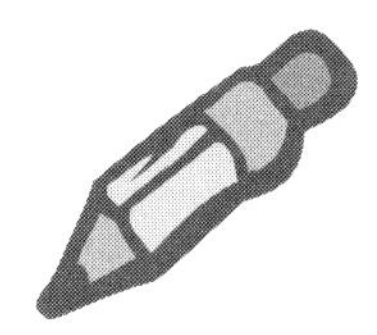

As a beginning or young farmer, choosing a financial strategy and financing alternatives may seem intimidating, especially if you haven't had the chance to build a credit history or an asset base. Several well-known funding sources for beginning farmers are listed in Figure 81. As you review these finance sources, don't ignore

Figure 81.
Financial Assistance Options for Beginning Farmers

Parental or family financing. Parents or other family members directly assist with financing through the gifting of assets or by providing down-payment money for land purchases.

Local banks. Local banks, with whom your family has a good working relationship, can be an excellent source of financing.

State government financing. In Minnesota, the Minnesota Rural Finance Authority (RFA) has established several programs to assist beginning farmers, including a low-interest and institution-backed land, machinery and breeding livestock purchase program.

Federal government financing. The Farm Service Agency (FSA) of the USDA offers direct and guaranteed farm ownership and operating loans. FSA often works with beginning farmers who don't qualify for conventional loans due to insufficient resources.

TASK 4

the opportunity to gradually build your business assets through partnership with a retiring farmer in your community. Retiring producers sometimes are willing to transfer their assets in exchange for sweat equity. Minnesota's Passing on the Farm Center offers a service to link retiring farmers with beginning farmers (see "Resources"). Check with your local Extension service to see if your state has a similar program.

You should also carefully consider your values and how they pertain to issues of control, cost, risk and maturity. Each of these financial issues are described in Figure 82.

There are many state and federal government programs available to help you finance or defer some of the start-up and long-term development costs associated with everything from new business development to natural resource and wildlife habitat improvement. The Natural Resources Conservation Service (NRCS), for example, offers cost-share payments as part of its Environmental Quality Incentives Program (EQIP) available to farmers who convert to organic production. Your local Extension office can help you determine whether or not EQP and other state and federal cost-share programs are appropriate based on your current farm resources and management goals.

Figure 82.
Financial Strategy Issues[64]

Control. How much control and independence do you want to have in the decision-making process? Many small businesses use internal equity as their major source of finances to maintain control and autonomy. This desire for control may hinder their ability to branch out into more unconventional methods of agricultural financing.

Cost. Which method of resource control will come at a lower cost? The standard comparison here is between lease and purchase options. But there are several other options including such methods as shared ownership and outside equity financing. Look beyond traditional ownership costs to include administrative and legal costs, taxes and licensing fees when evaluating financing opportunities.

Risk. Each financing method comes with its own level of financial risk. Some will expose you to claims on income from partners and investors. Others will place claims on the assets of your business, which may change the size and speed of your equity growth. Still others could open you to certain legal liabilities such as liability for the debts of business partners. And there is the final risk of failure, which can be influenced by the financial structure and method of financing that you choose.

Maturity. Some financing and business structures are short-term in nature and relatively easy to change or dissolve. Others, such as a corporate structure, are more permanent and can be very costly to dissolve. When selecting a finance strategy, consider the importance of business liquidity versus permanence.

64 *Planning the Financial/Organizational Structure of Farm and Agribusiness Firms: What Are the Options?,* Boehlje and Lins, 1998 (revised).

Operating			
Intermediate	*Ag Star*	*7.8%*	*Seven-year lease. Payments tax deductible. At end of lease, CSC will own all equipment*
	Local Bank	*8.2 %*	*Seven-year payments. SBA guarantee required.*
Long-term	*Ag Star*	*7.8%*	*Ten-year lease for building. Payments tax deductible. At end of lease, CSF will own the processing building.*
	Local Bank	*8.2 %*	*Ten-year payments. SBA guarantee required*
Real estate			

Figure 83. Excerpt from Cedar Summit Farm's Worksheet 4.27: Finance

As you consider financial alternatives, be creative. Regardless of whether you are a beginning or experienced business owner, you may be able to identify and employ several alternatives to meet your goals, limit risk, and increase financial flexibility. The Minars identified two finance strategies for needed equipment—lease agreements with Ag Star and debt financing from their local bank.

Use **Worksheet 4.27: Finance** to identify one or more financing strategies for your business. You may not be able to answer all the finance questions until after you've completed your business plan—particularly if your purpose for planning is to secure outside financing. Still, you should begin this research and identify the most plausible strategy alternatives for your business.

TASK 4

Develop a Strategic Financial Plan

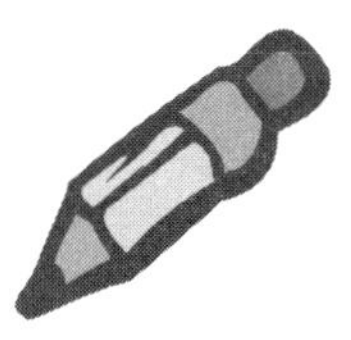

You've done a lot of research and brainstorming in this section about risk management, business organization, and capital financing strategies. Use **Worksheet 4.28: Financial Strategy Summary** to summarize your financial strategies for each enterprise into one strategic financial plan for the whole farm. If you are considering more than one whole-farm financial strategy at this point, describe both in the space provided. You may not be able to narrow down your alternatives until after completing a whole-farm evaluation.

Dave and Florence Minar initially recorded two external capital financing options—leasing and debt financing. In Worksheet 4.27, they described the advantages and disadvantages of each alternative. However, it wasn't until they had consulted with a financial advisor that they made their final decision to finance the business through a lease agreement with Ag Star.

The Minars then went back and summarized their financial strategy, highlighting their legal organization and borrowing components.

Figure 84. Excerpt from Cedar Summit Farm's Worksheet 4.28: Financial Strategy Summary

Business Plan Input–Financial Strategy Summary:

We plan to organize the processing portion of our business [Cedar Summit Creamery] as an LLC so that we can gradually transfer shares and ownership to our children in preparation for retirement. The Creamery will finance all start-up and annual equipment costs. Cedar Summit Farm will finance and own the processing building.

All start-up, intermediate, and long-term equipment and building needs will be financed using 7-10 year lease arrangements from Ag-Star. All future growth will be financed through retained earnings from the Creamery business.

Whole Farm Strategy

Throughout this Guide, we've asked you to break out your business into marketing, operations, human resources and finance components. Now, it's time to pull all of these components together—to make sure that the strategies you've chosen for each functional area are compatible as an integrated system.

If you've identified more than one strategy for each functional area, then think about how each strategic alternative might impact the business and other strategies. Dave and Florence Minar considered two operations strategies—the use of new versus used processing equipment. By evaluating how each of these equipment alternatives would affect the marketing, human resources, and finance components of their business, they temporarily ruled out used equipment as an operations strategy and pursued on-farm processing with the use of a new Mini-Dairy equipment package. They reasoned that although the new equipment package was more expensive, it was also more compatible with their overall vision. The new equipment package (which included training and product recipes) would enable them to begin processing and marketing a full line of products from the start, while creating immediate jobs for all of their children who wanted to return to the farm. In contrast, the used equipment alternative would cost the Minars time, sales, and potentially more money in the long-run as they searched for and fit the equipment to their operation, learned how to use the equipment, and experimented with inputs to develop their own products and recipes.

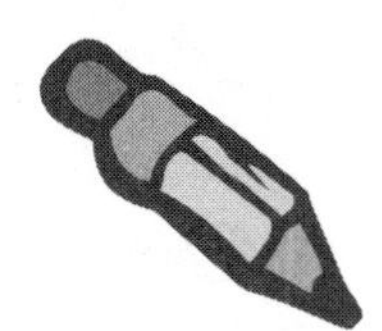

Think about these types of system-wide connections before you move on to the evaluation section. Then use **Worksheet 4.29: Summarize a Whole Farm Strategic Plan of Action** to shape one or more whole farm strategies for your business. If you've completed the Summary Worksheets throughout the Planning Tasks (Worksheets 4.9, 4.17, 4.23 and 4.28) this final task should be relatively easy. With a whole farm strategy you will be ready to analyze your business for long-term profitability and cash flow.

If you haven't already researched product and enterprise expenses for each of the individual strategies you've developed (marketing, operations, human resources, finance), do so now. Secure "certified bids" for all equipment and machinery from manufacturers, dealers or representatives. Certified bids come directly from the equipment representative and are often required by lenders when applying for a loan. When certified bids are unavailable, look for published cost estimates (available for the Upper Midwest through the Center for Farm Financial Management—see "Resources") or talk with other producers who purchased similar inputs or who have initiated a similar business strategy.

Worksheet 4.29 Summarize a Whole Farm Strategic Plan of Action

Ask yourself if each of the marketing, operations, human resources, and finance strategy alternatives you've identified are compatible as a system. If you are considering more than one functional strategy (such as two marketing strategies or two finance strategies), be sure to explore on paper how these different strategies will affect the business as a whole. How will they affect other functional areas of the business? Rule out those strategies that are not compatible with one another or your business vision as a whole. Then, use the space below to name one or more system-wide business strategies for your whole farm and describe, in one to two paragraphs, how each strategy addresses your critical planning needs, vision, mission and goals.

Whole Farm Strategy Alternative # 1:

The idea of processing milk from grass-fed cows using the new Mini-Dairy equipment package and family staffing all seem compatible as a system and will, we believe, fulfill our primary planning purpose: the creation of jobs and income for any family member who wants to join the operation. Although our plan to use new equipment from Pladot will be more expensive, the training and product recipes (provided by Pladot) will enable us to market a full line of products - something that we feel will enhance our ability to reach our projected sales volume and secure future markets.

Figure 85. Example from Cedar Summit Farm—Worksheet 4.29: Summarize a Whole Farm Strategic Plan of Action

Dave and Florence Minar obtained certified bids for new processing equipment directly from the Israeli manufacturer, Pladot. Start-up and annual operating expense estimates for items like bottles, crates, flavorings, labor and labels came from business plans shared by other on-farm processors and regional suppliers. The Minars also spoke with local processor Mike Hartman, owner of Minnesota's Organic Milk (MOM's) about the cost and availability of local processing supplies.

Once you've secured realistic cost estimates, you can properly allocate direct (variable) and overhead (fixed) expenses for the whole farm. Knowing your costs and your cost structure will improve your overall knowledge of the operation and will prove invaluable as you make decisions over time. The difference between direct and overhead expenses as well as a method for allocating overhead expenses among enterprises is explained in Figure 86.

Try to break down your costs between annual direct or variable expenses (those costs that vary with production volume) and annual overhead or fixed expenses (those costs that will be incurred no matter how much you produce). One time start-up costs may be prorated as fixed expenses when developing long-term income projections and as intermediate expenses in your first-year cash flow.

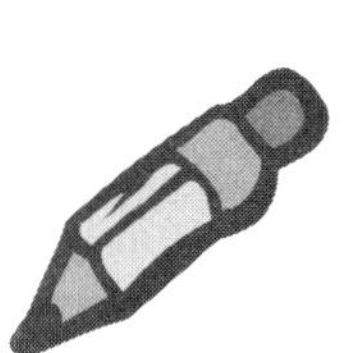

Use **Worksheet 4.30: Annual Operating Expenses for the Whole Farm** to record and total your annual variable costs and fixed expenses for each whole-farm strategy alternative.

Figure 86.

Allocating Whole Farm Expenses

Direct expenses. Direct or variable expenses typically include annual crop inputs (such as seed, soil amendments and crop insurance) and livestock inputs (feed, pasture maintenance, veterinary expenses) as well as any hired labor, utilities, fuel, interest on operating (12-month) loans, and equipment repairs. In addition, your estimate of variable costs should include product-specific marketing expenses.

Direct input expense estimates are available for a wide range of traditional Upper Midwest crop and livestock enterprises from the Center for Farm Financial Management's website, or for other crops from the USDA National Agricultural Statistics Service's *Agricultural Prices* publication (see "Resources"). However, if you plan to produce a specialty crop, use an alternative livestock management systems or offer a highly specialized service, you may have to do a little more digging to develop realistic cost estimates. Talk with other farmers, Extension educators and farm business management consultants, as well as equipment and input dealers to begin putting together cost estimates for organic seed, livestock fencing and watering systems, and other inputs for which price histories do not exist.

TASK 4

Overhead expenses. Overhead or fixed expenses include permanent hired labor (including your own labor and that of other family members), machinery and building leases, farm insurance, dues and professional fees, utilities, and advertising.

When estimating the value of machinery and equipment, be sure to include capital ownership costs such as depreciation, interest, repairs, taxes and insurance estimates rather than the cost of capital itself. Your interest, repairs, taxes, and insurance rates will vary considerably. However, depreciation is fairly standard and can be easily calculated.

Calculating Depreciation. Straight-line depreciation, in which an asset is depreciated annually in equal amounts over the asset's projected life, is commonly used for farm machinery and equipment. The straight-line depreciation formula, listed below, can be used when estimating the depreciation value of machinery and equipment for your overhead cost analysis. In the example below, taken from Barry, et al., a new tractor worth $30,000 is depreciated equally over ten years.[65] The tractor's salvage value at the end of the ten-year period is $2,000. Using the straight-line calculation, a depreciation charge of $2,800 should be added to the interest, repair, tax, and insurance costs of the tractor for annual enterprise accounting purposes.

Depreciation Formula:	Depreciation Example:
D = (OC – SV)/N	D = (30,000 – 2,000) / 10 D = $2,800
Where:	
OC = original cost	OC = cost of new tractor, $30,000
SV = salvage value	SV = value of tractor after 10 years, $2,000
N = asset's expected life	N = book life of tractor, 10 years

Evaluate Strategic Alternatives

You know what you're going to market, who's going to buy it and why, how you're going to produce it, and where your finances will come from. The next question is, will your business actually make it? Will you accomplish your personal and environmental goals, cover costs, generate the income needed to cover family living expenses, service debt, and build equity in the long run?

The evaluation process can be as sophisticated and comprehensive as you like, and there are a wide range of helpful tools available. This Guide presents just a few tools here to help you study whether your whole farm strategy is financially feasible.

65 *Financial Management in Agriculture, 7th Edition*, Barry, et al., 2002.

Financial evaluation is critical regardless of your goals and planning purpose. This information, along with the goals that you developed in Planning Task Three (Vision, Mission, Goals), will help you choose between whole farm strategies (if you are considering more than one). It will help you evaluate whether your new business strategy is an improvement over your present business approach in the long run.

In this section, you will evaluate the financial feasibility of each whole-farm strategy (or strategies) by preparing long-range and transition period performance projections. Specifically, you will work through a whole farm evaluation to look at projected profitability, liquidity, solvency and risk.

Once you've completed the financial evaluation, you may decide to further test and evaluate your strategy for environmental, market, community and quality of life or personal benefits. For instance, notebook and computer software programs, like Farm*A*Syst, are available to help you study the impact of your operations strategy on soil and water quality. Similarly, nonprofit organizations like the Land Stewardship Project can assist with field monitoring for conservation benefits, such as increased amphibian and bird populations. Other organizations like the Agricultural Utilization and Research Institute in Minnesota, can assist with the product development and market testing. These and other evaluation tools and organizations are listed in the "Resources" section. Be your own guide when deciding which additional business strategy components to evaluate.

Long-Term Outlook

Market expansion, operational transitions, and human resources shifts likely will impact output and expenses, and consequently income levels, for more than one year. A long-term evaluation is therefore critical to help you decide whether or not to adopt a new marketing, operations, human resources, finance or whole farm strategy.

Figure 87.

Tips for Analyzing Strategic Plans

The following guidelines will help you develop more accurate and realistic financial projections:

Use average production levels and prices that realistically can be expected over the long run. Don't be overly optimistic or conservative. It seems that it is human nature to be one or the other. If you are overly optimistic, you may be fooling yourself into making a major mistake. But if you are overly conservative, you may steer yourself away from a real opportunity.

Estimate costs on a per unit basis first, then calculate totals. Estimate variable costs, those that will vary directly with your production levels, on a per acre or per unit of production basis. Then calculate totals for each alternative. For overhead costs, start with the average expense levels from your past history for what you are doing now. Then adjust them as best you can for your alternative plans.

Include the annual ownership costs of capital investments, not the capital investments themselves. These costs are sometimes called the DIRTI costs (depreciation, interest, repairs, taxes and insurance).

Allocate home-produced feed properly. For home-produced feeds, estimate your total production in an average year and the total livestock requirements. If the balance is positive, include the balance in crop sales. If the balance is negative, include it in feed purchases.

Be consistent between alternatives. Try not to let your emotions or your desires favor one plan over the other. Your desires will obviously impact your final decisions, but first, get the facts so you can make an informed decision.

Realize that your plans will not be perfect. Don't agonize over an individual income or expense item too long. But keep your assumptions, and how sure you are about them, in mind when you consider the results.

You will analyze the financial impact of your potential business change using the same financial criteria or performance measurements that you used when assessing your current financial situation in Planning Task Two (see "Glossary" for definitions).

- Profitability: Will this new strategy significantly increase net income from the farm?
  —Enterprise Evaluation: Net returns and break-evens
  —Whole Farm Evaluation: Partial budgeting and long-range planning
- Liquidity: Will this new strategy help generate cash flow sufficient to pay back debts in a timely fashion?
- Solvency: Will this new strategy facilitate continued growth in net worth?
- Risk: Will this new strategy affect the risks faced by the farm business and family?

Profitability: Will this new strategy significantly increase net income from the farm?

TASK 4

Before you can begin to address this question on a whole-farm basis, you may need to do some preliminary evaluation. If your new strategy includes the addition of a new product enterprise, you should begin by analyzing each enterprise separately, using the net return and break-even calculations.

Enterprise Evaluation for Profitability: Net returns and break-evens. Most financial planning and evaluation begins at the enterprise level. Whether you are considering the addition of one or more products (enterprises) to your business, an evaluation at this level can help you settle on profitable pricing strategies, crop and livestock mixes, and risk management tactics. Moreover, if you intend to seek outside debt financing for a traditional or specialty operation, farm lenders will request an enterprise budget to evaluate the relative credit worthiness of the enterprise.

An enterprise budget is simply a look at the net returns contributed to the business by each enterprise. It often includes an estimate of the enterprise's break-even sales price and volume.

Net return. The net return to an enterprise represents returns to (unpaid) operator labor, management and equity capital. It is a measure of profitability, which over the long run should be large enough to justify using unpaid labor and equity capital.

Net returns are easily calculated, particularly if you have already estimated sales revenue, output and expenses (marketing, operations, human resources and finance) in previous Worksheets. Your net return to the enterprise is calculated by subtracting total expenses from gross returns. **Worksheet 4.31: Enterprise Budget Break-even Analysis** can be used to calculate enterprise returns.

Break-evens. A break-even analysis is probably one of the most useful calculations that you will perform when considering alternative business strategies. Break-even numbers can be used to instantly identify those enterprises that don't cover variable and fixed costs of production.

If you intend to sign a market contract or lock in a future price for your product, crunch some numbers to determine what level of production is necessary at that price to break even. Make sure you can cover your variable and fixed costs of production. On the flip side, if your output or production volume is fixed, try calculating a break-even value to determine what product price is necessary to break even on production and marketing-related costs. If neither your price nor output is fixed, these calculations can be used to develop production and price floors for each enterprise—something that will be useful for future monitoring and decision-making.

$$\textit{Break-even Volume} = \frac{\textit{overhead expenses}}{\left[\frac{\textit{market price}}{\textit{unit}} - \frac{\textit{direct expenses}}{\textit{unit}}\right]}$$

$$\textit{Break-even Value} = \frac{\textit{overhead expenses} + \textit{direct expenses}}{\textit{production volume}}$$

Calculating a break-even volume. Break-even volumes will tell you the minimum production volume necessary to cover your costs of production. You might consider this a lower size limit for your business. The break-even volume is calculated by dividing total annual fixed costs for the enterprise by the difference between your estimated market value and variable costs for each enterprise. Substitute the DIRTI costs of capital ownership (depreciation, interest, repairs, taxes, and insurance) for the actual cost when estimating the ownership costs of annual fixed expenses. Use the cost estimates that you developed in Worksheet 4.28 along with market values developed in Worksheet 4.9 to calculate break-even volumes. Try experimenting with a range of market prices to see how they affect your break-even production levels.

Calculating a break-even value. If your production volume is fixed—either because of production capacity or sales contracts—calculate a break-even value for your product; in other words, determine what market price is needed to cover your variable and fixed costs. Break-even values are calculated by dividing your total costs for the product or enterprise by the total quantity you expect to produce or sell. Again, your total costs are the sum of your direct and overhead expenses for the enterprise.

Worksheet 4.31 will walk you through a break-even analysis. The Worksheet is not reproduced for the Minars' bottled milk enterprise for confidentiality reasons. Instead, an example is presented in Figure 88 for an imaginary bed and breakfast business whose annual direct and overhead expenses average $800 and $4,000, respectively. Both a break-even volume and

Figure 88.
Example for Bed and Breakfast Enterprise—Break-even Analysis

Break-even Volume Example

Direct expenses/unit (a)	= $10/room (including breakfast when occupied)
Overhead expenses (b)	= $4,000
Market price/unit (c)	= $75/room
Break-even output (b) / (c – a)	= 4,000 / (75 – 10) = 62 rooms/year

Break-even Value Example

Average direct expenses (a)	= $800
Average overhead expenses (b)	= $4,000
Production volume (c)	= 80 rooms
Break-even value (a + b) / (c)	= (4,000 + 800) / 80 = $60/room

a break-even value are calculated to determine what level of sales and market price would be necessary for the business to cover its full operating costs. In the first example, where the owner expects to charge $75/room, he or she must sell a minimum of 62 rooms each year before breaking even on direct and overhead expenses. In the second example, where the owner's sales volume is fixed at 80 rooms per year, he or she must charge a minimum of $60/room in order to cover costs.

Once you've calculated one or more break-even numbers for each enterprise or product, compare these numbers against your sales projections (Worksheet 4.2) and your upper limit for production capacity (Worksheet 4.16) or your projected market price (Worksheet 4.6). Are your sales goals financially feasible? Can you produce the break-even volume? Will the market, based on your research, support your minimum break-even value?

Worksheet 4.31 provides the skeleton of an enterprise budget. Use this Worksheet to calculate net returns and break-even numbers for each year during your transition period and for your long run or expected outlook.

If your enterprise doesn't break even, then you'll need to take another look at the market or your cost structure. Is there a way to boost your projected market price or to cut input costs? If not—if you can't break even on your costs—then your business idea for this enterprise is not financially feasible. Stop here, return to your vision and rethink your plan. Is there another way to reach your goals or are you willing to sacrifice income from this enterprise to achieve your vision? On the other hand, if calculations suggest that your enterprise will more than break even, you're ready to perform a profitability assessment for the whole farm.

Whole Farm Evaluation for Profitability: Partial budgeting and long range planning. Even more important than the enterprise evaluation is the whole farm financial evaluation. This is where you pull everything together and evaluate whether or not, when all is said and done, the farm will make the profit that you and your family want.

There are two types of financial planning tools available to analyze whole farm profitability: partial budgeting and long-range planning. Both the partial budgeting and long-range planning approaches allow you to compare the outlook of your present farm operation with that of one or more proposed strategic alternatives.

The first tool, partial budgeting, is most useful if your current business is financially sound and the change that you are considering is relatively simple. For instance, Greg Reynolds' plan to add a staff member and a walk-in cooler would be best analyzed using the partial budget approach since his strategy to relieve seasonal labor constraints does not involve a major change in business operations.

The second tool, long-range planning, is used to project whole farm profitability and cash flow when you are considering substantial reorganization of the business or operations. Long-range planning is different from partial budgeting in that you project the financial status of the business after the change is in place instead of just the financial impact of the change. This planning approach is recommended if your whole farm strategy involves a major change in operations (like the Minars' addition of an on-farm processing plant and home delivery service) or if you are a beginning farmer with no business history. Long-range planning generally takes more effort than partial budgeting, but there are many advantages to using this tool. After completing a long-range planning analysis you gain a complete financial picture of the farm after implementation and determine if your alternative plans are likely to put your operation on a sound financial course.

Partial budgeting. The partial budget approach uses annual income and expense changes to simultaneously study the impact of a new business idea on your present business' profitability and cash flow.

The real-life example in Figure 89 illustrates how partial budgeting can be used to evaluate the financial impact of hoop house and farrowing livestock purchases on a small-scale hog enterprise.[66] In this example, the farmer currently purchases and finishes 620 pigs—this is considered her base plan. Alternatively, she would like to farrow and finish 388 pigs in a hoop house (and continue purchasing and finishing out another 230 pigs). With the hoop house and livestock purchases, total costs or outflows for the whole farm increase by $13,026 per year. At the same time, the owner can expect an annual increase in cash inflows equal to $1,875 worth of culled breeding livestock.

The net result shows that the hog operation's owner will generate $4,369 additional profits from the addition of hoop-house farrowing. The farm owner has captured the ownership cost of the hoop house and breeding livestock by

66 Example prepared by the Center for Farm Financial Management using actual records from a Minnesota farm.

including depreciation and interest on the new investment under the "profit" or long-range income projection. In the cash flow projection depreciation was left out and instead the full value of debt repayment (principal and interest) is added. Dividing the additional income by the $28,750 of new capital, this investment is projected to generate a 21.2 percent annual return on investment.

Worksheet 4.32: Partial Budget provides a partial budget format that will help you project the changes in both income and cash flow for relatively minor business changes in marketing, operations, human resources, or finance.

Figure 89. Example from Hog Finishing Operation—Worksheet 4.32: Partial Budget

Worksheet 4.32 Partial Budget

If appropriate, calculate and record the impact of each whole farm business strategy using the partial budget approach. Begin by estimating additional income (added inflows) and new expenses (additional outflows). Next, estimate any reduction in your annual expenses (reduced outflows) and income (reduced inflows) that will occur as a result of your proposed strategy or business change. Lastly, total up the positive impact of your business strategy (e) and the negative impact (f). What is the net effect on profit and cash flow? What is your return on assets?

Whole Farm Strategy: *Hog finishing*

Added Inflows	Profit	Cash Flow	Added Outflows	Profit	Cash Flow
Cull breeding stock	*$ 1,875*	*$ 1,875*	*Feed*	*$ 8,187*	*$ 8,187*
			Veterinary	*1,250*	*1,250*
			Supplies	*500*	*500*
			Marketing	*150*	*150*
			Utilities	*200*	*200*
			Depreciation	*1,000*	
			Interest	*1,739*	
			Debt repayment		*4,967*
			Income taxes		*1,883*
Subtotal (a) =	*1,875*	*1,875*	**Subtotal** (b) =	*13,026*	*17,137*

Reduced Outflows	Profit	Cash Flow	Reduced Inflows	Profit	Cash Flow
Feeder pigs	*15,520*	*15,520*			
Subtotal (c) =	*15,520*	*15,520*	**Subtotal** (d) =	*0*	*0*
Total (a + c) = (e)	*17,395*	*17,395*	**Total** (b + d) = (f)	*13,026*	*17,137*
			Net (e – f) = (g)	*4,369*	*258*
			Added Interest (h) =	*1,739*	
			Total Investment (i) =	*28,750*	
			Return on Assets [(g + h) / i] =	*21.2%*	

Long-Range planning. The long-range planning approach suggested here is based on the FINPACK software long-range planning module (known as FINLRB). It is designed to project the average expected net farm income for each whole-farm strategy you are considering. Since, in an average year, there will be no inventory change, the format is reasonably simple. Total expenses (variable and fixed) are subtracted from total farm revenue to arrive at net farm income. Cash flow is considered separately and discussed later, when you are measuring liquidity.

If you choose the long-range planning evaluation method, use **Worksheet 4.33: Long-Range Projected Income Statement** to project income and cash flow. Figure 90 shows this Worksheet filled out for the same hog enterprise analyzed in Figure 89.

The base plan projects income and cash flow should the owner continue to purchase and finish out 620 feeder pigs. Strategy 1 reflects the projected income and expenses from farrowing 388 pigs in the hoop house and finishing up to 620 hogs.

Strategy 1 looks slightly more profitable when compared to the base plan. But, there are two other questions that this producer must ask before making a final decision about whether or not to go ahead with plans to farrow and finish in the hoop.

First, will the additional return justify the added investment? While the methodology is not shown here, the hog producer's FINLRB result shows that the projected rate of return on the added investment is 19.6 percent and that their whole farm rate of return will increase from 6.8 percent to 7.4 percent.

Second, does the projected income and profit from the business satisfy goals for business income? Profitability estimates from the income statement can be compared to the income and quality of life goals (Worksheet 3.3). At a minimum, will the alternative cover a portion or all estimated family living expenses?

Worksheet 4.33 Long-Range Projected Income Statement

Use the space below to record average income and expenses (variable and fixed costs) for your present business (base plan) and the whole farm strategy alternative you are considering. The base plan should project the average expected future results for your current farm operation. Do this column first based on past history (Worksheet 2.10) and then build on it for each of your alternative strategies using information from your gross sales revenue projections (Worksheet 4.8) and the whole farm cost analysis (Worksheet 4.27). Then, calculate the net farm income for each alternative by subtracting total expenses from total revenue. How do your proposed alternatives compare to your present business income? Remember, when projecting the income for each strategy alternative, assume that your strategy has been fully implemented.

		Base Plan	Strategy #1	Strategy #2
Revenues:				
Gross product sales	*Hay sales*	*$ 18.022*	*$ 18,022*	
	Corn sales	*80,670*	*80,670*	
	Soybean sales	*70,121*	*70,121*	
	Pig sales	*89,100*	*89,100*	
Cull breeding livestock			*1,875*	
Other income		*2,200*	*2,200*	
Total revenue (a)		*260,113*	*261,988*	
Expenses:				
Annual variable expenses	*Seed*	*12,718*	*12.718*	
	Fertilizer	*15,053*	*15,053*	
	Chemicals	*11,025*	*11,025*	
	Other direct crop expense	*10,582*	*10,582*	
	Feeder livestock purchases	*24,800*	*9,280*	
	Feed	*10,124*	*18,311*	
	Breeding fees			
	Veterinary	*3,100*	*4,350*	
	Livestock supplies	*4,960*	*5,460*	
	Livestock marketing	*2,000*	*2,150*	
	Fuel and oil	*5,500*	*5,500*	
	Repairs	*8,400*	*8,400*	
	Hired labor	*5,480*	*5,480*	
Annual fixed expenses	*Rent and leases*	*44,993*	*44,993*	
	Real estate taxes	*3,586*	*3,586*	
	Insurance	*2,612*	*2,612*	
	Utilities	*3,000*	*3,200*	
	Interest	*22,436*	*24,175*	
	Depreciation	*12,000*	*13,000*	
Other farm expenses		*3,890*	*3.890*	
Total expenses (b)		*206,259*	*203,765*	
Net farm income (a – b)		*53,854*	*58,223*	

Figure 90. Example from Hog Finishing Operation—Worksheet 4.33: Long-Range Projected Income Statement

TASK 4

Liquidity: Will this new strategy help generate cash flow sufficient to pay back debts in a timely fashion?

Your next task is to look at cash flow for each strategy alternative as well as your base plan. Just because an investment or idea is profitable does not mean that it will generate cash flow to meet debt repayment. The cash flow analysis takes into account owner withdrawals and projected income taxes that were not included in profitability projections.

Figure 91. Example from Hog Finishing Operation—Worksheet 4.34: Long-Range Projected Cash Flow

Worksheet 4.34 Long-Range Projected Cash Flow

Use the space below to calculate and compare your business' present cash flow and its cash flow under the alternative whole-farm strategies that you are considering. Begin by estimating total cash inflows and outflows. Then subtract outflows from inflows. If the projected net cash flow is positive, then the plan will cash flow—it will be able to make debt payments on time. On the other hand, if the net cash flow is negative, the business alternative will have trouble servicing short-term debt.

		Base Plan	Strategy #1	Strategy #2
Projected Cash Flow:				
Net farm income		*$ 53,854*	*$ 58,223*	
Depreciation expense		*12,000*	*13,000*	
Interest expenses on term debt		*16,886*	*18,625*	
Nonfarm income		*18,000*	*18,000*	
Total cash inflows	(a)	*100,740*	*107,848*	
Owner withdrawals		*40,000*	*40,000*	
Income and social security taxes		*20,796*	*22,679*	
Principal and interest payments on term debt				
Loan *Existing payments*		*38,533*	*38,533*	
Loan *Hoop house*			*4,967*	
Loan				
Loan				
Loan				
Loan				
Total cash outflows	(b)	*99,329*	*106,179*	
Projected net cash flow	(a – b)	*1,411*	*1,669*	

If you used the partial budget evaluation, return again to Worksheet 4.32 (Partial Budget) and complete the cash flow columns. On the other hand, if you used Worksheet 4.33 (Long-Range Projected Income Statement) work through this section using Worksheet 4.34 (Long-Range Projected Cash Flow). Figure 91 shows the projected cash flow for our real-life hog finishing operation and the farrowing alternative.

As you complete **Worksheet 4.34: Long-Range Projected Cash Flow**, be sure to add depreciation expenses and term debt interest payments to net farm income—this will get you back to a starting cash position. You will have the opportunity to subtract out the full value of principal and interest payments further down on the Worksheet.

Solvency: Will this new strategy lead to growth in net worth?

When implementing alternative plans you will frequently need to plan for the purchase of additional equipment, machinery, buildings or land. You may plan to sell machinery, land or breeding livestock. Alternative plans that involve these types of capital investments and sales will change the balance sheet and, therefore, the solvency position of the business when they have been implemented.

As discussed in Planning Task Two (History and Current Situation), the balance sheet is a summary of the business' assets and liabilities at a specific point in time. Your assets, liabilities and possibly net worth as reported on the balance sheet will change significantly with major investment changes (purchases, expansions and reorganizations).

Preparing **Worksheet 4.35: Projected Balance Sheet** will help you work out the impact of your alternative business strategies on equity or future net worth growth. Complete Worksheet 4.35 using either cost or market asset valuation (whichever you used in Planning Task Two). Record "new investments," "capital sales," and "liabilities" for your base plan and each whole farm alternative. When doing so, include only the "one-time" changes necessary to move from the base plan to the alternative under consideration. These one-time changes may include the purchase or sale of machinery, buildings and land as well as new investments[67] in breeding stock beyond current numbers (including herd sires and additional replacements). Do not include machinery and equipment replacements that are necessary to maintain the existing operation. Moreover, do not include purchases of breeding livestock used to replace cull animals. This Worksheet is only for one-time purchases that are necessary to implement an alternative business plan.

How much equity will your strategy alternative generate in the future compared to your base plan? If your business strategy does not return the level of profit and equity desired or if it cannot service debt, return to your expense estimates, output projections and price forecasts. Is there another alternative you previously ruled out that may be worth reconsidering? The Minars, for instance, could have re-evaluated their plan substituting used equipment for the more expensive, new equipment package had their initial plan failed to cash flow. Is there something you can do differently?

On the other hand, if your strategy appears financially healthy—it yields the profit and equity that you desire and can service debt in a timely manner—then you are ready to shock the analysis. See what happens to your financial picture when market prices decline or input expenses increase. In other words, run through a quick risk analysis of your proposed strategy.

TASK 4

67 New investments must be financed by the proceeds from asset sales, through increased liabilities or by withdrawals from cash accounts. Funds generated from asset sales must be used either to finance new investments, reduce existing liabilities, or to build cash accounts.

Risk: Will this new strategy affect the risks faced by the farm business and family?

Like it or not, despite all of your planning, certain aspects of your business are not in your control. Crop yields are subject to weather and disease conditions and other unknowns. Therefore, it's a good idea to analyze business performance under a range of uncertainties. One way to do this is to *project your income and cash flow under the best and worst case scenarios*—varying those elements of your business that seem the most vulnerable to uncertainty.

Mabel Brelje, the organic grain farmer, projected income for the four crops in her rotation under best and worst case scenarios. She varied market prices and yields based on her own experience and on conversations with other organic producers. Figure 92 shows how her income for each enterprise will vary with yields (her high and low yield estimates from Worksheet 4.16). Mabel planned for the worst-case yield scenario in her analysis, since she was relatively new to organic production. She also looked for market price contracts, where possible, to secure a profitable market price.

TASK 4

Another way to judge the feasibility of your plan under conditions of uncertainty is to *shock the plan.* See how sensitive it is to fluctuations in market prices, interest rates, and expenses. Worksheet 4.36 (Risk Analysis) provides a format recommended by Dr. David Kohl of Virginia Tech University.[68] His approach is to ask what will happen to the financial results if you experience: a five percent reduction in prices; a five percent increase in expenses; or a three percent increase in interest rates?

[68] Presentation in Morris, MN: "Credit and Marketing in the New Era", Kohl, 1998.

Figure 93 shows the Risk Analysis Worksheet 4.36 for our example hog enterprise. Note that the base plan and alternative strategy do not cash flow with any of the proposed changes in market price and input expense conditions. The owners of this business would need to consider which plan is more likely to

Figure 92. Income Sensitivity Analysis Prepared by Mabel Brelje

	Yield/Acre	Avg. Projected Market Price/ Unit	Gross Income/Acre	Input Cost/Acre	Net Profit/Acre
Best Case Yield					
Alfalfa	6 tons	90	540	142	398
Soybeans	55 bushels	10	550	68	482
Wheat	50 bushels	3.5	175	73	102
Corn	150 bushels	3.0	450	94	356
Worst Case Yield					
Alfalfa	3 tons	90	270	142	128
Soybeans	30 bushels	10	300	68	232
Wheat	30 bushels	3.5	105	73	32
Corn	100 bushels	3.0	300	94	206

experience a financial shock and make adjustments to reduce their risk.

In the Minars' case, the dairy processing alternative was financially superior to their base plan. But which plan is more uncertain? Most would probably agree that the un-established markets assumed in the dairy processing alternative make it more uncertain. So, that uncertainty was something they had to consider in their final decision about whether or not to pursue the milk processing strategy.

Worksheet 4.36 Risk Analysis

Use the space below to record and compare the results of a five percent decrease in market prices, a five percent increase in expenses, or a two percent increase in interest rates for each whole-farm strategy alternative. You will need to use software or another sheet of paper to calculate the effect of these very real market uncertainties. How do these market and finance-related shocks affect your present business and its future under the whole-farm strategy alternatives that you are considering?

	Base Plan	Strategy #1	Strategy #2
Effect of a 5% decrease in prices			
Net farm income	$40,848	$45,124	
Net cash flow	-7,303	-7,107	
Effect of a 5% increase in expenses			
Net farm income	43,541	48,035	
Net cash flow	-5,499	-5,157	
Effect of a 3% increase in interest rates			
Net farm income	47,631	51,500	
Net cash flow			

Figure 93. Example from Hog Finishing Operation—Worksheet 4.36: Risk Analysis

Use **Worksheet 4.36: Risk Analysis** to analyze the financial risk associated with each whole farm strategy that you are considering. If you develop best and worst case scenarios, vary whatever factor seems least controllable—input costs, output, market prices? Likewise, if you choose to shock your original plan, adjust the recommended shocking rate (five percent) based on your own research. Organic producers, for example, have experienced dramatic and steady increases in organic market prices over the past five years as a result of fast growing demand. Conversely, as organic supplies begin to catch up with demand, organic growers could face an equally dramatic decline in prices. What do you think is a reasonable shock based on your own experience?

Transition Period Evaluation

Almost any strategy that you consider will take time to implement and may involve some trade-offs. *Sustainable Agriculture* author John Mason (see "Resources) advises new and existing business owners to expect disruption, even some losses, when transitioning into a new business or management strategy. As you move along the learning curve, things may get worse before they get better. Low yields, high debt payments, unusually high family living

Figure 94.
What to Do if Your Strategy Isn't Feasible in the Long Run [69]

Financial management specialists recommend the following:

- Change production plans
- Change marketing plans
- Reduce costs
- Reduce consumption
- Refinance
- Institute alternative financing sources and methods
- Consider leasing new capital items
- Postpone expenditures
- Introduce new equity capital
- Seek off-farm income
- Sell highly liquid financial assets and inventories
- Downsize the scale of operations

TASK 4

69 *Financial Management in Agriculture*, Financial Planning and Feasibility Analysis, 7th Ed., Barry, et al., 2002.

Worksheet 4.37 Transitional Cash Flow

Use the space below to project the business' first three years' cash flow. Begin by recording gross income from sales of products. Then, record other farm and nonfarm income as well as borrowed funds that will be used by the business. Record total projected income or total inflows (a) for each year. Next, record all cash outflows (b), including annual farm expenses, owner withdrawals (for family living), taxes, and debt payments. Subtract total cash outflows (b) from total cash inflows (a) to calculate net cash flow for the year.

Whole Farm Strategy:

		Year 1	Year 2	Year 3
Projected Cash Inflows:				
Gross product sales	*Hay sales*	$ 18,000	$ 18,000	$ 18,000
	Corn sales	75,445	75,445	75,445
	Soybean sales	67,946	67,946	67,946
	Pig sales	87,718	89,100	89,100
	Cull sows and boars	438	750	750
	Government payments	9,790	9,790	9,790
		2,200	2,200	2,200
Other income				
		18,000	18,000	18,000
Nonfarm income				
Capital sales		25,000		
New borrowings				
Total Cash inflows (a)		304,537	281,231	281,231
Projected Cash outflows:				
Farm expenses (excluding interest)		171,391	168,333	168,333
Owner withdrawals		40,000	40,000	40,000
Income and social security taxes		15,000	15,000	15,000
Capital purchases		26,250	450	450
Debt payments	*Existing payments*	38,533	37,541	34,152
	Hoop house loan	2,483	4,967	4,967
	Operating loan interest	17,262	12,042	11,918
Total cash outflows (b)		310,919	278,333	274,820
Net cash flow (a – b)		-6,382	2,898	6,411
Cumulative net cash flow		-6,382	-3,484	2,927

Figure 95.
Example from Hog Finishing Operation—Worksheet 4.37: Transitional Cash Flow

expenses, or unexpected machinery replacement needs may cause the cash flow for a profitable farm to be insufficient in a given year.

If you are putting together a loan proposal, your lender will probably be more interested in your transitional plans than your long-range plans. The best long-range strategy can be undermined by short-term roadblocks. You need to convince yourself and your external business partners that you can get from here to there.

Your transition plan will be different than the long-range plans that you have already completed.

First, you will prepare a projected cash flow plan for a specific year or years rather than a "typical" or average year in the future. Second, you will use your best estimates of short-term prices and costs instead of long-range averages. Finally, your transition plans will be affected by your current inventories of crops for sale, feed, market livestock and other products. In your long-range plans, this Guide assumed that you would sell an average year's production. In transitional planning, you need to work through your projected inventory changes.

Including the change in current inventories is an essential part of developing an accurate cash flow plan. A cash flow plan, which only considers cash transactions without inventory changes, can grossly misrepresent the actual farm financial situation. For example, if two years of crop production are sold in one year, the cash flow will look excellent but the change in current inventories would adjust for the reduction in crop held in storage. Another example might be a livestock expansion where the inventories are being built up during the first year but no cash sales occur.

Use **Worksheet 4.37: Transitional Cash Flow** to record your income and expenses during the transition period. You'll find some of this information on Worksheet 4.31 (Enterprise Budget) where you first recorded expenses.

Figure 95, on the preceding page, shows a summary of the hog producer's transitional cash flow plan for the first three years of on-farm farrowing. Note that this plan projects that it will take three years before the business will begin to show a positive cash flow. If the hog producer decides to go ahead with her hoop house purchase and farrowing enterprise, she will have to subsidize the business through cash reserves or operating credit during the transition.

There is software available to help you develop transitional cash flow information. The Center for Farm Financial Management's FINFLO component of FINPACK and most similar software will walk you through a monthly cash flow projection for the next year and then, if need be, push that forward for one or two more years (see "Resources").

Choose the Best Whole Farm Strategy

After all of the brainstorming, analysis and discussion, the final component of strategy formulation is to make a decision—choose a future direction and then implement it. At the end of this section, you will need to make a decision to:

- Stay with the business base plan (make no changes in business).
- Adopt the alternative strategy (implement your new plan).
- Reconsider or brainstorm new alternatives.

If you have done a complete job of laying the foundation and evaluating strategic alternatives, this may be the easiest part. If, for example, you identified a strategic direction that is in tune with your values, moves you toward your personal and family goals, and is technically and financially feasible, it will probably be easy to make this final decision and to get everyone in your family or business on board.

If your decision about which business strategy to pursue is not so clear, you may want to do some more research or explore additional strategy alternatives.

Figure 96.
Strategy "Best Fit" Tests [70]

Vision Consistency Test. How well does the proposed strategy fit with your whole farm and personal vision? If the strategy does not lead toward your personal and business vision or embrace the core values of your planning team, it should be rejected. Success and enthusiasm will be low and the plan is unlikely to succeed otherwise.

Goodness of Fit Test. How well does the proposed strategy fit with your external analysis of the industry and the internal analysis of your farm? Does the proposed strategy explain how it will build on your business' current strengths and opportunities while managing for weaknesses and threats? Recall your SWOT analysis from Worksheet 2.18 (in Planning Task Two).

Building for the Future Test. How well does the proposed strategy build for the future? Recall your vision from Planning Task Three. Will your business strategy help get you there? Moreover, will your strategy generate resources, such as soil quality and financial equity, for the next generation? If a strategy uses but does not generate resources, it should receive a low score for this test.

Feasibility and Resource Test. How realistic are the business' start-up and long-term resource needs? In other words, are resources available to implement your whole farm strategy? Review your current list of resources (Worksheet 2.3) and compare them to your resource needs (Worksheet 4.14 in Planning Task Four). Is your soil type appropriate for the crops that you want to grow? Can people be hired to do the work needed? Can financing be obtained?

Performance Test. How well does the proposed strategy help accomplish your marketing, operations, human resources and financial goals for the farm business? What are the projections for income, rates of return, and net worth growth? Most importantly, can your business survive the transition period?

Importance Test. How well does the strategy address the important or critical planning issues that you identified in Introduction Worksheet? Does your strategy focus on these important issues or on the trivial? If a proposed strategy does not address important issues then it should be rejected as written.

Confidence Test. How high is the confidence of your planning team in the anticipated outcomes of the proposed strategy? How high is the risk that events will occur that will change the expected results—particularly in a negative direction?

Without clarity, each management decision will require a round of agonizing debate and it will be difficult for everyone in your organization to see where the business is headed. These are the types of situations that breed conflict between family members and partners. Your strategic plan should be something that you, your family, and any other stakeholders, can embrace and move toward decisively.

Minnesota economist Kent Olson recommends testing your business strategy or strategies from several perspectives before making the final decision to implement it. Olson outlines a series of subjective "tests" that can be used to rank each of the major strategy alternatives that you are considering (including your base plan) and help you choose the best strategy for your business (Figure 96). He suggests giving each strategy a subjective score, from one to five (five being the highest) for each test. The strategy with the highest score is apparently the best for the farm and for you and your family. You will need to be brutally honest. Take into account the research and evaluation that you have conducted as a team thus far when scoring each whole farm business strategy.

The Minars used the tests to score their base plan and the alternative milk processing strategy (on Worksheet 4.38 as shown in Figure 97). They gave a high score to the processing alternative. It appeared to offer the most promise for future business stability and job creation—objectives that the Minars, as a family, place great importance on. Conversely, the base plan, which reflected their present business, received low scores in all areas related to the family's future vision. Only those

70 *A Strategic Management Primer for Farmers*, Olson, 2001.

tests related to feasibility and resources (those factors that are known to the Minars) ranked well. Based on this final series of tests, the Minars were very ready to move ahead with their idea to process milk products on the farm.

Use **Worksheet 4.38: Scoring and Deciding on a Final Business Strategy** to score your base plan and whole-farm business strategies. How does your new strategy rank? If more than one strategy ranks similarly, then spend more time researching and evaluating the remaining strategies before making a final decision about what direction to take your business. Conversely, if your new strategy is a clear "winner," move on and begin developing a brief contingency plan for the business.

Worksheet 4.38 Scoring and Deciding on a Final Business Strategy

Use each of the strategy tests (described in Figure 96) to assess your whole farm business alternatives. Give each strategy a subjective score, from one to five (five being the highest), for each test. Once each strategy is scored, sum the scores across all tests. The strategy with the highest score is apparently the best for the farm and your planning team. If more than one strategy ranks similarly, then spend more time researching and evaluating the remaining strategies before making a final decision about which direction to take your business.

Proposed Strategy:	Base Plan	Strategy #1 *Processing Alternative*	Strategy #2
Strategy Tests (high = 5, low = 1)			
Vision Consistency	*2*	*5*	
Goodness of Fit	*2*	*4*	
Building for Future	*2*	*5*	
Performance	*2*	*5*	
Importance	*2*	*5*	
Feasibility	*2*	*5*	
Resources	*5*	*4*	
Confidence	*5*	*4*	
Total Score	*22*	*37*	

Which whole farm or enterprise strategy will we pursue?

Figure 97. Example from Cedar Summit Farm—Worksheet 4.38: Scoring and Deciding on a Final Business Strategy

TASK 4

Develop a Contingency Plan

You have confidently chosen a final whole farm strategy based on your thorough research and evaluation. Now, one of your last steps in the planning process is to develop a contingency plan—an action plan for how to cope should conditions within and outside the business change. They will. Contingency planning is important to assure that your business plan will be implemented smoothly.

Throughout the planning process you've used your research to inform and make a number of realistic assumptions about the industry, prices, productivity and labor. Assumptions, however, are just that—best guesses that can change. No matter how carefully you plan, the likelihood of everything working out precisely as planned is small.[71] A contingency plan can help you prepare for those situations when things don't go as planned—when market or economic conditions that are out of your control change.

TASK 4

Consider how the following problems, for example, could change your cash flow during the transition period:

- New construction costs 20 percent more than planned.
- Funds are borrowed but income flows are delayed for six months.
- Construction is stopped because of a missing regulatory permit.
- Livestock productivity is stunted due to dry pasture conditions.
- The person you hire to manage operations is incompetent or untrustworthy.
- You do not obtain a sales contract for your first year's production.
- Market prices sink to 15 percent below average historical values.
  A sound business plan will lay out what needs to be done to avoid or address these delays, inefficiencies, and bottlenecks in the form of a contingency or control plan.

Contingency plans need not be long or complicated. If you intend to share your written business plan with lenders or other external business partners, contingency plans simply need to convince readers that you've done a thorough job of planning and that the business is prepared to respond successfully should internal and external conditions change. If your business plan is strictly for family or internal planning purposes, a contingency plan can be used as something to fall back on should marketing prices, labor supplies, family goals, and institutional requirements change unexpectedly.

71 *Planning for Contingencies*, in Business Owners' Toolkit online, CCH Incorporated, 2002.

Authors of *Planning for Contingencies* note that there are several ways to incorporate contingency plans into your final business plan: "For example, your financial statements can incorporate a footnote explaining that the projected interest rate can go up by as much as three percent before your profit margin is seriously affected. Or, your discussion of how many employees you'll need can state that an additional production person will be hired when sales of $X are achieved."[72]

Begin your contingency planning by identifying events that may throw your strategy off track and necessitate a major change in your business plan—like a change in government policy, market prices, organic certification rules. The Minars, for instance, identified new competition—other farmers or businesses that begin offering non-homogenized or glass-bottled milk—as a source of uncertainty. Their contingency plan could include a number of ideas, such as "frequent customer" discounts, for coping with increased competition. Conversely, the Minars' contingency plan might include plans to cope with labor and production constraints should home delivery sales exceed their expectations. If for example, 150 customers—rather than the projected 75—sign up for home delivery during the Minars' first three months of processing, how would they respond? Additional milk would be available for processing, but Dave and Florence might need to hire and train new staff to fill orders or risk losing potential customers.

TASK 4

As stated earlier, your contingency plan need not be complicated. You simply need to show that you have thought through and planned for a range of future scenarios. Take a look at the contingency plan prepared by Greg Reynolds, owner of Riverbend Farm:

"If CSA sales do not materialize, I will sell the produce to restaurants and co-ops. The lack of up-front money will delay the plans to build a root cellar. The need for help and a cooler are crucial to expanding the business. Without the CSAs, weekly sales [to restaurants and co-ops] will have to reach $1,000/week [in order to meet financial goals]. That is about 40 cases per week, harvesting two cases per hour per person or 20 hours of additional labor."

What are your contingency plans for the business? Take some time to discuss with your planning team how internal and external conditions may change in the future. Then use **Worksheet 4.39: Contingency Statement** to develop a brief contingency plan for the business.

72 *Planning for Contingencies*, in Business Owners' Toolkit online, CCH Incorporated, 2002.

Prepare the Strategy Section of Your Business Plan

The executive summary is, perhaps, the most important section of your written business plan since many readers, including lenders, will not look beyond the executive summary if it does not communicate careful planning and promise.

TASK 4

The work that you've done in this Planning Task is very much about the planning process. But the culmination of all of your work is the development of a very specific business strategy. This strategy, along with the research that supports it, will become the crux of your written business plan. Take time now to summarize your business strategy for the whole farm.

One way to do this is to draft the Executive Summary for your business plan—to summarize your principal business planning objective, goals, and your strategy (or strategies) for reaching them. Authors of *The Executive Summary* say "The executive summary is, perhaps, the most important section of your written business plan since many readers, including lenders, will not look beyond the executive summary if it does not communicate careful planning and promise."[73]

An Executive Summary typically includes information about the business:

- **Identity:** Who you are (and the name of your business).
- **Location:** Where the business is located.
- **History:** How long the business has been in operation.
- **Ownership:** Current ownership structure.
- **Industry and Competition:** Brief description of the business' competitive position.
- **Product:** What type of product you now offer and plan to market in the future.
- **Marketing:** Who your potential customers are and what they will value.
- **Operations:** How you will produce.
- **Human Resources:** Who will manage and staff the business.
- **Finances:** How much profit and equity the business will generate, how you intend to finance the business and how you will cope with and manage risk.

The Executive Summary is a snapshot of your business and its strategy. It can be as short as you like but generally no longer than two pages. Most importantly, your Executive Summary should convey credibility and excitement, particularly if you are seeking external financing or new business partners. As an example, the Executive Summary prepared by Dave and Florence Minar for Cedar Summit Farm is reproduced in Figure 98. Look at how they incorporated information about their values, vision, research, and financial analysis into a concise, positive and realistic summary of their strategy to process milk on the farm.

73 *The Executive Summary,* in Business Owners' Toolkit online, CCH Incorporated, 2002.

Figure 98. Example from Cedar Summit Farm—Worksheet 4.40: Executive Summary

Worksheet 4.40 Executive Summary

Use the space below to draft an executive summary for your business plan. Remember, this is perhaps the most important section of your plan—it should provide a snapshot of what the business is about and how it will be successful. At the very least, your executive summary should communicate information about goals, market potential and sales volume, production management and capacity, expenses, profitability, cash flow and risk management.

Cedar Summit Farm will build a milk processing plant as a natural extension of our dairy business. We are located just north of New Prague and within 25 miles of the Minneapolis-St. Paul area including the suburbs of Edina, Minnetonka, Eden Prairie, Burnsville and Apple Valley. By capturing more of the consumer dollar we can afford to bring our farm-oriented children into the business. We feel that our grass-fed cows produce a superior product that has much value to the health conscious. We value producer to consumer relationships. The past few years that we have direct marketed our meat products have shown us that consumers value knowing where their food comes from. This past spring we sent out 450 brochures to past customers.

We will distribute our products from delivery trucks and a storefront with a drive up window that will be part of our processing plant. Our distribution will be home delivery, drop off sites at churches, co-op food stores, and restaurants that cater to locally produced food. The plant and store will be located near the intersection of Scott Co. roads 2 and 15.

We plan to process and sell 30 percent of the milk produced on our farm the first year. Processing will then be increased by five percent each month, until May 2004, when all our milk will be processed. Until we reach capacity, milk not processed in our plant will continue to be sold to Davisco of Le Sueur, MN., which has agreed to buy it at grade A prices.

Cedar Summit Farm will build the plant and lease it to Cedar Summit Creamery, LLC. Cedar Summit Creamery, LLC, will purchase all the necessary equipment and supplies for operation, and be responsible for production, marketing and distribution. According to the requirements in this business plan, and based on what we feel are sound business assumptions, our initial capital requirements are for:

(1) Cedar Summit Farm -- $XXX,000 for a 4,800 square foot concrete block building, with all infrastructures in place.
(2) Cedar Summit Creamery LLC -- $XXX,000 for the purchase of supplies and start-up costs.

We do not anticipate additional investment requirements. We will plan our growth through retained earnings.

We have children with many abilities and envision this business as a future for them and their families, and a valued asset to our community.

Use **Worksheet 4.40: Executive Summary** to draft an executive summary for your business plan. With an executive summary in hand, you're ready to write the rest of your plan! Move on to Planning Task Five—Present, Implement, and Monitor Your Business Plan!

Worksheet 4.1 Customer Segmentation

Complete this Worksheet for each major product you plan to produce. Develop a profile of the customer(s) you intend to target by market segment. Note the geographic, demographic, and psychographic characteristics of each segment. Be sure to describe your customers' needs and preferences and what they value. Use additional sheets of paper if this product has more than three major market segments.

Product: ____________________

Customer Segment: 1 ____________ 2 ____________ 3 ____________

Geographic

Demographic

Psychographic

Needs/Preferences

Worksheet 4.2 Potential Sales Volume

Complete this Worksheet for each major product you plan to produce. Use your information about average product consumption, geographic location, and customer preferences to develop simple sales projections for each segment of your market. Be sure to specify the timeframe (month, season, year) for each projection. You may want to calculate your potential sales volume for best and worst case scenarios—adjusting the estimated sales volume per customer and the potential number of customers as market conditions may change. If you decide to look at more than three customer segments, more than one sales season, or best and worst case sales projections, use additional paper or Worksheets to calculate and record your business' potential sales volume. Finally, describe any assumptions upon which your sales estimates are based. Be sure to list data sources (such as surveys, market reports, sourcebooks, etc.).

Product: ______________________________

Time Frame: ______________________________

	1	2	3
Customer Segment:			
Potential number of customers: (a)			
Estimated volume per customer (b)			
Potential sales volume (a x b) =			

Market Assumptions/Research Results

Describe your marketing assumptions and research. Include information about general industry conditions, competition, and future market potential for your product.

Worksheet 4.3 Product and Uniqueness

Complete this Worksheet for each major product you plan to produce. Describe your product and why it will appeal to each market segment. Begin by noting industry trends and general market conditions. Describe supply and demand market trends for this product. Discuss whether they are short-term fads or long-term, emerging trends. Note perceived marketing opportunities that may exist locally, regionally, nationally or internationally. Include evidence that supports your ideas. Then, describe the unique features that distinguish this product within the marketplace. For which customer segments are these unique features important? How easily could competitors imitate these features?

Product: ______________________________

Industry Trends/Changing Market Conditions:

____

____

____

____

____

Characteristic 1 ______________________________

Appeals to which segments? ______________________________

Easy for competitors to imitate? Yes/No ____________

Characteristic 2 ______________________________

Appeals to which segments? ______________________________

Easy for competitors to imitate? Yes/No ____________

Characteristic 3 ______________________________

Appeals to which segments? ______________________________

Easy for competitors to imitate? Yes/No ____________

Summarize the unique characteristics of this product and why it is valuable to your target market:

____

____

____

____

____

____

____

____

____

____

____

____

____

____

Worksheet 4.4 Competition

Complete this Worksheet for each major product you plan to produce. List your competitors in each market segment for this product. Describe competitors' product marketing strategies and the prices they charge for each product. Note any advantages and disadvantages you may have with respect to your competition. Then, develop and describe your strategy for competing or positioning your business in the marketplace.

Product: ____________________

Customer Segment:	1	2	3
Competitor names			
Competitor products			
Major characteristics			
Product price range			
Our advantages			
Our disadvantages			

Competition strategy:

TASK 4

Worksheet 4.5 Distribution and Packaging

Complete this Worksheet for each major product you plan to produce. Describe how you intend to move and package this product for each target market segment. Note where and how the product will be shipped (location and scope) and what type of distribution channel you will utilize (movement). Next, based on each distribution plan, research and describe one or more packaging strategies for this product. Consider what type of packaging might be valued by customers (e.g. convenience) or even required by intermediaries and distributors. Describe a delivery and handling schedule by period (month, season, year). Then, summarize your distribution and packaging strategies for this product.

Product: ____________________ **Period:** ____________________

Customer Segment: ____

Location: ____

Scope: ____

Movement (distribution channel): ____

Industry packaging requirements: ____

Packaging ideas: ____

Delivery schedule & handling: ____

CONTINUED

TASK 4

Worksheet 4.5 Distribution and Packaging

CONTINUED

Complete this Worksheet for each major product you plan to produce. Describe how you intend to move and package this product for each target market segment. Note where and how the product will be shipped (location and scope) and what type of distribution channel you will utilize (movement). Next, based on each distribution plan, research and describe one or more packaging strategies for this product. Consider what type of packaging might be valued by customers (e.g., convenience) or even required by intermediaries and distributors. Describe a delivery and handling schedule by period (month, season, year). Then, summarize your distribution and packaging strategies for this product.

Product: ____________ **Period:** ____________

Customer Segment: ____________

Location: ____________

Scope: ____________

Movement (distribution channel): ____________

Industry packaging requirements: ____________

Packaging ideas: ____________

Delivery schedule & handling: ____________

TASK 4

Worksheet 4.6 Pricing

Complete this Worksheet for each major product you plan to produce. List the price range for similar products offered by competitors (Worksheet 4.4) or industry buyers. Next, think about how you might price this product. Consider how much power you have to set the price for this product and how sensitive the demand for this product is to price changes. Then describe your pricing strategies for this product and list your low, expected, and high product price under each pricing strategy alternative. Finally, summarize your pricing strategy in the space provided.

Product: ______________________

Competitor/Industry Price Range: ______________________

____

Our Power to Set Prices: ____**Low** ____**Some** ____**High**

Demand Sensitivity to Price Changes: ____**Low** ____**Some** ____**High**

	Price Range: Low	Expected	High
Pricing Strategies			
Strategy #1: ______	______	______	______
______	______	______	______
______	______	______	______
______	______	______	______
______	______	______	______
______	______	______	______
______	______	______	______
Strategy #2: ______	______	______	______
______	______	______	______
______	______	______	______
______	______	______	______
______	______	______	______
______	______	______	______
______	______	______	______

Pricing Strategy:

____

____

____

____

____

____

____

____

____

____

____

TASK 4

Worksheet 4.7 Promotion

Complete this Worksheet for each major product you plan to produce. Choose an advertising approach (product, image, total) for each customer segment. Then use your information about customer needs and preferences (Worksheet 4.1) to develop a promotional message for this product. Next, think about what advertising tools and delivery methods you can use to communicate your message. Describe how often you intend to promote your product and communicate with customers (timing and frequency). It may be helpful to use a calendar or blank sheet of paper to map out an advertising plan that corresponds with slow demand periods or peak product availability. Finally, summarize your promotion strategy for this product.

Product: ____________________

Customer Segment:	1	2	3
Approach (product, image, total):			
Message:			
Tools:			
Delivery:			
Timing/frequency:			

Promotion strategy:

TASK 4

Worksheet 4.8 Inventory and Storage Management

Using the space below, describe how you will store and manage inventories for each product. Consider any regulations or industry standards that might apply to your business (Worksheet 4.11). Note how you will comply with any standards for product quality.

Product: ______________________________

Industry regulations/standards:

Product storage:

TASK 4

Inventory management:

Quality control:

Worksheet 4.9 Marketing Strategy Summary

Complete this Worksheet for each major product you plan to produce. Compile your market research (Worksheets 4.1–4.7) for each year in your transition period and for your long run or expected market outlook, as appropriate. Begin with a description of your target market (by segment). Then summarize product characteristics and competition, as well as your plans for distribution, pricing and promotion. Next, use the space below to estimate gross sales revenue and to record marketing expense estimates. You will use this expense information when evaluating the business' projected financial performance in the Evaluation section of Planning Task Four. Finally, summarize your marketing strategies for this product or the whole farm. Be sure to include a SWOT (strengths, weaknesses, opportunities, threats) analysis. This will be the start of your marketing strategy section for the written business plan.

Product: ______	**Long Run (Expected)**	**Transition Period** Year 1	Year 2	Year 3
Target Market Segments				
Number of Customers (a)				
Sales Volume/Customer (b)				
Potential Sales Volume (c) = (a x b)				
Product Characteristics (appeal and value)				
Competition				
Distribution				
Packaging				

CONTINUED

Worksheet 4.9 Marketing Strategy Summary

CONTINUED

	Long Run (Expected)	Transition Period Year 1	Year 2	Year 3
Promotion				
Price Range/Unit (d)				
Gross Sales Revenue (e) = (c x d)				
Marketing Expenses:				
Distribution & Handling				
Storage				
Packaging				
Advertising				
Other Promotion				
Licensing and Legal Fees				
Membership Fees				
Market Research/Consultant				
Other				
Total Expenses				

Business Plan Input—Marketing Strategy Summary:

TASK 4

Worksheet 4.10 Production System and Schedule

Use the space below to describe the production management system(s) that you use for each enterprise. You may have more than one enterprise for each product that you plan to produce. Be sure to detail your management plans for all enterprises. If you plan to gradually transition into a new management system, complete this Worksheet for each year or season during the transition period. You might find it helpful to use a map or calendar to describe any seasonal or transition-related management plans.

Enterprise ______________________________

Year ______________

System

Schedule/Rotation

TASK 4

Worksheet 4.11 Regulations and Policies

List any permits, institutional requirements, and other government policies that will affect your operations. When noting permit requirements, be sure to describe any ongoing compliance issues such as annual permit renewals and fees. Next, describe your ability to meet these conditions.

Permit/License/Policy ______________________

Issued by: ______________________

Conditions and compliance issues: ______________________

Fees: ______________________

Can we meet these conditions? ______________________

Permit/License/Policy ______________________

Issued by: ______________________

Conditions and compliance issues: ______________________

Fees: ______________________

Can we meet these conditions? ______________________

Permit/License/Policy ______________________

Issued by: ______________________

Conditions and compliance issues: ______________________

Fees: ______________________

Can we meet these conditions? ______________________

TASK 4

Worksheet 4.12 Describing Potential Crop Production Systems

Complete this Worksheet for each major crop enterprise. Be as specific and accurate as you can, since this information will be the basis for the resource acquisition strategies that you consider.

Crop Enterprise: ______________________ Current Acreage: ______________

Month	Machinery Operations				Operating Input				Labor	
	Operation	Hrs/ Acre	Machine 1	Machine 2	Item	Quantity/ Acre	Units	Price/ Unit	Hrs/ Acre	Type

TASK 4

Worksheet 4.13 Describing Potential Livestock Production Systems

Complete this Worksheet for each major livestock enterprise. Be as specific and accurate as you can, since this information will be the basis for the acquisition strategies you consider.

Livestock/Poultry Production System: ______________________ Projected Number of Units: ______________

Month or Period	Facility Space Req.	Labor		Feed Required	Vet & Medications Items & Amounts	Machinery & Equipment Req.	Other Inputs
		Hours	Type				

Worksheet 4.14 Resource Needs and Acquisition

Return to Worksheets 2.3 (Tangible Working Assets), 2.5 (Describing Crop Production Systems), and 2.6 (Describing Livestock Production Systems) where you described your current resource base and use. Study these Worksheets and compare them to Worksheets 4.12 and 4.13. Think about how your resource needs will change as you add a new enterprise, expand markets, or reallocate resources. If you used a map in Planning Tasks Two and Three to describe your current situation and future vision, then you may want to do so again here. Illustrate which parcels of land will be devoted to buildings, crops, livestock, recreation, education and wildlife according to your operations management strategy. Then, using the space below, describe any gaps between current resource availability and future resource needs. Lastly, develop your acquisition strategy for meeting or filling future resource needs. Will you redirect or make better use of current resources? Will you purchase or rent additional resources (new or used)? Or will you gain access to resources through agreements, custom-hire or contracting services? List your acquisition strategy alternatives in the space provided.

Enterprise ______________________________

Resource Needs:	Acquisition Strategy 1	Acquisition Strategy 2
Land		
Buildings		
Machinery and equipment		
Breeding livestock		
Supplies		

TASK 4

Worksheet 4.15 Institutional Considerations

Describe institutional factors that will affect your ability to use and manage physical resources under your new operations strategies. Include any long-term leasing arrangements, conservation easements, permit requirements, legal restrictions, and production or marketing contracts.

Long-term Leasing Arrangements for Real Estate

Specify whether items will be leased in for your use or leased out for the use of others.

Long-term Agreements and Easements

TASK 4

Permit and Legal Restrictions

Specify the agency responsible for issuing permits, conditions and compliance factors, fees, and your ability to meet these conditions.

Long-term Production Contracts and Marketing Agreements

Worksheet 4.16 Estimating Output and Capacity

Complete this Worksheet for each major product you plan to produce. Compile your market research (Worksheets 4.1–4.7) for each year in your transition period and for your long run or expected market outlook, as appropriate. Begin with a description of your target market (by segment). Then summarize product characteristics and competition, as well as your plans for distribution, pricing and promotion. Next, use the space below to estimate gross sales revenue and to record marketing expense estimates. You will use this expense information when evaluating the business' projected financial performance in the Evaluation section of Planning Task Four. Finally, summarize your marketing strategies for this product or the whole farm. Be sure to include a SWOT (strengths, weaknesses, opportunities, threats) analysis. This will be the start of your marketing strategy section for the written business plan.

Enterprise: ______________________

	Long Run (Expected)	Transition Period Year 1	Year 2	Year 3
Typical output				
Expected output				
High output				
Low output				
Production capacity				

At the whole-farm level, we plan to (grow/maintain/contract) our business:

TASK 4

Worksheet 4.17 Operations Strategy Summary

Complete this Worksheet, using your research from Worksheets 4.9–4.16, for each new enterprise or an existing one that will change. Begin with a brief description of the management system and implementation (describe your crop rotation, pasture layout and rotation, milking schedule, etc.). Next, list new resource needs and your strategy for acquiring them. Then record all operating expenses associated with this enterprise, including the overhead value of new equipment, machinery, and breeding livestock that may be needed. Try to allocate your overhead costs across this and other enterprises in proportion to use. Finally, summarize your operations strategies for this enterprise and the whole farm in the space provided. This will be the start of your operations strategy section for the written business plan. Be sure to include a SWOT (strengths, weaknesses, opportunities, threats) analysis.

Enterprise: ______________________

	Transition Period		
	Year 1	**Year 2**	**Year 3**
Production System and Rotation			
Resource Needs and Acquisition			
Land			
Buildings			
Machinery & equipment			
Breeding livestock			

TASK 4

CONTINUED

Worksheet 4.17 Operations Strategy Summary

CONTINUED

Enterprise: ______________________

	Transition Period		
	Year 1	Year 2	Year 3
Labor			
Supplies			
Other inputs			
Permits			
Output			
Storage			
Operations Expenses			
Seed			
Fertilizer			
Chemicals			
Irrigation energy			
Other direct crop expenses			
Feeder livestock expenses			

CONTINUED

TASK 4

Worksheet 4.17 Operations Strategy Summary

CONTINUED

Enterprise: ______________________

	Year 1	**Transition Period** **Year 2**	**Year 3**
Feed and forages			
Breeding fees			
Veterinary			
Livestock supplies			
Fuel and oil			
Repairs and maintenance			
Storage			
Processing			
Dues and professional fees			
Office supplies			
Utilities			
Rent and leases			
Equipment/ machinery			
Breeding livestock			
Buildings			
Land			
Other			
Total expenses			

Business Plan Input - Operations Strategy Summary:

TASK 4

Worksheet 4.18 Tasks and Workload

Use the space below to describe the marketing, operations, human resources and finance tasks associated with each new enterprise. Refer to Worksheets 4.11–4.12 (Describing Potential Crop and Livestock Systems) for operations workload estimates. Then estimate the workload (hours) associated with each task. If your business tends to be seasonal, distribute the total hours for each activity by periods of the year. Use a separate sheet of paper if more space is needed or make copies of this Worksheet to detail workload changes for each year in your transition period, as appropriate.

Enterprise ______________________ **Timeframe** ______________________

Hours/Month

Tasks	**Jan**	**Feb**	**Mar**	**Apr**	**May**	**June**	**July**	**Aug**	**Sep**	**Oct**	**Nov**	**Dec**
Marketing:												
Operations												
Management:												
Finances:												
Total Hrs/Month												

TASK 4

Worksheet 4.19 Filling Workforce Needs

Use the space below to flesh out new position titles and task descriptions for each new enterprise or existing enterprise that is short on labor. Next, if adding labor, describe the type of position that will be created—full-time or part-time, temporary or permanent, seasonal or year-round—as well as the skills desired for each position. Lastly, describe your strategy for addressing workforce gaps and acquiring and training labor. Workforce strategies may include: reassigning current labor; adding new labor (family, employees, volunteers, interns); hiring out work to custom operators or consultants; or developing work trade arrangements with neighbors or relatives. You might also consider reducing some of your labor needs through the use of additional equipment and machinery or through new business arrangements.

Position/Task (title)	**Type of Position** (full time/part time, temporary/permanent)	**Skills/Experience Desired**	**Acquisition Strategy**

TASK 4

CONTINUED

Worksheet 4.19 Filling Workforce Needs

CONTINUED

Position/Task (title)	Type of Position (full time/part time, temporary/permanent)	Skills/Experience Desired	Acquisition Strategy

TASK 4

1. Describe training that may be required for new positions or new members of the workforce:

2. How will training be accomplished?

Worksheet 4.20 Compensation

Research and record standard wage, salary and benefits for each new job or position. If you plan to create more than four new positions, make copies of this Worksheet or use additional sheets of paper.

	Position/Job 1	Position/Job 2	Position/Job 3	Position/Job 4
Average industry wage/salary/fees ($/hour):				
Typical industry benefits:				
Tax rate:				

TASK 4

Worksheet 4.21 Human Resources Expense Estimates

Use the space below to estimate and record your human resources input expenses for all family members and hired labor. Make these estimates as realistic as possible—use your research about industry standards and tax rates as well as your own compensation goals.

	Position/Job 1	Position/Job 2	Position/Job 3	Position/Job 4
Job title/description				
Name				
Wages/salary/fees ($/hour)				
Benefits (health care, retirement)				
Taxes				
Insurance (workers compensation)				
Other				
Total labor expenses (a)				
Total hours worked (b)				
Total labor expenses/hour (a) / (b)				

TASK 4

Worksheet 4.22 Management Strategy

Return to your skills assessment in Worksheet 2.7. Are you ready to manage the operation? If not, who will? As you answer the following questions, try to be honest and realistic. Then, develop a strategy for whole farm business management.

1. Are you willing and ready to manage the operation and hired labor? If so, what skills do you bring to the management position? Are you a good communicator?

2. Will you share management responsibilities? If so, how will you divide tasks? Will you develop a written management agreement? What skills do other management team members bring to the business?

TASK 4

3. Can the business function without you? Who will manage the operation when you are gone or ill? Who is your back-up?

4. How often will you check in with family and other members of your workforce?

5. Our management strategy can be summarized as follows:

Worksheet 4.23 Human Resources Strategy Summary

Complete this Worksheet for each major enterprise. Compile your research (from Worksheets 4.18–4.22) for each year in your transition period (if appropriate) and for the long run or expected market outlook. Begin with a description of workload requirements. Next, describe your labor and management strategy for meeting workload requirements. Use additional paper if needed. Next, record your human resources expenses for this enterprise. You will use this expense information when evaluating the business' projected financial performance. Finally, summarize your human resources strategies for this enterprise or the whole farm. Be sure to include a SWOT (strengths, weaknesses, opportunities, threats) analysis for each strategy. This will be the start of your human resources strategy section for the written business plan.

Enterprise:	**Long Run**		**Transition Period**	
______________	**(Expected)**	**Year 1**	**Year 2**	**Year 3**
Workload (hours/month)				
Labor and Acquisition				
Management				
Expenses				
Recruitment				
Wages				
Fees				
Training				
Education				
Salary				
Benefits				
Taxes				
Insurance				
Other				

Business Plan Input - Human Resources Strategy Summary:

Worksheet 4.24 Risk Management

Complete this Worksheet for each enterprise or the whole farm as appropriate. Briefly rank your business' exposure to market, production, environmental and personal risk. Talk over risk management ideas with members of your planning team, a financial consultant, or an accountant. List tools that you might use to reduce future risk. Then, summarize your strategy for managing and minimizing your business' risk exposure.

Enterprise: ______________________________

Production Risk

Exposure to production risk: ____**Low** ____**Medium** ____**High**

Type of production risk: ______________________________

____

Tools to minimize production risk: ______________________________

____

Market Risk

Exposure to market risk: ____**Low** ____**Medium** ____**High**

Type of market risk: ______________________________

____

TASK 4

Tools to minimize market risk: ______________________________

____

Financial Risk

Exposure to financial risk: ____**Low** ____**Medium** ____**High**

Type of financial risk: ______________________________

____

Tools to minimize financial risk: ______________________________

____

Personal Risk

Exposure to personal risk: ____**Low** ____**Medium** ____**High**

Type of personal risk: ______________________________

____

Tools to minimize personal risk: ______________________________

____

Our risk management strategy can be summarized as follows:

____

____

____

____

____

____

Worksheet 4.25 Business Organization

Use the space below to record information about the organizational alternatives that you are considering for the business. Your state's Small Business Association is an excellent place to begin your research. If you are planning a major reorganization of the business, be sure to consult a lawyer regarding necessary documentation and tax ramifications. Be sure to note advantages and disadvantages of each alternative as it pertains to your current situation, business vision and personal goals.

Organizational Alternative 1 ______________________________

Ownership: ______________________________

Tax rates: ______________________________

Filing requirements: ______________________________

Advantages: ______________________________

Disadvantages: ______________________________

Organizational Alternative 2 ______________________________

Ownership: ______________________________

Tax rates: ______________________________

Filing requirements: ______________________________

Advantages: ______________________________

Disadvantages: ______________________________

Organizational Alternative 3 ______________________________

Ownership: ______________________________

Tax rates: ______________________________

Filing requirements: ______________________________

Advantages: ______________________________

Disadvantages: ______________________________

Worksheet 4.26 Farmland Affordability

Use this Worksheet to estimate what price you can afford to pay for farmland.

Gross cash farm income	=	______________
Cash expenses (excluding interest)	–	______________
Income taxes	–	______________
Principal payments on term debt	–	______________
Depreciation reserve	–	______________
Social security taxes	–	______________
Total cash family living investments & nonfarm capital purchases	–	______________
Nonfarm income	+	______________
Cash available for principal and interest on added land debt	=	______________
Down payment on land	+	______________
Maximum financially feasible land price	=	______________

This worksheet was adapted from *Analyzing Land Investments*, videotape, Gayle S. Willett, 1988.

Worksheet 4.27 Finance

Use the space below to begin developing your financing strategy for any start-up, annual operating, and longer-term capital and real estate needs associated with each major business strategy alternative (for marketing, operations, and human resources). Begin by having each member of your planning team (if appropriate) evaluate the importance of the financing criteria described in Figure 82 (control, cost, risk, liquidity). Next list money that will be needed to finance start-up, operating, and long-term needs as well as one or more financing strategy for each. If any of your strategies include the use of external financing, be sure to research and record interest rates and financing conditions in the space provided. Be sure to talk with your local lender, accountant or Extension educator—they can help you locate and evaluate which finance strategy best fits your personal criteria and business needs.

Strategy Criteria

Rank the importance of each of the following finance strategy criteria:

Control	_____Low	_____Medium	_____High
Cost	_____Low	_____Medium	_____High
Risk	_____Low	_____Medium	_____High
Liquidity	_____Low	_____Medium	_____High

Financing Needs

List money needed for each expense category. Then, briefly describe one or more financing strategies for each.

	Value	Strategy One	Strategy Two
One-time start-up needs	$		
Annual operating needs	$		
Intermediate needs (5-7 years)	$		
Long-term needs (7-10 years)	$		
Real estate needs	$		

Finance Options

If you plan to seek outside financing (including government cost-share payments), research interest rates and other financing conditions (such as easement terms) from up to three sources for each financial need.

Need	Source/Institution	Interest Rate	Conditions
Start-up			
Operating			
Intermediate			
Long-term			
Real estate			

TASK 4

Worksheet 4.28 Financial Strategy Summary

Complete this Worksheet for each enterprise or for the whole farm. Use information from Worksheets 4.24–4.26 to record information about your strategies for risk management, organization and financing. If appropriate, describe how your strategies will change throughout your transition period. Then, list available financial expense information. Last, summarize your financial strategy for this enterprise and the whole farm. Be sure to include a SWOT (strengths, weaknesses, opportunities, threats) analysis in your strategy summary.

Enterprise: ______________	Long Run (Expected)	Transition Period Year 1	Transition Period Year 2	Transition Period Year 3
Risk exposure and management				
Organization and taxes				
Financing needs ($) and strategy				
Financial Expenses				
Consultant				
Filing fees				
Software				
Membership fees/collateral				
Interest on operating loan				
Interest on intermediate debt				
Interest on long-term debt				
Insurance				
Other				

Business Plan Input–Financial Strategy Summary:

TASK 4

Worksheet 4.29 Summarize a Whole Farm Strategic Plan of Action

Ask yourself if each of the marketing, operations, human resources, and finance strategy alternatives you've identified are compatible as a system. If you are considering more than one functional strategy (such as two marketing strategies or two finance strategies), be sure to explore on paper how these different strategies will affect the business as a whole. How will they affect other functional areas of the business? Rule out those strategies that are not compatible with one another or your business vision as a whole. Then, use the space below to name one or more system-wide business strategies for your whole farm and describe, in one to two paragraphs, how each strategy addresses your critical planning needs, vision, mission and goals.

Whole Farm Strategy Alternative # 1:

Whole Farm Strategy Alternative # 2:

TASK 4

Worksheet 4.30 Annual Operating Expenses for the Whole Farm

Using your current tax records (if applicable), estimate total variable and fixed expenses for your base plan—for your business as is. Then, list annual operating expenses for each major whole-farm strategy alternative that you are considering. Be sure to calculate and include (1) annual ownership costs of machinery, equipment, and buildings (depreciation, interest, repairs, taxes and insurance); and (2) start-up costs as either one-time cash expenses or as part of annual debt or lease payments (it depends on how you decide to finance these costs). Try to break all of your annual whole farm expenses up into variable- and fixed-expense categories.

	Base Plan	Alternative One	Alternative Two
Direct Expenses			
Marketing			
Seed			
Fertilizer			
Chemicals			
Crop insurance			
Other direct crop expenses			
Feeder livestock purchases			
Feed and forages			
Breeding fees			
Veterinary			
Livestock supplies			
Other direct livestock expenses			
Custom hire			
Fuel and oil			
Repairs and maintenance			
Storage			
Processing			
Dues and professional fees			
Interest on operating loan			
Sales taxes			
Other operating expenses			
Total variable costs			
Overhead Expenses			
Utilities			
Rent			
Hired labor			
Depreciation			
Farm insurance			
Repairs and maintenance			
Taxes			
Interest on intermediate debt			
Interest on long-term debt			
Other fixed costs			
Total fixed costs			

TASK 4

Worksheet 4.31 Enterprise Budget Break-even Analysis

Calculate your break-even value or volume for each enterprise or product. If you plan to look at break-even volumes, use the cost estimates that you developed in Worksheet 4.25 along with market values developed in Worksheet 4.6. Try experimenting with a range of market prices to see how they affect your break-even volume. Then, compare your break-even volume to the sales volume projections and output capacity estimates that you generated in Worksheets 4.2 and 4.12, respectively.

Likewise, when calculating break-even values, look back at Worksheets 4.4 and 4.6—can you break even and still remain competitive? Is your break-even value below the projected market price that you identified in Planning Task Four?

Enterprise or Product: ______________________________

Annual fixed costs (a) = ____________________

Variable costs/unit (b) = ____________________

Estimated market value/unit (c) = ____________________

Break-even volume (a) / (c – b) = ____________________

Estimated sales volume = ____________________ (Worksheet 4.2)

Upper limit or output capacity = ____________________ (Worksheet 4.12)

How does our break-even volume for this product compare to our projected sales volume and production capacity estimates? Can we break even?

____

____

____

____

____

Enterprise or Product: ______________________________

Annual fixed costs (a) = ____________________

Variable costs/unit (b) = ____________________

Estimated market value/unit (c) = ____________________

Break-even volume (a) / (c – b) = ____________________

Estimated sales volume = ____________________ (Worksheet 4.2)

Upper limit or output capacity = ____________________ (Worksheet 4.12)

How does our break-even volume for this product compare to our projected sales volume and production capacity estimates? Can we break even?

____

____

____

____

____

TASK 4

Worksheet 4.32 Partial Budget

If appropriate, calculate and record the impact of each whole farm business strategy using the partial budget approach. Begin by estimating additional income (added inflows) and new expenses (additional outflows). Next, estimate any reduction in your annual expenses (reduced outflows) and income (reduced inflows) that will occur as a result of your proposed strategy or business change. Lastly, total up the positive impact of your business strategy (e) and the negative impact (f). What is the net effect on profit and cash flow? What is your return on assets?

Whole Farm Strategy: ______________________________

Added Inflows	Profit	Cash Flow	Added Outflows	Profit	Cash Flow
Subtotal (a) =			**Subtotal (b) =**		

Reduced Outflows	Profit	Cash Flow	Reduced Inflows	Profit	Cash Flow
Subtotal (c) =			**Subtotal (d) =**		
Total (a + c) = (e)			**Total (b + d) = (f)**		
			Net (e – f) = (g)		
			Added Interest (h) =		
			Total Investment (i) =		
			Return on Assets [(g + h) / i] =		

TASK 4

Worksheet 4.33 Long-Range Projected Income Statement

Use the space below to record average income and expenses (variable and fixed costs) for your present business (base plan) and the whole farm strategy alternative you are considering. The base plan should project the average expected future results for your current farm operation. Do this column first based on past history (Worksheet 2.10) and then build on it for each of your alternative strategies using information from your gross sales revenue projections (Worksheet 4.8) and the whole farm cost analysis (Worksheet 4.27). Then, calculate the net farm income for each alternative by subtracting total expenses from total revenue. How do your proposed alternatives compare to your present business income? Remember, when projecting the income for each strategy alternative, assume that your strategy has been fully implemented.

Revenues:		**Base Plan**	**Strategy #1**	**Strategy #2**
Gross product sales				
Cull breeding livestock				
Other income				
Total revenue (a)				
Expenses:				
Annual variable expenses				
Annual fixed expenses				
Other farm expenses				
Total expenses (b)				
Net farm income (a – b)				

TASK 4

Worksheet 4.34 Long-Range Projected Cash Flow

Use the space below to calculate and compare your business' present cash flow and its cash flow under the alternative whole-farm strategies that you are considering. Begin by estimating total cash inflows and outflows. Then subtract outflows from inflows. If the projected net cash flow is positive, then the plan will cash flow—it will be able to make debt payments on time. On the other hand, if the net cash flow is negative, the business alternative will have trouble servicing short-term debt.

		Base Plan	Strategy #1	Strategy #2
Projected Cash Flow:				
Net farm income				
Depreciation expense				
Interest expenses on term debt				
Nonfarm income				
Total cash inflows	**(a)**			
Owner withdrawals				
Income and social security taxes				
Principal and interest payments on term debt				
Loan				
Loan				
Loan				
Loan				
Loan				
Loan				
Total cash outflows	**(b)**			
Projected net cash flow	**(a – b)**			

TASK 4

Worksheet 4.35 Projected Balance Sheet

Construct a projected balance sheet for your business base plan and for each whole farm strategy alternative you are considering. Where possible, include itemized details under each asset and liability category. Then, calculate your overall change in wealth earned from farm and nonfarm income after adjusting for living expenses and partner withdrawals. You may want to use a computer software package, such as FINPACK (available from the Center for Farm Financial Management), to collect and process the information needed for your projected balance sheet.

Year: ____________________

		Base Plan	Strategy #1	Strategy #2
Assets				
Current Farm Assets				
Cash and checking balance		______	______	______
Prepaid expenses & supplies		______	______	______
Growing crops		______	______	______
Accounts receivable		______	______	______
Hedging accounts		______	______	______
Crops and feed		______	______	______
Crops under gov't loan		______	______	______
Market livestock		______	______	______
Other current assets		______	______	______
Total current assets	**(a)**	______	______	______
Intermediate Farm Assets				
Breeding livestock		______	______	______
Machinery and equipment		______	______	______
Other intermediate assets		______	______	______
Total intermediate assets	**(b)**	______	______	______
Long-term Farm Assets				
Farm land		______	______	______
Buildings and improvements		______	______	______
Other long-term assets		______	______	______
Total long term assets	**(c)**	______	______	______
Total Farm Assets	**(d) = (a + b + c)**	______	______	______
Nonfarm Assets	**(e)**	______	______	______
Total Assets	**(f) = (d + e)**	______	______	______

CONTINUED

TASK 4

Worksheet 4.35 Projected Balance Sheet (continued)

CONTINUED

Year: ____________

		Base Plan	Strategy #1	Strategy #2
Liabilities				
Current Farm Liabilities				
Accrued interest				
Accounts payable & accrued expense				
Current farm loans				
Principal on CCC loans				
Principal due on term loans				
Total Current Farm Liabilities	(g)			
Intermediate Farm Liabilities	(h)			
Long-term Farm Liabilities	(i)			
Total Farm Liabilities	**(j) = (g + h + i)**			
Nonfarm Liabilities	**(k)**			
Total Liabilities	**(l) = (j + k)**			
Net Worth	**(m) = (f – l)**			
Earned Net Worth Change Per Year				
Net Farm Income (from Worksheet 4.33)	(n)			
Nonfarm Income	(o)			
Family Living/Partner Withdrawals	(p)			
Income Taxes	(q)			
Earned Net Worth Change	**(r) = (n + o) – (p + q)**			

TASK 4

Worksheet 4.36 Risk Analysis

Use the space below to record and compare the results of a five percent decrease in market prices, a five percent increase in expenses, or a two percent increase in interest rates for each whole-farm strategy alternative. You will need to use software or another sheet of paper to calculate the effect of these very real market uncertainties. How do these market and finance-related shocks affect your present business and its future under the whole-farm strategy alternatives that you are considering?

	Base Plan	Strategy #1	Strategy #2
Effect of a 5% decrease in prices			
Net farm income			
Net cash flow			
Effect of a 5% increase in expenses			
Net farm income			
Net cash flow			
Effect of a 3% increase in interest rates			
Net farm income			
Net cash flow			

TASK 4

Worksheet 4.37 Transitional Cash Flow

Use the space below to project the business' first three years' cash flow. Begin by recording gross income from sales of products. Then, record other farm and nonfarm income as well as borrowed funds that will be used by the business. Record total projected income or total inflows (a) for each year. Next, record all cash outflows (b), including annual farm expenses, owner withdrawals (for family living), taxes, and debt payments. Subtract total cash outflows (b) from total cash inflows (a) to calculate net cash flow for the year.

Whole Farm Strategy:

		Year 1	Year 2	Year 3
Projected Cash Inflows:				
Gross product sales				
Other income				
Nonfarm income				
Capital sales				
New borrowings				
Total Cash inflows (a)				
Projected Cash outflows:				
Farm expenses				
(excluding interest)				
Owner withdrawals				
Income and social security taxes				
Capital purchases				
Debt payments				
Total cash outflows (b)				
Net cash flow (a – b)				
Cumulative net cash flow				

Worksheet 4.38 Scoring and Deciding on a Final Business Strategy

Use each of the strategy tests (described in Figure 96) to assess your whole farm business alternatives. Give each strategy a subjective score, from one to five (five being the highest), for each test. Once each strategy is scored, sum the scores across all tests. The strategy with the highest score is apparently the best for the farm and your planning team. If more than one strategy ranks similarly, then spend more time researching and evaluating the remaining strategies before making a final decision about which direction to take your business.

Proposed Strategy:	Base Plan	Strategy #1	Strategy #2
		________	________
		________	________
Strategy Tests (high = 5, low = 1)			
Vision Consistency	________	________	________
Goodness of Fit	________	________	________
Building for Future	________	________	________
Performance	________	________	________
Importance	________	________	________
Feasibility	________	________	________
Resources	________	________	________
Confidence	________	________	________
Total Score	________	________	________

Which whole farm or enterprise strategy will we pursue?

TASK 4

Worksheet 4.39 Contingency Statement

Describe future challenges and risks for the business. Think about what internal circumstances or external events might positively and negatively affect the business and how the business would respond to each. .

TASK 4

Worksheet 4.40 Executive Summary

Use the space below to draft an executive summary for your business plan. Remember, this is perhaps the most important section of your plan—it should provide a snapshot of what the business is about and how it will be successful. At the very least, your executive summary should communicate information about goals, market potential and sales volume, production management and capacity, expenses, profitability, cash flow and risk management.

TASK 4

TASK
4

Present, Implement and Monitor Your Business Plan—Which Route Will You Take, and How Will You Check Your Progress Along the Way?

By now you and your planning team have gone through a lot of work—hours of brainstorming, discussion, and research. Together you have completed more than a dozen Worksheets for each Planning Task. This final Planning Task is what you've no doubt been waiting for—writing up your business plan and implementing your new strategy.

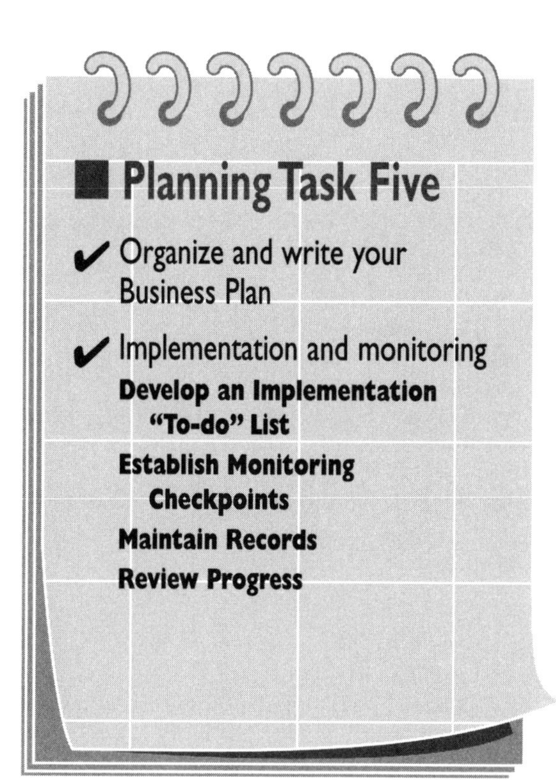

Organizing and Writing Your Business Plan

Finally! You are ready to pull all of your work together into a written business plan. All along you have probably been asking: What should I include in my business plan? What should my plan look like? How should I organize my plan? Your business plan should be organized in a way that is most useful for you. It should be organized in a way that meets your internal and external planning purposes and effectively communicates with your intended audience.

There is no single format that should be used for written business plans. That said, a grand strategy that is poorly communicated will be difficult to implement. There are some critical pieces of information that can help you stay on track and

See pages 243–245 for a complete set of blank worksheets for Task Five.

To print a complete set of blank worksheets, go to ***www.misa.umn.edu/publications/bizplan.html***

that your lender, shareholders or partners will expect to see. As you discuss which business plan formats to use with your planning team, think again about how you ultimately intend to use the plan—for internal organizing or for communicating externally to a lender or potential shareholders.

If you will present your plan to others outside the business (lenders, potential clients or investors, family or other planning team members), it should convince them of the feasibility of your strategy. Therefore it should clearly convey ideas, supporting research, financial evaluation, and a contingency plan. Documentation will be critical. You will need to justify your strategy with information from your research, particularly if you intend to seek financing, solicit funds from outside investors, or to offer stock. When discussing your pricing strategy, for instance, justify why your prices are set higher, lower or even with competitive products. State under what circumstances you might change the pricing structure for each product and service to gain a stronger position in the marketplace.

On the other hand, if your plan is strictly for internal organizing, you may want to emphasize your goals, vision, mission and the overall operating plan.

Plan A: Holistic

- Cover
- Executive Summary
- Table of Contents
- Business Mission
- Business Background (History and Current Situation)
- Vision and Goals
- Key Planning Assumptions
- Marketing Strategy
- Operations Strategy
- Management and Human Resources Strategy
- Financial Strategy
- Projected Income Statement and Cash Flow
- Appendices (relevant support information such as market research, resumes, brochures, letters of recommendation, tax returns, etc.)

A few of the most common business plan formats are shown here. Consider these with your planning team, and talk about which business plan formats seem most appropriate given your planning objectives. Use any one or a combination of these formats.

Figure 99 shows the Minar's business plan outline. Notice that they have combined elements from the above sample outlines to create their own business plan format. Specifically, they included three years' worth of prior tax statements, FINAN financial analyses, and a projected income/cash flow statement for the proposed processing business in an Appendix. Without this information, the Minars would not have been able to pursue the use of external funds to finance their new building and processing equipment.

TASK 5

Plan B: For Lender/Other Investors
(This is the format of the FINPACK Business Planning Software)

- Cover
- Executive Summary
- Farm Description (Business type and size, location, history and ownership structure)
- Strategic Plan (Mission, goals, industry analysis, competitive position, business strategy, implementation plan)
- Production and Operations Plan (Crop and livestock systems, other enterprises, risk management plan, environmental considerations, quality control systems)
- Marketing Plan (Marketing strategy and resources, promotion and distribution, inventory and storage management)
- Human Resources Plan (Management team, family and hired labor, consultants, personnel management)
- Financial Plan (Balance sheet, asset management, projected profitability, cash flow, long-range projections, historical trends, benchmarks, capital required)

Plan C: For Family

- Cover
- Mission
- Values
- Vision
- Goals
- History and Current Situation
- Whole Farm Business Strategy
- Human Resources Plan
- Contingency Plan
- Monitoring Checkpoints
- Timeline and To-do List

Plan D: New/Alternative Product

- Cover
- Executive Summary
- Statement of Goals and Objectives
- Background of Proposed Business Idea
- Technical Description of Product
- Description of Industry and Competition
- Marketing Analysis and Strategy
- Operations Analysis and Strategy
- Human Resources Analysis and Strategy
- Financial Analysis and Strategy
- Supporting Data and Assumptions
- Conclusions and Summary
- Appendix (Marketing surveys, certified bids, brochures, etc.)

Plan E: For Cooperative or Other Collaborative Marketing Group

- Cover
- Mission Statement
- Executive Summary
- Management Team
- Market Description
- Product Description
- Business Strategy
- Financial Plan
- Appendix (Articles of Incorporation, By-Laws, etc.)

Plan F: Beginning Farmer/ Start-Up Business

- Cover
- Mission Statement
- Goals and Personal History
- Whole Farm Business Strategy
- Performance/Market Assumptions
- Income Projections
- Cash Flow Projections
- Risk Analysis
- Contingency Plan

Figure 99. Example from Cedar Summit Farm— Worksheet 5.1: Business Plan Outline

Worksheet 5.1 Business Plan Outline

Use the space below to develop an outline for your business plan. Remember to think about how the plan will be used—who is going to see it and why.

a. Cover
b. Executive Summary
c. Values
d. Mission Statement
e. Farm History
f. Current Situation
g. Vision
h. Goals
i. Marketing Plan
j. Management Team
k. Board of Advisors
l. Operations Plan
m. Financial Plan
n. Monitoring/Controls
Appendix A: Project Cost Budget (with certified bids)
Appendix B: Five Year Cash Flow Plan (with assumptions)
Appendix C: Financial Analysis of Current Operation: 1998-2000
Appendix D: Tax Statements from Current Operation: 1998-2000
Appendix E: Resumes for Management Team Members

TASK 5

Use **Worksheet 5.1: Business Plan Outline** to draft an outline for your written plan. You might also consider using business planning software to begin drafting a written outline and plan. The FINPACK Business Planning Software developed by the Center for Farm Financial Management is one software alternative that allows you to input FINPACK financial analyses directly into a business plan outline (see "Resources").

You should also look at some of the common presentation "pitfalls" (Figure 100) and bear these in mind as you begin to compile a written business plan.

Figure 100.
Common Presentation Pitfalls[74]

Too much detail. There is a fine line between too little and too much detail in a business plan. Minute or trivial items that dilute or mask the critical aspects of the plan should be avoided.

Graphics without substance. With the sophisticated computer software available to the average user today, it is easy to over-emphasize aesthetics while compromising substance. Graphics should be a complement to, not a substitute for, logic and reasoning.

No executive summary. Many readers of business plans will not read past the executive summary. If it does not exist, they may not read the plan at all.

Inability to communicate plan. The business plan should clearly outline the proposal in understandable terms. Monumental ideas are worthless if they cannot be communicated.

Infatuation with product or service. Although a business plan should clearly explain the attributes of the business' key product or service, it should focus on the marketing plan. An entrepreneur can often become so intrigued by his or her ideas that he or she forgets about the big picture.

Focusing on production estimates. When making projections, the focus needs to be on sales estimates, not production estimates. Production is irrelevant if there are no buyers.

Unrealistic financial projections. Potential investors are certainly interested in profitability so that they earn a return on investment. However, unrealistic financial projections can cause a plan to lose credibility in the eyes of investors.

Technical language or jargon. Technical language, acronyms and jargon that would be unfamiliar to a person without experience in a particular industry should be avoided. The reader will be more impressed if he or she understands the plan.

Lack of commitment. The entrepreneur must show commitment to his or her business if he or she expects a commitment from others. Commitment is exhibited by timeliness and following up on all professional appointments. Investment of personal money is looked upon favorably because it shows that the owner is willing to make a financial commitment.

74 *Business Planning—A Roadmap for Success*, Wilson and Kohl, 1997.

Gigi DiGiacomo

Figure 101. The Minar family began processing their first batch of milk in March, 2002

Implementation and Monitoring

The success of your whole farm business strategy will be, to a large extent, dependent on timely and efficient implementation. This is sometimes the hardest part for many people who worry that they haven't done enough research or that their strategy won't go as planned. In fact, it probably won't. Most plans don't realize themselves perfectly; there are always uncertainties, like those discussed when you were developing your contingency plan. But there comes a time when you must, as the well-known marketing slogan goes, just do it!

Have you done a good job of researching your markets, gathering cost estimates, projecting profitability, risk analysis? Most importantly, do you have the confidence of your planning team behind the plan? Then you are ready to put your plan into action, and to begin monitoring the results.

Remember, business planning is an on-going process. You should develop checkpoints or "milestones" to help monitor progress and make effective management decisions down the road.

TASK 5

Monitoring involves tracking how your farm or business is progressing and taking action where necessary to make sure that it is on course to meet your goals. It means, as Allan Savory notes, "looking for deviations from the plan for the purpose of correcting them."[75] For instance, if you drew a map for Worksheet 4.2 to estimate direct market sales potential, try plotting the zip codes from your customers' checks to see just how far your customers travel to purchase your product. What does this tell you? Is your marketing strategy effective? Are you reaching your target market? Are there households within 20 miles of your business that aren't customers but who should be? You'll also want to ask yourself how does your work, accomplishments, output, etc., compare with desired goals and projections.

In order to track your progress, you should develop an implementation "to-do" list, establish checkpoints, keep records, and review progress with planning team members, board members, or management staff.

Develop an Implementation "To-do" List.

Describe how your strategy will be implemented, indicate who will be responsible for completing implementation tasks, and specify deadlines for completing each task. In other words, create a "to-do" list for strategy

75 *Holistic Management, A New Framework for Decision Making*, 2nd Ed., Savory and Butterfield, 1999.

Figure 102. Example from Cedar Summit Farm—Worksheet 5.2: Implementation To-do List

Worksheet 5.2 Implementation To-do List

Use the space below to develop an implementation "to-do" list for your business. You may find it helpful to develop a to-do list for each functional area of the business (marketing, operations, human resources and finance). Regardless of how you choose to organize your list, be sure to note who will be responsible for each task and a deadline for doing so.

Task	Person Responsible	Deadline
Approach lenders, secure financing	*Dave*	*March 2001*
Contact PLADOT, order Mini-Dairy	*Dave*	*May 2001*
Begin plant construction	*Dave to work with contractors*	*May 2001*
Complete logo design and send to bottle supplier	*Bob*	*June 2001*
Hire Mike to help with start-up	*Florence*	*June 2001*
Locate delivery truck	*Dave*	*July 2001*
Contact retailers with product availability date	*Mike*	*August 2001*
Contact potential home-delivery customers	*Mike*	*August 2001*
Revise sales and production projections	*Mike and Dave*	*September 2001*
Order supplies (crates, bottles with logo, flavorings, etc.)	*Mike*	*September 2001*
Hire Merrisue and Dan	*Florence*	*October 2001*
Begin training for all family members	*PLADOT consultant*	*October 2001*
Place ads in local paper, Cooperative newsletter	*Mike*	*October 2001*
Begin processing milk!	*Mike, Dave, Florence*	*November 2001*

implementation. This will help you stay on course as you begin implementing your whole-farm strategy.

A portion of the to-do list created by Dave and Florence Minar for their proposed processing business is presented in Figure 102. The first item on their to-do list, of course, is to contact lenders and secure financing for the new business strategy. Once financing was available at interest rates that allowed adequate repayment and profit, the Minars were ready to quickly move down their list and begin readying the business for its first day of milk processing.

Put someone in charge of overseeing the entire implementation process—particularly if a major change is being made or when several family members/partners are involved.

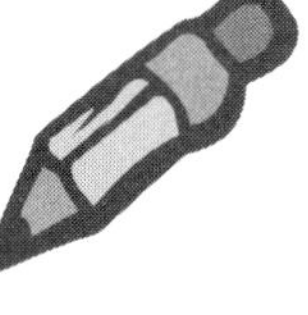

Use **Worksheet 5.2: Implementation To-do List** to create a simple to-do list. Make sure that you have the staff and time to successfully implement your business plan.

TASK 5

Worksheet 5.3 Monitoring

Briefly describe your plans for checking-in with your planning team to track and evaluate business progress. Then, list monitoring checkpoints for the business as a whole and for each functional business component.

Check-In Schedule ______

Whole Farm Checkpoints *Within two years: Have full-time orchard and propagation manager. Have an on farm sales room and part-time sales staff in place. Have another two acres of orchard fruit planted. Within five years: Meet our financial goals. Have the farm 'experience' operations, such as camping and picnic sites, trails, and fruit walks. Settle into a routine that will be enjoyable, sustainable, and reproducible.*

Marketing ______

Operations ______

Human Resources ______

Finance ______

Figure 103. Example from Northwind Nursery and Orchard—Worksheet 5.3: Monitoring

TASK 5

Establish Monitoring Checkpoints.

Next, develop a list of monitoring checkpoints. Monitoring checkpoints, also called "critical success factors" and "objectives," are those key events or accomplishments that must occur for your business to succeed. They measure progress and act as "early warning" signals that alert you to when, where, and how your goals and plans may need to change. In this way, note authors of the Land Stewardship Project's *Monitoring Tool Box*, "monitoring can act as a springboard for finding creative ways to adapt your management."[76]

Monitoring checkpoints are typically more detailed than your goals for the whole farm and are based on a shorter time frame. Monitoring checkpoints can be specific production targets, sales objectives, profit goals, wildlife counts, or whatever measure of success is important to you and your planning team.

Frank Foltz, owner of Northwind Nursery and Orchard, summarized monitoring checkpoints for his business into two- and five-year time frames. His checkpoints, reproduced above, should be easy to monitor as Frank and his family implement their plans.

76 *The Monitoring Tool Box*, Ahlers Ness (ed.), 1998.

Following are other examples of monitoring checkpoints taken from the business plans prepared by Mabel Brelje, Mary Doerr, Dave and Florence Minar, and Greg Reynolds:

- *Increase Community Supported Agriculture share sales by 20 percent this year*
- *Pay down debt by 15 percent this year*
- *Provide health care for all employees by December*
- *Identify buyer for farm within two years*

Of course, the goals that you outlined in Planning Task Three (Vision, Mission and Goals) can be used as long-term critical success factors. Likewise, the financial ratios described in Planning Task Two (History and Current Situation), as well as your long-range income and cash flow projections developed in Planning Task Four (Strategic Planning and Evaluation), can be used as monitoring benchmarks from which to track and compare the financial performance of your business over the long-run. In fact, FINFLO—the cash flow planning piece of FINPACK—includes a "Monitoring Worksheet" to help you monitor planned versus actual cash flows during the year. By monitoring cash flow performance, it may be possible to adjust your operating plan before experiencing financial adversity.

If you are interested in tracking natural resource benefits, check out the *Monitoring Tool Box* developed by the Land Stewardship Project. This publication provides Worksheets and practical suggestions on how to monitor some of those intangibles (quality of life), as well as the tangibles, (stream and soil quality) (see "Resources").

Use **Worksheet 5.3: Monitoring** to develop a checklist or calendar of timely objectives to help you track the immediate progress of your business.

Figure 104.
Record Keeping Ideas

You may decide to maintain records for everything from songbird counts to input expenses. Below are examples of just a few of the record-keeping possibilities for each functional area of your business.

Marketing. Maintain a customer database to track purchases, feedback and customer location. Addresses, phone numbers and email contact information for each customer can be obtained from personal checks or sign-up sheets at farmers' markets or local events.

Operations. Track the productivity of each enterprise—such as yields or rates of gain—as well as other indicators like pasture composition, soil composition, the protein content of feed, and wildlife populations on your farm. Use a simple notebook or chart to record this information for future use.

Human Resources. Record the number of hours that you spend on the job. This can be time consuming in itself, but one way to get a gauge of your labor time is to track your hours during a "typical" week or month—one that is representative of the different tasks that you perform during a typical year for each enterprise. From these records, you can estimate time spent working on the farm for the entire year.

Finances. Manual or computerized accounting systems can be used to develop an annual balance sheet, accrual income statement, monthly cash flow, enterprise cost/profit center reports, and a financial ratio summary (*FINPACK, Quicken for Farm Financial Records* or *Farm Biz*—see "Resources").

Maintain Records.

Keeping careful records! At the end of the year, with good records in hand, you will be able to compare actual yields, costs and sales to those projected figures in your business plan as well as any other monitoring checkpoints established by your planning team.

Records can be formal accounts of financial performance, productivity and sales. However, records can also take the form of "field" observations to help you track changes in wildlife populations, plant species and hours on the job. It's up to you to decide what records to keep depending on the type of management feedback you require.

Designate a file, box or log book in which to maintain your records. Manual and computerized record-keeping tools are described in the "Resources" section to help you with this task. Next, assign someone the task of record keeping and designate a time to regularly review your records. The information contained in your records will be meaningful only if it is maintained and put to use. If you need help getting organized or maintaining records, consider joining a farm management association or farm business education class. You might also hire a consultant or tap into the experience of another business owner.

The Full Circle of the Business Planning Process

Identify values

Review current situation

Draft vision, mission, goals

Research, develop, and evaluate business strategy

Implement and monitor business plan

Review Progress.

Finally, you may want to develop a written monitoring schedule that outlines when you will review your plan and checkpoints with planning team members—once per month or season? During a slow time of the year? At a regularly scheduled family retreat? Arrange a time when planning team members can meet to discuss what about the business has been successful and what has not using your critical success factors, goals and financial projections or ratios as guides.

If you were unsuccessful in some areas or in terms of several objectives, try to understand why. Ask whether or not circumstances have changed within the business or externally in the industry and market, or if your initial projections were unrealistic. Use both your successes and failures to learn more about your business. Time brings experience and makes you wiser about your business and the industry. For example, after a year, you may have a better sense of market prices or production potential. Always remember to adjust your prices and output projections as you gain experience.

Next, take time to re-evaluate your business plan. You've come full circle in the planning process. Review your goals, take stock of the business' current resources and competitive environment, and make strategy adjustments if necessary. Then you're ready to develop new checkpoints for your next season/year in business.

Worksheet 5.1 Business Plan Outline

Use the space below to develop an outline for your business plan. Remember to think about how the plan will be used—who is going to see it and why.

TASK 5

Worksheet 5.2 Implementation To-do List

Use the space below to develop an implementation "to-do" list for your business. You may find it helpful to develop a to-do list for each functional area of the business (marketing, operations, human resources and finance). Regardless of how you choose to organize your list, be sure to note who will be responsible for each task and a deadline for doing so.

Task	Person Responsible	Deadline

TASK 5

Worksheet 5.3 Monitoring

Briefly describe your plans for checking-in with your planning team to track and evaluate business progress. Then, list monitoring checkpoints for the business as a whole and for each functional business component.

Check-In Schedule ______________________________

Whole Farm Checkpoints ______________________________

Marketing ______________________________

Operations ______________________________

Human Resources ______________________________

Finance ______________________________

TASK 5

List of Footnote References

(18, 20, 24-25, 66-68 N/A)

1 *Financial Management in Agriculture,* 7th ed., Barry et al., Prentice Hall, 2002. Contact your local library or bookstore.

2 *FINPACK* software, Center for Farm Financial Management, University of Minnesota, updated annually. Contact CFFM, Department of Applied Economics, 130 Classroom Office Building, 1994 Buford Avenue, St. Paul, MN 55108-6040, (612) 625-1964, on-line: www.cffm.umn.edu.

3 Ibid.

4 *Financial Guidelines for Agricultural Producers,* Recommendations of the Farm Financial Standards Council, 1995 (revised). Contact the FFSC, 1212 S. Naper Boulevard, Suite 119, Naperville, IL 60540, (630) 637-0199, on-line: www.ffsc.org.

5 *Managing Risk in Farming: Concepts, Research and Analysis,* Harwood, et al., 1999. Report number AER 774. Contact the USDA Order Desk, 5285 Port Royal Road, Springfield, VA 22161, (800) 999-6779, web version: www.ers.usda.gov/publications/AER774/index.htm.

6 *Holistic Management: A New Framework for Decision Making,* 2nd Ed., Savory and Butterfield, 1999. Contact Allan Savory Center for Holistic Management, 1010 Tijeras NW, Albuquerque, NM 87102, (505)842-5252, on-line: www.holisticmanagement.org, e-mail: savorycenter@holisticmanagement.org.

7 *Organic Certification of Crop Production in Minnesota,* Gulbranson, 2001 (revised). Contact University of Minnesota Extension Service, 405 Coffey Hall, 1420 Eckles Ave., St. Paul, MN 55108-6068, (800) 876-8636, e-mail: order@extension.umn.edu.

8 *Making Your Small Farm Profitable,* Macher and Kerr Jr., 1999. Contact Storey Books, 210 Mass Moca Way, North Adams, MA 01247, (800) 335-3432, on-line: www.storeybooks.com.

9 *Goal Setting for Farm and Ranch Families,* Doye, 2001.Fact sheet WF-244. Contact Oklahoma Cooperative Extension Service, 139 Agriculture Hall, Oklahoma State University, Stillwater, OK 74078, (405) 744-5385, web version: www.agweb.okstate.edu/pearl/agecon/farm/wf-244.html.

10 *Business Planning for Your Farm—Setting Personal and Business Goals,* Saxowsky, et al., 1995. Contact Carol Jensen, Department of Agribusiness and Applied Economics, North Dakota State University, P.O. Box 5636, Fargo, ND 58105-5636, (701) 231-7441, e-mail: cjensen@ndsuext.nodak.edu.

11 See footnote 9.

12 *A Strategic Management Primer for Farmers,* Olson, 2001. Staff Paper number: P01-15. Contact the Department of Applied Economics, University of Minnesota, 231 Classroom Office Building, 1994 Buford Ave., St. Paul MN 55108-6040, (612) 625-1222, on-line: www.agecon.lib.umn.edu.

13 *Small Business Marketing for Dummies,* Schenck, Hungry Minds, Inc., 2001. Contact your local bookstore or library.

14 *The Marketing Plan: Step-by-Step,* O'Donnell, 1991. Contact the Center for Innovation, North Dakota State University, 4300 Dartmouth Dr., PO Box 8372, Grand Forks, ND 58202-8372, (701) 777-3132, on-line: www.innovators.net.

15 See footnote 13.

16 *Finding Customers: Market Segmentation,* Bull and Passewitz, 1994. Publication CDFS-1253-94. Contact Ohio State University Extension, 700 Ackerman Road, Suite 235, Columbus, OH 43202-1578, (614) 292-1607, e-mail: pubs@postoffice.ag.ohio-state.edu, web version: ohioline.osu.edu/cd-fact/1253.html.

17 See footnote 8.

19 *Buyers of Organic Products in the Upper Midwest,* Minnesota Department of Agriculture, 2002. Contact the Minnesota Department of Agriculture, 90 West Plato Boulevard, Saint Paul, MN 55107, (651) 297-1629, on-line: www.mda.state.mn.us.

21 *Collaborative Marketing: A Roadmap and Resource Guide for Farmers,* King and DiGiacomo, 2000. Publication BU-7539-S. Contact University of Minnesota Extension Service, 405 Coffey Hall, 1420 Eckles Ave., St. Paul, MN 55108-6068, (800) 876-8636, e-mail: order@extension.umn.edu.

22 *New Markets for Producers: Selling to Retail Stores,* Center for Integrated Agricultural Systems, 1999. Research Brief 38. Contact the Center for Integrated Agricultural Systems, 1450 Linden Drive, University of Wisconsin, Madison, WI 53706, (608) 262-5200, on-line: www.wisc.edu/cias/, e-mail: phaza@facstaff.wisc.edu.

23, 26 Ibid.

27 See footnote 7.

28 *Marketing,* Kurtz and Boone, Dryden Press. Chicago, IL. 1981. Contact your local library or bookstore.

29 *Cooperative Grocer,* Natural/Organic Industry Outlook, Southworth, September-October 2001, Number 96. Contact the Cooperative Grocer on-line at: www.cooperativegrocer.com.

30 *Contract Evaluation,* University of Illinois, 2001 (reviewed). Contact Burton Swanson, Project Director, Department of Agricultural and Consumer Economics, 1301 West Gregory Drive, Urbana, IL 61801, (217) 244-6978, e-mail: swansonb@uiuc.edu, view on-line: web.aces.uiuc.edu/value/contracts/contracts.htm.

31 *Marketing Strategies for Agricultural Commodities,* Weness, 2001 (reviewed). Marketing Fact Sheet #13. Contact University of Minnesota Extension Service, 405 Coffey Hall, 1420 Eckles Ave., St. Paul, MN 55108-6068, (800) 876-8636, e-mail: order@extension.umn.edu, web version: swroc.coafes.umn.edu/SWFM/Files/mrkt/marketing_strategies.pdf.

32 Ibid.

33 See footnote 14.

34 See footnote 28.

35 See footnote 15.

36 See footnote 22.

37 See footnote 7.

38 *A Guide to Starting a Business in Minnesota,* Minnesota Small Business Assistance Office, updated annually. Contact Minnesota Department of Trade and Economic Development, 500 Metro Square, 121 Seventh Place East, St. Paul, MN 55101-2146, (651) 297-1291 or toll-free (800) 657-3858, on-line: www.dted.state.mn.us.

39 *Sharing Farm Machinery,* Weness, 2001. Contact University of Minnesota Extension Service, 405 Coffey Hall, 1420 Eckles Ave., St. Paul, MN 55108-6068, (800) 876-8636, on-line: order@extension.umn.edu.

40 *Analyzing Land Investments, Business Management in Agriculture* videotape series, Willett, 1988. Contact: Lisa Scarbrough, Iowa State University Extension Communications, 1712 ASB, Ames, IA 50011, (515) 294-4972, e-mail: lscarb@iastate.edu.

41 *Acquiring and Managing Resources for the Farm Business,* Thomas, 2001. Part four of a planned six-part series: *Business Management for Farmers.* Contact MidWest Plan Service, 122 Davidson Hall, Iowa State University, Ames, IA 50011-3080, (800) 562-3618, on-line: www.mwpshq.org.

42 Ibid.

43 FINBIN database (online), Center for Farm Financial Management, 2002. Contact CFFM, Department of Applied Economics, 249 Classroom Office Building, 1994 Buford Avenue, St. Paul, MN 55108-6040, (612) 625-1964, on-line: www.agrisk.umn.edu/GettingStarted.asp.

44 *Farm Business Management Annual Report,* 2002. Contact: John Murray, Farm and Small Business Management Programs, 851 30th Ave. S.E., Rochester, MN 55904-4999, (507) 280-3109, on-line: www.mgt.org/fbm, view online at: www.mgt.org/fbm/reports/2001/state/state.htm

45 See footnote 7.

46 *Filling a Position in the Farm Business,* Zoller, 1997. Fact sheet HRM-1-97. Contact Ohio State University Extension, 385 Kottman Hall, 2021 Coffey Rd., Columbus, OH 43210-1044, (614) 292-1607, e-mail: pubs@postoffice.ag.ohio-state.edu, web version: ohioline.osu.edu/hrm-fact/0001.html.

47 *Labor Laws and Regulations,* Miller, 1997. Fact sheet number: HRM-5-97. Contact Ohio State University Extension, 385 Kottman Hall, 2021 Coffey Rd., Columbus, OH 43210-1044, (614) 292-1607, e-mail: pubs@postoffice.ag.ohio-state.edu, web version: ohioline.osu.edu/hrm-fact/0005.html.

48 *Economic and Business Principles in Farm Planning and Production,* James and Eberle, 2000. Contact Iowa State University Press, PO Box 570, Ames, IA 50010-0570, (800) 862-6657, on-line: www.isupress.com.

49 See footnote 41.

50 See footnote 48.

51 *Overcoming Barriers to Communication,* Erven, 2001 (reviewed). Contact the Department of Agricultural, Environmental, and Development Economics, Ohio State University, 2120 Fyffe Road, Columbus, OH 43210, (614) 292-7911, web version: www.cce.cornell.edu/issues/cceresponds/Work/Milligan/Communication.pdf.

52 *Making It Work,* Passing on the Farm Center, 1999. Part One in a Farm Transitions video series. Contact Passing on the Farm Center, 140 Ninth Avenue, Granite Falls, MN 56241, (320) 564-4808 or toll-free (800) 657-3247, e-mail: pofc@kilowatt.net.

53 See footnote 51.

54–55 See footnote 5.

56 *Managing Production and Marketing Systems,* Thomas, 2000. Part three of a planned six-part series: Business Management for Farmers. Publication NCR-610C. Contact Midwest Plan Services, 122 Davidson Hall, Iowa State University, Ames, IA 50011-3080, (800) 562-3618, on-line: www.mwpshq.org.

57 *Sustainable Agriculture,* John Mason, Kangaroo Press, 1997. Contact your local bookstore or library

58 See footnote 5.

59 See footnote 1.

60 *Planning theFinancial/Organizational Structure of Farm and Agribusiness Firms: What Are the Options?,* Boehlje and Lins, 1998 (revised). Publication NCR-568. Contact Midwest Plan Services, 122 Davidson Hall, Iowa State University, Ames, IA 50011-3080, (800) 562-3618, on-line: www.mwpshq.org, e-mail: mwps@iastate.edu.

61 Ibid.

62 See footnote 38.

63–64 See footnote 60.

65 See footnote 1.

69 See footnote 1.

70 See footnote 12.

71 *Planning for Contingencies,* in Business Owners' Toolkit online, CCH Incorporated, 2002. View on-line: www.toolkit.cch.com/text/P02_5201.asp.

72 Ibid.

73 *The Executive Summary,* in Business Owners' Toolkit online, CCH Incorporated, 2002. View on-line: www.toolkit.cch.com/text/P02_5531.asp.

74 *Business Planning—A Roadmap for Success,* Wilson and Kohl, 1997. Contact Virginia Cooperative Extension, on-line: www.ext.vt.edu.

75 See footnote 6.

76 *The Monitoring Tool Box,* Ahlers Ness (ed.), 1998. Contact Land Stewardship Project, 2200 4th St., White Bear Lake, MN 55110, (651) 653-0618, on-line: www.landstewardshipproject.org.

Resources

Keep in mind that web site addresses change frequently. Some resources are specific to Minnesota or the Upper Midwest. Contact your local University Extension Service or state Department of Agriculture to see if similar programs exist in your state.

General Business Planning

Publications, Software and Videos

The Business Plan: A State-of-the-Art Guide. Michael O'Donnell. Center for Innovation, University of North Dakota. 1988. Contact the Center for Innovation, PO Box 8372, UND, Grand Forks, ND 58202-8372, phone: (701) 777-3132, on-line: www.Innovators.net.

Business Planning: A Roadmap for Success. *Farm Business Management Update.* Troy D. Wilson and David M. Kohl. Department of Agricultural and Applied Economics, Virginia Tech. 1997. Contact Virginia Cooperative Extension, on-line: www.ext.vt.edu.

The Complete Holistic Management Planning and Monitoring Guide. Allan Savory Center for Holistic Management. Various updates. Contact the Allan Savory Center for Holistic Management, 1010 Tijeras NW, Albuquerque, NM 87102, phone: (505) 842-5252, on-line: www.holisticmanagement.org, e-mail: savorycenter@holisticmanagement.org.

Developing a Longer-Range Strategic Farm Business Plan. Part One of planned six part series: *Business Management for Farmers*. Ken Thomas. Midwest Plan Services, Iowa State University, Ames, IA. 1999. Publication number: NCR-610A. Contact Midwest Plan Services, 122 Davidson Hall, Iowa State University, Ames, IA 50011-3080, phone: (800) 562-3618, on-line: www.mwpshq.org, e-mail: mwps@iastate.edu.

Economic and Business Principles in Farm Planning and Production. Sydney C. James and Phillip R. Eberle. Iowa State University Press. 2000. Contact Iowa State University Press, PO Box 570, Ames, IA 50010-0570, phone: (800) 862-6657, on-line: www.isupress.com.

Family/Farm Business Planning. Part Three in a *Farm Transitions* video series. 91 minutes. 1999. Contact Passing on the Farm Center, 140 Ninth Avenue, Granite Falls, MN 56241, phone: (320) 564-4808 or toll-free (800) 657-3247, e-mail: pofc@kilowatt.net.

Farming Alternatives: A Guide to Evaluating the Feasibility of New Farm-Based Enterprises. Nancy Grudens Schuck, Wayne Knoblauch, Judy Green and Mary Saylor. 1988. Natural Resource, Agriculture, and Engineering Service, Cornell University. 1988. Publication number: NRAES-32. Contact Natural Resource, Agriculture, and Engineering Service, Cooperative Extension, 152 Riley-Robb Hall, Ithaca, New York 14853-5701, phone: (607) 255-7654, on-line: www.nraes.org, e-mail: NRAES@cornell.edu.

Farm Planning Process. Part Two in a *Farm Transitions* video series. 71 minutes. 1999. Contact Passing on the Farm Center, 140 Ninth Avenue, Granite Falls, MN 56241, phone: (320) 564-4808 or toll-free (800) 657-3247, e-mail: pofc@kilowatt.net.

FINPACK Business Planning Software. Center for Farm Financial Management. Updated annually. Contact CFFM, Department of Applied Economics, 130 Classroom Office Building, 1994 Buford Avenue, St. Paul, MN 55108, phone: (612) 625-1964 or toll-free (800) 234-1111, on-line: www.cffm.umn.edu, e-mail: cffm@umn.edu.

A Guide to Starting a Business in Minnesota. Charles A. Schaffer, Madeline Harris, and Ann M. Wilczynski (editors). Minnesota Small Business Assistance Office. Minnesota Department of Trade and Economic Development. Updated annually. Contact Minnesota Department of Trade and Economic Development, 500 Metro Square, 121 Seventh Place East, St. Paul, MN 55101-2146, phone: (651) 297-1291 or toll-free (800) 657-3858, on-line: www.dted.state.mn.us.

How to Really Create a Successful Business Plan. David E. Gumpert. Boston Inc. Magazine Publishing. 1994. Contact your local library or bookstores.

Making Your Small Farm Profitable. Ron Macher and Howard W. Kerr Jr., Storey Books. 1999. Contact Storey Books, 210 Mass Moca Way, North Adams, MA 01247, phone: (800) 335-3432, on-line: www.storeybooks.com.

Succession Planner. Linda Kirk Fox. University of Idaho Cooperative Extension System. 1997. Publication number: CIS 1058. Contact University of Idaho Cooperative Extension System, Moscow, ID 83844, on-line: www.uidaho.edu/extension.

Agencies, Organizations and Networks

Agricultural Utilization Research Institute (AURI). Grants available to fund business plan development, product development, and market research. Assists with the development of business and marketing plans. Address: 1380 Energy Lane, Suite 112 West, St. Paul, MN 55108, phone: (651) 603-8108, on-line: www.auri.org.

Cooperative Development Grant Program. Grants available to fund market research, feasibility studies and business plans for value-added cooperative ventures. Contact Terry Dalbec, Minnesota Department of Agriculture (MDA), 90 West Plato Boulevard, Saint Paul, MN 55107, phone: (651) 297-1629, on-line: www.mda.state.mn.us.

Minnesota Dairy Business Planning Grant Program. Grants of up to $5,000 are available to cover consulting fees associated with the development of a comprehensive business plan for dairy producers. Contact David Weinand, Minnesota Department of Agriculture (MDA), 90 West Plato Boulevard, Saint Paul, MN 55107, phone: (651) 297-1629, on-line: www.mda.state.mn.us.

Minnesota Small Business Development Centers. Provides business owners with financial and technical assistance as well as information about licenses, permits and targeting market segments. Contact Minnesota Small Business Development Centers, Administrative Office, 500 Metro Square, 121 7th Place East, St. Paul, MN 55101-2146, phone: (651) 297-5770 or toll-free: (800) 657-3858, on-line: www.dted.state.mn.us.

NxLEVEL Courses. Provides training curriculums for starting and existing businesses. Topics covered include micro-businesses, alternative agriculture, e-business, and doing business abroad or in the U.S. In Minnesota, contact Jim Soncrant, West Central Minnesota Initiative Fund, 220 West Washington, Suite 205, Fergus Falls, MN 56537, phone: (218) 287-3847, on-line: www.wcif.org, e-mail: jsoncrant@earthlink.net. Nationally, for more information visit www.nxlevel.org or call (800) 873-9378.

Planning Task One: Identify Values

Publications

Upper Midwest Organic Resource Directory. Available from Midwest Organic and Sustainable Education Services (MOSES), P.O. Box 339, Spring Valley, WI, 54767, phone: (715) 772-3153, on-line: www.mosesorganic.org, e-mail: moses@wwt.net.

Planning Task Two: History, Current Situation

Publications, Software and Videos

Developing a Balance Sheet. Ross O. Love, Harry G. Haefner, and Damona G. Doye. Oklahoma Cooperative Extension Service. 1998. Publication number: F-752. Contact Oklahoma Cooperative Extension Service, 139 Agriculture Hall, Oklahoma State University, Stillwater, OK 74078, phone: (405) 744-5385, on-line: www.dasnr.okstate.edu/oces, web version: agweb.okstate.edu/pearl/agecon/tax/f-752.pdf.

Developing an Income Statement. Lori J. Shipman and Damona G. Doye. Oklahoma Cooperative Extension Service. 1998. Publication number: F-753. Contact Oklahoma Cooperative Extension Service, 139 Agriculture Hall, Oklahoma State University, Stillwater, OK 74078, phone: (405) 744-5385, on-line: www.dasnr.okstate.edu/oces, web version: agweb.okstate.edu/pearl/agecon/tax/f-753.pdf.

Evaluating Financial Performance and Position. Harry P. Mapp and Ross O. Love. Oklahoma Cooperative Extension Service. 1998. Publication number: F-790. Contact Oklahoma Cooperative Extension Service, 139 Agriculture Hall, Oklahoma State University, Stillwater, OK 74078, phone: (405) 744-5385, on-line: www.dasnr.okstate.edu/oces, web version: http://agweb.okstate.edu/pearl/agecon/tax/f-790.pdf.

FINPACK Software. Center for Farm Financial Management. Updated annually. Contact CFFM, 130 Classroom Office Building, 1994 Buford Avenue, St. Paul, MN 55108, phone: (612) 625-1964 or toll-free (800) 234-1111, on-line: www.cffm.umn.edu, e-mail: cffm@umn.edu.

The Monitoring Tool Box. Julia Ahlers Ness (editor). Land Stewardship Project and the Minnesota Institute for Sustainable Agriculture. 1998. Contact the Land Stewardship Project, 2200 4th St., White Bear Lake, MN 55110, phone: (651) 653-0618, on-line: www.landstewardshipproject.org.

Agencies, Organizations and Networks

Center for Farm Financial Management. Develops educational software and training programs for farmers, agricultural lenders, and educators that apply the principles and concepts of farm planning, financing, and analysis in a practical manner. Contact CFFM, 130 Classroom Office Building, 1994 Buford Avenue, St. Paul, MN 55108, phone: (612) 625-1964 or toll-free (800) 234-1111, on-line: www.cffm.umn.edu, e-mail: cffm@umn.edu.

Farm Business Management, Education Programs (Minnesota). Offers courses and individual instruction/consultation for long-range financial monitoring and planning. Contact Farm Business Management Education Programs, State Director John Murray, Rochester Community and Technical College, 851 30th Ave. SE, Rochester, MN 55904-3109, phone: (507) 280-3109, on-line: www.mgt.org/fbm, e-mail: john.murray@roch.edu.

United States Department of Agriculture Natural Resources Conservation Service. To locate the service center nearest you, go to www.nrcs.usda.gov and click on "Local Service Centers."

Planning Task Three: Vision, Goals, Mission

Publications, Software and Videos

Business Planning for Your Farm—Setting Personal and Business Goals. David M. Saxowsky, Cole R. Gustafson, Laurence M. Crane, and Joe C. Samson. Department of Agricultural Economics, North Dakota State University. 1995. Contact Carol Jensen, Department of Agribusiness and Applied Economics, North Dakota State University, P.O. Box 5636, Fargo, ND 58105-5636, phone: (701) 231-7441, e-mail: cjensen@ndsuext.nodak.edu.

Establishing and Reaching Goals. Suzanne Karberg. Department of Agricultural Economics, Purdue University. 1993. Publication number: EC-669. Contact Purdue University Cooperative Extension Service, 1140 Ag. Administration Bldg., West Lafayette, IN 47907, phone: (765) 494-8499, on-line: www.admin.ces.purdue.edu, web version: agecon.uwyo.edu/RiskMgt/generaltopics/EstablishingAndReachingGoals.pdf.

Goal Setting for Farm and Ranch Families. Damona Doye. Oklahoma Cooperative Service Extension Service. 2001. Fact sheet number: WF-244. Contact Oklahoma Cooperative Extension Service, 139 Agriculture Hall, Oklahoma State University, Stillwater, OK 74078, phone: (405) 744-5385, on-line: www.dasnr.okstate.edu/oces, web version: www.agweb.okstate.edu/pearl/agecon/farm/wf-244.html.

Holistic Management: A New Framework for Decision Making. Allan Savory and Jody Butterfield. Island Press. 2nd Edition. 1999. Contact Allan Savory Center for Holistic Management, 1010 Tijeras NW, Albuquerque, NM 87102, phone: (505)842-5252, on-line: www.holisticmanagement.org, e-mail: savorycenter@holisticmanagement.org.

How to Establish Goals: A Group Project for Farmers and Their Families. John Lamb. Minnesota Project, Whole Farm Planning Interdisciplinary Team and the Minnesota Institute for Sustainable Agriculture. 2000. Contact Minnesota Project, 1885 University Ave. W., Suite 315, St. Paul, MN 55104, phone: (651) 645-6159, on-line: mnprojct@gte.net.

Whole Farm Planning: Combining Family, Profit and Environment. David Mulla, Les Everett, and Gigi DiGiacomo. Minnesota Institute for Sustainable Agriculture. 1998. Publication number: BU-06985. Contact University of Minnesota Extension Service, 405 Coffey Hall, 1420 Eckles Ave., St. Paul, MN 55108-6068, phone: (800) 876-8636, on-line: order@extension.umn.edu, web version: www.extension.umn.edu/distribution/businessmanagement/DF6985.html.

Whole Farm Planning: What It Takes. Dana Jackson (editor). Land Stewardship Project, Minnesota Department of Agriculture, and University of Minnesota Extension Service. 1997. Contact Land Stewardship Project, 2200 4th St., White Bear Lake, MN 55110, phone: (651) 653-0618, on-line: www.landstewardshipproject.org.

Whole Farm Planning at Work: Success Stories of Ten Farms. Jill MacKenzie and Loni Kemp. Minnesota Project. 1999. Contact Minnesota Project, 1885 University Ave. W., Suite 315, St. Paul, MN 55104, phone: (651) 645-6159, on-line: mnprojct@gte.net.

Agencies, Organizations and Networks

Agricultural Mediation Program. Offers confidential mediation services in each state to assist with conflict resolution among family and business partners over goals and other issues. Conducted by the USDA's Farm Service Agency. Contact Chester A. Bailey, Farm Service Agency, USDA Agricultural Mediation Program, USDA/FSA/EDSO, STOP 0539/Rm. 6724-S, Washington, DC 20250-0539, phone: (202) 720-1471, on-line: www.fsa.usda.gov/pas/publications/facts/html/mediate01.htm, e-mail: cbailey@wdc.fsa.usda.gov.

Allan Savory Center for Holistic Management. Provides resources and consultation to assist farmers and other individuals with a goals-based decision-making process that can be applied to personal and business planning. Contact the Allan Savory Center for Holistic Management, 1010 Tijeras NW, Albuquerque, NM 87102, phone: (505)842-5252, on-line: www.holisticmanagement.org, e-mail: savorycenter@holisticmanagement.org.

Planning Task Four: Strategic Planning

Publications, Software and Videos

Agricultural Prices—Annual. National Agricultural Statistics Service. 2002 (updated annually). Contact: NASS, phone: (800) 727-9540, online: www.usda.gov/nass, e-mail: nass@nass.usda.gov, view online at: jan.mannlib.cornell.edu/reports/nassr/price/zap-bb/.

Analyzing Land Investments. *Business Management in Agriculture* videotape series. Gayle Willett. 1988. Iowa State University Extension. Contact: Lisa Scarbrough, Iowa State University Extension Communications, 1712 ASB, Ames, IA 50011, phone: (515) 294-4972, e-mail: lscarb@iastate.edu.

Contract Evaluation. Value Project, University of Illinois. 2000 (reviewed). Contact Burton Swanson, Project Director, Department of Agricultural and Consumer Economics, 1301 West Gregory Drive, Urbana, IL 61801, phone: (217) 244-6978, e-mail: swansonb@uiuc.edu, view on-line: web.aces.uiuc.edu/value/contracts/contracts.htm.

Developing a Longer-Range Strategic Farm Business Plan. Part One of a planned six part series: *Business Management for Farmers*. Ken Thomas. Midwest Plan Services, Iowa State University, Ames, IA. 1999. Publication number: NCR-610A. Contact Midwest Plan Services, 122 Davidson Hall, Iowa State University, Ames, IA 50011-3080, phone: (800) 562-3618, on-line: www.mwpshq.org.

Evaluating a Rural Enterprise. Preston Sullivan and Lane Greer. Appropriate Technology Transfer for Rural Areas (ATTRA). 2000. Contact ATTRA, PO Box 3657, Fayetteville, AR 72702, phone: (800) 346-9140, on-line: www.attra.org.

The Executive Summary. In *Business Owners' Toolkit* online. CCH Incorporated. 2002. View on-line: www.toolkit.cch.com/text/P02_5201.asp.

Farm Business Management Annual Reports. Crop Information. 2002 (updated annually). Contact: John Murray, Farm and Small Business Management Programs, 851 30th Ave. S.E., Rochester, MN 55904-4999, phone: (507) 280-3109, on-line: www.mgt.org/fbm, view online at: www.mgt.org/fbm/reports/2001/state/state.htm.

Farming Alternatives: A Guide to Evaluating the Feasibility of New Farm-Based Enterprises. Nancy Grudens Schuck, Wayne Knoblauch, Judy Green and Mary Saylor. Natural Resource, Agriculture, and Engineering Service, Cornell University. 1988. Publication number: NRAES-32. Contact Natural Resource, Agriculture, and Engineering Service, Cooperative Extension, 152 Riley-Robb Hall, Ithaca, New York 14853-5701, phone: (607) 255-7654, on-line: www.nraes.org, e-mail: NRAES@cornell.edu.

In the Eyes of the Law: Legal Issues Associated with Direct Farm Marketing. Richard F. Prim and Kaarin K. Foede. University of Minnesota Extension Service. 2002. Product number: BU-07683. Contact the University of Minnesota Extension Service, 405 Coffey Hall, 1420 Eckles Ave., St. Paul, MN 55108-6068, phone: (800) 876-8636, e-mail: order@extension.umn.edu.

Planning for Contingencies. In *Business Owners' Toolkit* online. CCH Incorporated. 2002. view online: www.toolkit.cch.com/text/P02_5531.asp.

Primer for Selecting New Enterprises for Your Farm. Tim Woods and Steve Isaacs. Agricultural Economics, University of Kentucky. 2000. Publication number: 00-13. Contact University of Kentucky Agricultural Economics Cooperative Extension, College of Agriculture, University of Kentucky, Lexington, Kentucky 40546-0091,on-line: www.uky.edu/Ag/AgEcon/extension, web version: www.uky.edu/Ag/AgEcon/publications/ext2000-13.pdf.

Rural Resource Management: Problem Solving for the Long Term. Sandra E. Miller, Craig W. Shinn, and William R. Bentley. 1994. Contact Iowa State University Press, PO Box 570, Ames, IA 50010-0570, phone: (800) 862-6657, on-line: www.isupress.com.

A Strategic Management Primer for Farmers. Kent Olson. Department of Applied Economics, University of Minnesota. 2001. Staff Paper number: P01-15. Contact the Department of Applied Economics, University of Minnesota, 231 Classroom Office Building, 1994 Buford Ave., St. Paul MN 55108-6040, phone: (612) 625-1222, on-line: www.agecon.lib.umn.edu.

Strategic Planning: A Conceptual for Small and Midsize Farmer Cooperatives. James J. Wadsworth, Jim J. Staiert, and Beverly Rotan. Agricultural Cooperative Service, US Department of Agriculture. Research Report number: 112. 1993. Contact your local USDA Agricultural Cooperative Service or find the closest one on-line at www.rurdev.usda.gov/recd_map.html. View the publication on-line at: www.rurdev.usda.gov/rbs/pub/rr112.pdf.

Transferring Your Farm Business to the Next Generation. Jim Polson, Robert Fleming, Bernie Erven, and Warren Lee. Ohio State University Extension. 1996. Bulletin 862. Contact Ohio State University Extension Media Distribution, 385 Kottman Hall, 2021 Coffey Rd., Columbus, OH 43210-1044, phone: (614) 292-1607, e-mail: pubs@postoffice.ag.ohio-state.edu, web version: ohioline.osu.edu/b862.

Agencies, Organizations and Networks

Farm*A*Syst. Identifies potential environmental risks posed by farmstead operations, especially in regard to groundwater. Fact sheets provide educational information and list reference people to contact if questions arise. Contact Farm*A*Syst, 1545 Observatory Drive, 303 Hiram Smith Hall Madison, WI 53706-1289, phone: (608) 262-0024, on-line: www.uwex.edu/farmasyst, e-mail: farmasyst@uwex.edu.

National Ag Risk Education Library. A USDA initiative offering information, tools, and assistance for risk management planning. Visit on-line at: www.agrisk.umn.edu.

Planning Task Five: Implementation and Monitoring

Publications, Software and Videos

Holistic Management: A New Framework for Decision Making. Allan Savory and Jody Butterfield. Island Press. 2nd edition. 1999. Contact Allan Savory Center for Holistic Management 1010 Tijeras NW, Albuquerque, NM 87102, phone: (505) 842-5252, on-line: www.holisticmanagement.org, e-mail: savorycenter@holisticmanagement.org.

The Monitoring Tool Box. Julia Ahlers Ness (editor). Land Stewardship Project. 1998. Contact Land Stewardship Project, 2200 4th St., White Bear Lake, MN 55110, phone: (651) 653-0618, on-line: www.landstewardshipproject.org.

Functional Areas: Marketing

Publications, Software and Videos

Adding Value to Farm Products: An Overview. Janet Bachman. Appropriate Technology Transfer for Rural Areas (ATTRA). 1999. Contact ATTRA, PO Box 3657, Fayetteville, AR 72702, phone: (800) 346-9140, on-line: www.attra.org.

Alternative Enterprises and Agritourism Tool Kit: Farming for Sustainability and Profit. Resource Economics and Social Sciences Division and Resource Conservation and Community Development Division, US Department of Agriculture. 2000. Contact USDA/NRCS National Agritourism, Recreation and Alternative Enterprises, Director Jim Maetzold, PO Box 2890, Washington, DC 20013, phone: (202) 720-0132, on-line: www.nhq.nrcs.usda.gov/RESS/econ/ressd.htm.

Alternative Meat Marketing. Holly Born. Appropriate Technology Transfer for Rural Areas (ATTRA). 2000. Contact ATTRA, Appropriate Technology Transfer for Rural Areas, PO Box 3657, Fayetteville, AR 72702, phone: (800) 346-9140, on-line: www.attra.org.

Bacon's Directories: *The Newspaper/Magazine Directory* and *The Radio/TV/Cable Directory.* BACON. Updated annually with media and editorial contacts for U.S. and Canadian media. Contact your local library.

CACI Market System Group Sourcebooks: *The Sourcebook of ZIP Code Demographics* and *The Sourcebook of County Demographics*. CACI. Updated annually with consumer demographic information. Contact your local library reference desk.

Collaborative Marketing: A Roadmap and Resource Guide for Farmers. Robert P. King and Gigi DiGiacomo. Minnesota Institute for Sustainable Agriculture. 2000. Publication number: BU-7539-S. Contact University of Minnesota Extension Service, 405 Coffey Hall, 1420 Eckles Ave., St. Paul, MN 55108-6068, phone: (800) 876-8636, e-mail: order@extension.umn.edu.

Community Supported Agriculture . . . Making the Connection. University of California Cooperative Extension, Placer County and UC Small Farm Center. 1995. Contact University of California Cooperative Extension, 11477 E Ave., Auburn, CA 95603, phone: (530) 889-7385, on-line: www.ceplacer.ucdavis.edu.

Community Supported Agriculture: The Producer/ Consumer Partnership. Colorado State University. 1995. Publication number: XCM-189. Contact Colorado State University Cooperative Extension Resource Center, Colorado State University, 115 General Services Bldg., Ft. Collins, CO 80523-4061, phone: (970) 491-6198, on-line: www.cerc.colostate.edu/.

Contract Evaluation. Value Project, University of Illinois. 2000 (reviewed). Contact Burton Swanson, Project Director, Department of Agricultural and Consumer Economics, 1301 West Gregory Drive, Urbana, IL 61801, phone: (217) 244-6978, e-mail: swansonb@uiuc.edu, view on-line: web.aces.uiuc.edu/value/contracts/contracts.htm.

Cooperative Grocer On-line. www.cooperativegrocer.com.

Developing a Marketing Plan. Stan Bevers, Mark Waller, Steve Amosson, and Dean McCorkle. Texas Agricultural Extension Service. 1998. Publication number: RM3-3.0. Contact Texas Agricultural Extension Service, Texas A&M University, Department of Agricultural Economics, College Station, Texas 77843-2124, phone: (409) 845-4911, on-line: www.agextension.tamu.edu.

Developing a Sensible and Successful Marketing Attitude. Suzanne Karberg. Department of Agricultural Economics, Purdue University. 1993. Publication number: EC-673. Contact Purdue University Cooperative Extension

Service, 1140 Ag. Administration Bldg., West Lafayette, IN 47907, phone: (765) 494-8499, on-line: www.admin.ces.purdue.edu, web version: www.aae.wisc.edu/jones/aae320hand/PurdueMarket1.pdf.

Developing and Implementing a Successful Marketing Plan. Suzanne Karberg. Department of Agricultural Economics, Purdue University. 1993. Publication number: EC-674. Contact Purdue University Cooperative Extension Service, 1140 Ag. Administration Bldg., West Lafayette, IN 47907, phone: (765) 494-8499, on-line: www.admin.ces.purdue.edu.

Direct Farm Marketing and Tourism Handbook. Russell Tronstad and Julie Leones. University of Arizona, Cooperative Extension Service. 1995. Contact the Arizona Cooperative Extension Service, Department of Agricultural and Resource Economics, PO Box 210023, University of Arizona, Tuscon, AZ 85721, phone: (520) 621-6241, on-line: www.ag.arizona.edu/AREC.

Doing Your Own Market Research: Tips on Evaluating the Market for New Farm-Based Enterprises. Judy Green. Cornell University. 2003 (reviewed). Contact the Community Food & Agriculture Program, Department of Rural Sociology, 216 Warren Hall, Cornell University, Ithaca, NY 14853, on-line: www.cfap.org. Available only online at: www.cals.cornell.edu/agfoodcommunity/fap/DYOMResearch.pdf.

Dynamic Farmers' Marketing: A Guide to Successfully Selling Your Farmers' Market Products. Jeff W. Ishee. Bittersweet Farmstead. 1997. Contact Bittersweet Farmstead, PO Box 52, Middlebrook, VA 23116, phone: (540) 248-3938, e-mail: farmstead@cfw.com.

Farmers' Markets: Consumer Trends, Preferences, and Characteristics. Ramu Govindasamy, Marta Zurbriggen, John Italia, Adesoji Adelaja, Peter Nitzsche, and Richard VanVraken. New Jersey Agricultural Experiment Station. University of New Jersey, Rutgers. 1998. Publication number: P-02137-7-98. Contact Rutgers Cooperative Extension, Cook College, Rutgers, The State University of New Jersey, 88 Lipman Dr., New Brunswick, NJ 08901-8525, phone: (732) 932-9306.

Farmers' Markets: Producers' Characteristics and Status of Their Businesses. Ramu Govindasamy, Marta Zurbriggen, John Italia, Adesoji Adelaja, Peter Nitzsche, and Richard VanVraken. New Jersey Agricultural Experiment Station. University of New Jersey, Rutgers. 1998. Publication number: P-02137-6-98. Contact Rutgers Cooperative Extension, Cook College, Rutgers, The State University of New Jersey, 88 Lipman Dr., New Brunswick, NJ 08901-8525, phone: (732) 932-9306.

Finding Customers: Market Segmentation. Nancy H. Bull and Gregory R. Passewitz. Ohio State University Extension. 1994. Publication number: CDFS-1253-94. Contact Ohio State University Extension, 700 Ackerman Road, Suite 235, Columbus, OH 43202-1578, phone: (614) 292-1607, e-mail: pubs@postoffice.ag.ohio-state.edu, web version: ohioline.osu.edu/cd-fact/1253.html.

Food Labeling Fact Sheet. Minnesota Department of Agriculture Dairy & Food Inspection Division. 1999. Contact Minnesota Department of Agriculture, 90 West Plato Boulevard, Saint Paul, MN 55107, phone: (651) 296-1592, on-line: www.mda.state.mn.us, web version: www.mda.state.mn.us/dairyfood/labeling.pdf

Household Spending: Who Spends How Much on What. The New Strategist Editors, 7th edition. 2002. Contact New Strategist Publications, PO Box 242, Ithaca, NY 14851, phone: (800) 848-0842, on-line: www.newstrategist.com

The Legal Guide for Direct Farm Marketing. Neil Hamilton. Drake Agricultural Law Center, Drake University. 1999. Contact Drake Agricultural Law Center, Drake University, Cartwright Hall, 2507 University Ave., Des Moines, IA 50311-4505, phone: (515) 271-2947 or toll-free (800) 443-7253, on-line: www.drake.edu.

Market Farm Forms: Spreadsheet Templates for Planning and Organization Information on Diversified Farms. Full Circle Farm. 2000. Contact Full Circle Farm, 3377 Early Times Lane, Auburn, CA 95603, phone: (530) 885-9201, on-line: fullcircle@jps.net.

Marketeer: The Crop Market Planning Tool. Center for Farm Financial Management (CFFM) and Country Hedging Inc. 2001. Contact CFFM, 130 Classroom Office Building, 1994 Buford Avenue, St. Paul, MN 55108, phone: (612) 625-1964 or toll-free (800) 234-1111, on-line: www.cffm.umn.edu, e-mail: cffm@umn.edu.

Marketing. David L. Kurtz and Louise E. Boone. Dryden Press. Chicago, IL. 1981. Contact your local library or bookstore.

The Marketing Plan: Step-by-Step. Michael O'Donnell. 1991. Contact the Center for Innovation, North Dakota State University, 4300 Dartmouth Dr., PO Box 8372, Grand Forks, ND 58202-8372, phone: (701) 777-3132, on-line:www.innovators.net.

Marketing Strategies for Agricultural Commodities. Erlin J. Weness. University of Minnesota Extension Service. 2001 (reviewed). Marketing Fact Sheet # 13. Contact University of Minnesota Extension Service, 405 Coffey Hall, 1420 Eckles Ave., St. Paul, MN 55108-6068, phone: (800) 876-8636, e-mail: order@extension.umn.edu, web version: swroc.coafes.umn.edu/SWFM/Files/mrkt/marketing_strategies.pdf.

The Minnesota Grown Directory. Contact Minnesota Grown, Minnesota Department of Agriculture, 90 West Plato Boulevard St. Paul, MN 55107-2094, phone: (651) 297-4648, on-line: www.mda.state.mn.us/mngrown.

Natural/Organic Industry Outlook. George Southworth. Cooperative Grocer. September-October 2001. Number 96. Contact the Cooperative Grocer on-line at: www.cooperativegrocer.com.

New Markets for Producers: Selling to Retail Stores. Center for Integrated Agricultural Systems. 1999. Research Brief number: 38. Contact the Center for Integrated Agricultural Systems, 1450 Linden Drive, University of Wisconsin, Madison, WI 53706, phone: (608) 262-5200, on-line: www.wisc.edu/cias/, e-mail: chaza@facstaff.wisc.edu.

Practical Marketing Research. Jeffrey L. Pope. American Management Association. 1993. Contact American Management Association, 1601 Broadway, New York, NY 10019-7420, phone: (800) 262-9699, on-line: www.amanet.org.

Reap New Profits: Marketing Strategies for Farmers and Ranchers. USDA, Sustainable Agriculture Network (SAN). 2001. Contact SAN, USDA, Attn: Abiola Adeyemi, USDA National Agriculture Library, 10301 Baltimore Ave., Room 304, Beltsville, MD 20904, phone: (301) 504-5422, on-line: www.sare.org.

Resources for Organic Marketing. Holly Born. Appropriate Technology Transfer for Rural Areas (ATTRA). 2001. Contact ATTRA, PO Box 3657, Fayetteville, AR 72702, phone: (800) 346-9140, on-line: www.attra.org.

Sell What You Sow! Eric Gibson. New World Publishing. 1993. Contact New World Publishing, 11543 Quartz Dr. #1, Auburn CA 95602, phone: (530) 823-3886, on-line: www.nnwpub.net.

Small Business Marketing for Dummies. Barbara Findlay Schenck. Hungry Minds, Inc. 2001. Contact your local bookstore or library.

SRDS Lifestyle Market Analyst. SRDS. Updated annually with demographic and lifestyle data; organized by geographic market area, lifestyle preferences, and consumer profiles. Contact your local library.

Agencies, Organizations and Networks

Agricultural Direct Marketing Email Discussion Group. Information about agricultural direct marketing. Join by sending an e-mail with the message: subscribe direct-mkt to majordomo@reeusda.gov.

Altmarketing Listserve. Discussion list for farmers, educators and others interested in alternative and direct marketing. Join by sending an e-mail with the message: SUBSCRIBE altmarketing Firstname Lastname to listserv@crcvms.unl.edu.

Agricultural Marketing Service (AMS), USDA. Includes six commodity programs—Cotton, Dairy, Fruit and Vegetable, Livestock and Seed, Poultry, and Tobacco. Programs employ specialists who provide standardization, grading, and market news services for these commodities. Also oversee marketing agreements and orders, administer research and promotion programs, and purchase commodities for Federal food programs. For specific contact information, visit AMS on-line at: www.ams.usda.gov/.

Association of Official Seed Certifying Agencies (AOSCA). International organization dedicated to identity-preserved seed certification. Contact AOSCA, 55 SW Fifth Ave., Suite 150 Meridian, ID 83642, phone: (208) 884-2493, on-line: www.aosca.org.

Agricultural Utilization and Research Institute (AURI). Assists with the development and financing of marketing plans. Contact Agricultural Utilization and Research Institute (AURI), 1380 Energy Lane, Suite 112, West St. Paul, Minnesota 55108, phone: (651) 603-8108, on-line: www.auri.org.

Buyers of Organic Products in the Upper Midwest. A listing of more than 65 buyers and processors of organic grains, oilseeds, fruits, vegetables, herbs, milk, and maple syrup. Contact Minnesota Department of Agriculture, 90 West Plato Boulevard, Saint Paul, MN 55107, phone: (651) 297-1629, on-line: www.mda.state.mn.us.

Cooperative Development Services (CDS). Develops marketing plans for cooperatives on a fee-for-service basis. Contact your local USDA Agricultural Cooperative Service or find the closest one online at: http://www.rurdev.usda.gov/recd_map.html.

Internet Marketing Center. Offers tips and strategies, resources, and a free monthly newsletter about marketing on-line. Contact Internet Marketing Center, 1123 Fir Ave., Blaine, WA 98230, phone: (604) 730-2833, on-line: www.marketingtips.com.

Minnesota Grown. Partnership between the Minnesota Department of Agriculture and farmers that produces and distributes a directory of Minnesota-grown products. Contact Minnesota Grown, Minnesota Department of Agriculture, 90 West Plato Boulevard St. Paul, MN 55107-2094, phone: (651) 297-4648, on-line: www.mda.state.mn.us/mngrown.

US Department of Agriculture (USDA), Department of Rural Development. Provides technical and financial assistance for marketing research. Contact your local USDA Department of Rural Development or find the closest one on-line at: www.rurdev.usda.gov/recd_map.html.

Wholesale Produce Dealers Licensing and Bonding Program. Minnesota Department of Agriculture. Updated annually. Contact MDA, John Malmberg, auditor, Wholesale Produce Dealers Licensing and Auditing, Minnesota Department of Agriculture, 90 West Plato Boulevard, Saint Paul, MN 55107, phone: (651) 296-8620, e-mail: John.Malmberg@state.mn.us. View on-line at: www.mda.state.mn.us/wholedeal/default.htm.

Functional Areas: Operations

Publications, Software and Videos

Alternative Agronomic Crops. Patricia Sauer and Preston Sullivan. Appropriate Technology Transfer for Rural Areas (ATTRA). 2000. Contact ATTRA, Appropriate Technology Transfer for Rural Areas, PO Box 3657, Fayetteville, AR 72702, phone: (800) 346-9140, on-line: www.attra.org.

Farm Business Management Annual Reports. Crop Information. 2002 (updated annually). Contact: John Murray, Farm and Small Business Management Programs, 851 30th Ave. S.E., Rochester, MN 55904-4999, phone: (507) 280-3109, on-line: www.mgt.org/fbm, view online at: www.mgt.org/fbm/reports/2001/state/state.htm.

Grazing Systems Planning Guide. Kevin Blanchet, Howard Moechnig, and Jodi Dejong-Hughes. University of Minnesota Extension. 2000. Publication number: BU-7606-GO. Contact University of Minnesota Extension, 405 Coffey Hall, 1420 Eckles Ave., St. Paul, MN 55108-6068, phone: (800) 876-8636, e-mail: order@extension.umn.edu.

Integrated Pest Management. Rex Dufour and Janet Bachmann. Appropriate Technology Transfer for Rural Areas (ATTRA). March 1998. Contact ATTRA, Appropriate Technology Transfer for Rural Areas PO Box 3657, Fayetteville, AR 72702, phone: (800) 346-9140, on-line: www.attra.org.

Making the Transition to Sustainable Farming. Burt Hall and George Kuepper. Appropriate Technology Transfer for Rural Areas (ATTRA). December 1997. Contact ATTRA, PO Box 3657, Fayetteville, AR 72702, phone: (800) 346-9140, on-line: www.attra.org.

Managing Production and Marketing Systems. Part three of a planned six-part series: *Business Management for Farmers.* Midwest Plan Services, Iowa State University, Ames, IA. July 2000. Publication number: NCR-610C. Contact Midwest Plan Services, 122 Davidson Hall, Iowa State University, Ames, IA 50011-3080, phone (800) 562-3618, on-line: www.mwpshq.org.

Managing Your Land for Wildlife: Opportunities for Farmers and Rural Land Owners. Gigi DiGiacomo, Les Everett, James Kitts, and Kevin Lines. University of Minnesota Extension Service. 1998. Publication number: FO-7067-S. Contact University of Minnesota Extension Service, 405 Coffey Hall, 1420 Eckles Ave., St. Paul, MN 55108-6068, phone: (800) 876-8636, e-mail: order@extension.umn.edu.

Natural Resource Management Practices: A Primer. Peter Folliott and Luis A. Bojorquez-Navarez. 2000. Iowa State Press. Contact Iowa State Press, PO Box 570, Ames, IA 50010-0570, phone: (800) 862-6657, on-line: www.isupress.com.

The New Farmers' Market: Farm Fresh Ideas for Producers, Managers, and Communities. Vance Corum, Marcie Rosenzweig, and Eric Gibson. Hotline Printing and Publishing. 2001. Contact Hotline Printing and Publishing, PO Box 161132, Altamonte Springs, FL 32716-1132, phone: (407) 628-1377.

Organic Certification of Crop Production in Minnesota. Lisa Gulbranson. Minnesota Institute for Sustainable Agriculture. 2001. Publication number BU-07202. Contact University of Minnesota Extension Service, 405 Coffey Hall, 1420 Eckles Ave., St. Paul, MN 55108-6068, phone: (800) 876-8636, e-mail: order@extension.umn.edu.

Overview of Agroforestry. Alice Beetz. Appropriate Technology Transfer for Rural Areas (ATTRA). October 1999. Contact ATTRA, PO Box 3657, Fayetteville, AR 72702, phone: (800) 346-9140, on-line: www.attra.org.

Overview of Organic Crop Production. George Kuepper. Appropriate Technology Transfer for Rural Areas (ATTRA). November 2000. Contact ATTRA, PO Box 3657, Fayetteville, AR 72702, phone: (800) 346-9140, on-line: www.attra.org.

Overview of Organic Fruit Production. Guy K. Ames and George Kuepper. Appropriate Technology Transfer for Rural Areas (ATTRA). February 2000. Contact ATTRA, PO Box 3657, Fayetteville, AR 72702, phone: (800) 346-9140, on-line: www.attra.org.

Rotational Grazing. Alice E. Beetz. Appropriate Technology Transfer for Rural Areas (ATTRA). 1999. Contact ATTRA, PO Box 3657, Fayetteville, AR 72702, phone: (800) 346-9140, on-line: www.attra.org.

Sharing Farm Machinery. Erlin Weness. University of Minnesota Extension Service. 2001. Available on-line: swroc.coafes.umn.edu/SWFM/Files/fin/sharing_machinery.htm.

haring the Harvest: A Guide to Community Supported griculture. Elizabeth Henderson with Robyn Van En. helsea Green Publishing Company, Vermont. 1999. ontact Chelsea Green Publishing Company, PO Box 428, /hite River Junction, VT 05001, phone: (800) 639-4099, n-line: www.chelseagreen.com.

ustainable Agriculture. John Mason. Kangaroo Press. 997. Contact your local bookstore or library.

ustainable Corn and Soybean Production. Preston ullivan. Appropriate Technology Transfer for Rural Areas ATTRA). 2000. Contact ATTRA, PO Box 3657, ayetteville, AR 72702, phone: (800) 346-9140, on-line: ww.attra.org.

ustainable Soil Management. Preston Sullivan. ppropriate Technology Transfer for Rural Areas ATTRA). 1999. Contact ATTRA, PO Box 3657, ayetteville, AR 72702, phone: (800) 346-9140, on-line: ww.attra.org.

Ipper Midwest Organic Resource Directory. Midwest rganic and Sustainable Education Services (MOSES). rd edition, 2001. Contact MOSES, N7834 County Road , PO Box 339, Spring Valley, WI 54767, phone: (715) 72-3153, on-line: www.mosesorganic.org.

Agencies, Organizations and Networks

lternative Farming Systems Information Center AFSIC), National Agricultural Library, USDA. nformation center specializing in the location, collection, nd provision of information about sustainable and lternative agricultural systems. Contact Alternative arming Systems Information Center (AFSIC), National gricultural Library, 10301 Baltimore Ave., Rm. 304, eltsville, MD 20705-2351, phone: (301) 504-6559, onine: www.nal.usda.gov/afsic.

ppropriate Technology Transfer for Rural Areas ATTRA). A national sustainable farming information enter that provides technical assistance information free f charge to farmers and farm support groups. They have number of excellent up-to-date publications on lternative crops, livestock, and sustainable farming ractices. Check their listing of available publications online, or for more information, contact ATTRA, P.O. Box 657, Fayetteville, AR 72702, phone: (800) 346-9140, online: www.attra.org.

enter for Rural Affairs, Beginning Farmer ustainable Agriculture Project. A nonprofit farm dvocacy and support information provider. The eginning Farmer Sustainable Agriculture Project xposes beginning farmers to low-input, low capital, lternative, and knowledge-based farming systems that re environmentally sustainable. The Center has umerous publications and information about sustainable agriculture. Contact Center for Rural Affairs, 101 S Tallman St., P.O. Box 406, Walthill, NE 68067, phone: (402) 846-5428, on-line: www.cfra.org.

Energy and Sustainable Agriculture Program (ESAP), Minnesota Department of Agriculture. ESAP's purpose is to demonstrate and promote alternative agricultural practices that are energy efficient, environmentally sound, and enhance the self-sufficiency of Minnesota farmers. ESAP sponsors a loan program, demonstration grant program, on-farm research, workshops, and speakers. Contact MDA-ESAP, 90 West Plato Boulevard, Saint Paul, MN 55107, phone: (651) 296-7673, on-line: www.mda.state.mn.us/esap/.

Farm Beginnings Program (Minnesota). Production and finance-related business training for beginning farmers offered by the Land Stewardship Project (LSP) with support from the Minnesota Extension Service. Contact LSP, 2200 4th St., White Bear Lake, MN 55110, phone: (651) 653-0618, on-line: www.landstewardshipproject.org.

Land Stewardship Project. A nonprofit that fosters an ethic of stewardship for farmland, and promotes sustainable agriculture and sustainable communities. Contact the Land Stewardship Project, 2200 4th St., White Bear Lake, MN 55110, phone: (651) 653-0618, online: www.landstewardshipproject.org.

Minnesota Institute for Sustainable Agriculture (MISA). A partnership between the College of Agricultural, Food and Environmental Sciences at the University of Minnesota, and the Sustainers' Coalition (a group of community nonprofit organizations, which includes the Institute for Agricultural and Trade Policy, the Land Stewardship Project, the Minnesota Food Association, the Minnesota Project, and the Minnesota Sustainable Farming Association). MISA operates a website with current sustainable agriculture information, including a calendar of sustainable agriculture events, and announcements, a searchable database of resources, and links to many related sites and resources. Contact MISA, 411 Borlaug Hall, 1991 Buford Circle, St. Paul, MN 55108, phone: (612) 625-8235 or toll-free (800) 909-MISA (6472), on-line: www.misa.umn.edu.

National Organic Program, USDA. Provides information, contacts, and forms for organic certification in each state. At the national level, contact Richard Mathews, Program Manager, USDA-AMS-TMP-NOP, Room 4008-South Building, 1400 Independence Avenue SW, Washington, DC 20250-0020, phone: (202) 720-3252, e-mail: NOP.Webmaster@usda.gov. To find state contacts, visit online at: www.ams.usda.gov/nop/StatePrograms/StateContacts.html.

Sustainable Agriculture Research and Education (SARE). SARE is a U.S. Department of Agriculture-funded initiative that sponsors competitive grants for sustainable agriculture research and education in a regional process nationwide. SARE works to increase knowledge about and help farmers and ranchers to adopt practices that are economically viable, environmentally sound, and socially responsible. Nationally, SARE devotes significant resources to ongoing outreach projects. SARE's Professional Development Program offers learning opportunities to a variety of agricultural extension and other field agency personnel. SARE's Sustainable Agriculture Network (SAN) disseminates information relevant to SARE and sustainable agriculture through electronic and print publications. Contact SARE, website: www.sare.org

Sustainable Farming Association of Minnesota, regional chapters throughout the state of Minnesota. The Sustainable Farming Association of Minnesota (SFA) provides a support network for farmers and networks with other organizations and agencies. The SFA facilitates educational opportunities for both members and the public about economically and environmentally sound agriculture practices. Each chapter plans and organizes various field days and workshops. For more information contact the Central Minnesota SFA, c/o DeEtta Bilek, Rt. 1 Box 4, Aldrich, MN 56434, phone: (218) 445-5475, on-line: www.sfa-mn.org.

Functional Areas: Human Resources

Publications, Software and Videos

Acquiring and Managing Resources for the Farm Business. Part four of a planned six-part series: *Business Management for Farmers.* Kenneth Thomas. MidWest Plan Service, Ames, IA. 2001. Contact MidWest Plan Service, 122 Davidson Hall, Iowa State University, Ames, IA 50011-3080, phone: (800) 562-3618, on-line: www.mwpshq.org.

Agribusiness Management Series: The Role of a Manager. David W. Park. Oklahoma Cooperative Extension Service. 1986. F-169. Contact Oklahoma Cooperative Extension Service 139 Agriculture Hall, Oklahoma State University, Stillwater, OK 74078, phone: (405) 744-5385, on-line: www.dasnr.okstate.edu/oces, web version: agweb.okstate.edu/pearl/agecon/agribiz/f-169.pdf.

Checking Your Farm Business Management Skills. Michael Boehlje, Craig Dobbins, Alan Miller, Janet Bechman, Aadron Rausch. Purdue University Cooperative Extension. 2000. Publication number: ID-237. Contact Purdue University Cooperative Extension, 1140 Ag. Administration Bldg., West Lafayette, IN 47907, phone: (765) 494-8499, on-line: www.admin.ces.purdue.edu.

Filling a Position in the Farm Business. Chris Zoller. Ohio State University Extension. 1997. Fact sheet number: HRM-1-97. Contact Ohio State University Extension, 385 Kottman Hall, 2021 Coffey Rd., Columbus, OH 43210-1044, phone: (614) 292-1607, e-mail: pubs@postoffice.ag.ohio-state.edu, web version: ohioline.osu.edu/hrm-fact/0001.html.

Labor Laws and Regulations. David Miller. Ohio State University Extension. 1997. Fact sheet number: HRM-5-97. Contact Ohio State University Extension, 385 Kottman Hall, 2021 Coffey Rd., Columbus, OH 43210-1044, phone: (614) 292-1607, e-mail: pubs@postoffice.ag.ohio-state.edu, web version: ohioline.osu.edu/hrm-fact/0005.html.

Making It Work. 1999. 59 minutes. Part One in a Farm Transitions video series. Focuses on family communication and conflict resolution for business planning. Contact Passing on the Farm Center, 140 Ninth Avenue, Granite Falls, MN 56241, phone: (320) 564-4808 or toll-free (800) 657-3247, e-mail: pofc@kilowatt.net.

Overcoming Barriers to Communication. Bernard Erven. Department of Agricultural, Environmental, and Developmental Economics, Ohio State University. 2001 (reviewed). Contact the Department of Agricultural, Environmental, and Development Economics, 2120 Fyffe Road, Columbus, OH 43210, phone: (614) 292-7911, web version: www.cce.cornell.edu/issues/cceresponds/Work/Milligan/Communication.pdf.

Paying Wages to Family Members. Bev Rawn. Ontario Agriculture and Rural Division. 1995. To order, contact Publications Ontario, 50 Grosvenor Street, Toronto, ON Canada M7A 1N8, phone: (800) 668-9938.

Performance Appraisal of Farm Employees. Kenneth D Simeral. Ohio State University Extension. 2001. Publication number: HRM-4-97. Contact Ohio State University Extension, 385 Kottman Hall, 2021 Coffey Rd., Columbus, OH 43210-1044, phone: (614) 292-1607, e-mail: pubs@postoffice.ag.ohio-state.edu, web version: ohioline.osu.edu/hrm-fact/0004.html.

Transferring Your Farm Business to the Next Generation. Jim Polson, Robert Fleming, Bernard Erven, and Warren Lee. Ohio State University Extension. 1996. Bulletin number: 862. Contact Ohio State University Extension, 385 Kottman Hall, 2021 Coffey Rd., Columbus, OH 43210-1044, phone: (614) 292-1607, e-mail: pubs@postoffice.ag.ohio-state.edu, web version: ohioline.osu.edu/b862/index.html.

Transferring the Farm Series. Series of 15 articles on farm succession planning. Minnesota Extension Service. 1994. Publication number: PC-6317-S. Contact University of Minnesota Extension Service, 405 Coffey Hall, 1420 Eckles Ave., St. Paul, MN 55108-6068, phone: (800) 876-8636, e-mail: order@extension.umn.edu.

Agencies, Organizations and Networks

Minnesota Farm Connection. Connects young and beginning farmers with retiring farmers through computerized lists. Contact Passing on the Farm Center, 140 Ninth Avenue, Granite Falls, MN 56241, phone: (320) 564-4808 or toll-free (800) 657-3247, e-mail: pofc@kilowatt.net.

Passing on the Farm Center. Offers a variety of services including estate planning, family communication building, succession planning, and goal setting, as well as workshops on farm transitioning. Contact Passing on the Farm Center, 140 Ninth Avenue, Granite Falls, MN 56241, phone: (320) 564-4808 or toll-free (800) 657-3247, e-mail: pofc@kilowatt.net.

Functional Areas: Finance

Publications, Software and Videos

Analyzing Land Investments. *Business Management in Agriculture* videotape series. Gayle Willett. 1988. Washington State University Extension. Contact: Lisa Scarbrough, Iowa State University Extension Communications, 1712 ASB, Ames, IA 50011, phone: (515) 294-4972, e-mail: lscarb@iastate.edu.

Approaching Your Banker for a Loan. 20 minutes. Minnesota Bankers Association. 1998. Contact the Minnesota Bankers Association, Suite 200, 7601 France Ave. South, Edina, MN 55435-5998, phone: (952) 835-3900, on-line: www.minnbankcenter.org.

Better Farm Accounting. Herbert B. Howell. Iowa State Press. 4th edition, 1980. Contact Iowa State Press, PO Box 570, Ames, IA 50010-0570, phone: (800) 862-6657, on-line: www.isupress.com.

Capital Leases. Harry Haefner and Damona G. Doye. Oklahoma Cooperative Extension Service. 1998. Publication number: WF-935. Contact Oklahoma Cooperative Extension Service, 139 Agriculture Hall, Oklahoma State University, Stillwater, OK 74078, phone: (405) 744-5385, on-line: www.dasnr.okstate.edu/oces, web version: www.agweb.okstate.edu/pearl/agecon/resource/wf-935.pdf

Cash Flow Planning in Agriculture. James D. Libbin, Lowell B. Catlett, and Michael L. Jones. Iowa State Press. 1994. Contact Iowa State Press, PO Box 570, Ames, IA 50010-0570, phone: (800) 862-6657, on-line: www.isupress.com.

Developing a Balance Sheet. Ross O. Loye, Harry G. Haefner, and Damona G. Doye. Oklahoma Cooperative Extension Service. 1998. Publication number: F-752. Contact Oklahoma Cooperative Extension Service, 139 Agriculture Hall, Oklahoma State University, Stillwater, OK 74078, phone: (405) 744-5385, on-line: www.dasnr.okstate.edu/oces, web version: agweb.okstate.edu/pearl/agecon/tax/f-752.pdf.

Developing a Cash Flow Plan. Damona G. Doye. Oklahoma Cooperative Extension Service. 1998. Publication number: F-751. Contact Oklahoma Cooperative Extension Service, 139 Agriculture Hall, Oklahoma State University, Stillwater, OK 74078, phone: (405) 744-5385, on-line: www.dasnr.okstate.edu/oces, web version: www.agweb.okstate.edu/pearl/agecon/tax/f-751.pdf.

Developing an Income Statement. Lori J. Shipman and Damona G. Doye. Oklahoma Cooperative Extension Service. 1998. Publication number: F-753. Contact Oklahoma Cooperative Extension Service, 139 Agriculture Hall, Oklahoma State University, Stillwater, OK 74078, phone: (405) 744-5385, on-line: www.dasnr.okstate.edu/oces, web version: agweb.okstate.edu/pearl/agecon/tax/f-753.pdf.

Estate Planning Principles, the first title in the *Estate Planning* series. Erlin J. Weness. University of Minnesota Extension Service. Web version only: swroc.coafes.umn.edu/SWFM/Files/estate/planning_principles.pdf.

Farm Biz Software. Specialized Data Systems, Inc. 2002. Contact: Specialized Data Systems, P.O. Box 346, Parsons, KS 67357, phone: (800) 438-7371, online: www.farmbiz.com, e-mail: info@farmbiz.com.

Financial Guidelines for Agricultural Producers: Recommendations of the Farm Financial Standards Council (FFSC). 1995 (revised). Contact the FFSC, 1212 S. Naper Boulevard, Suite 119, Naperville, IL 60540, phone: (630) 637-0199, on-line: www.ffsc.org.

Financial Management in Agriculture. Peter J. Barry, Paul N. Ellinger, John A. Hopkin and C.B. Baker. Prentice Hall. 7th edition, 2002. Contact your local library or bookstore.

Financing the Farm Operation. Phillip L. Kunkel and Scott T. Larison. University of Minnesota Extension Service. 2002. Publication number FS-02589. Contact the University of Minnesota Extension Service, 405 Coffey Hall, 1420 Eckles Ave., St. Paul, MN 55108-6068, phone: (800) 876-8636, e-mail: order@extension.umn.edu.

FINBIN. A searchable on-line database providing benchmark whole-farm and enterprise financial information from thousands of Minnesota and North Dakota farmers who use FINPACK for farm business analysis. Contact the Center for Farm Financial Management, 130 Classroom Office Building, 1994 Buford Avenue, St. Paul, MN 55108, phone: (612) 625-

1964 or toll-free (800) 234-1111, on-line: www.cffm.umn.edu, e-mail: cffm@umn.edu, on-line: www.agrisk.umn.edu/GettingStarted.asp.

FINPACK Software. Center for Farm Financial Management. Updated annually. Contact CFFM, 130 Classroom Office Building, 1994 Buford Avenue, St. Paul, MN 55108, phone: (612) 625-1964 or toll-free (800) 234-1111, on-line: www.cffm.umn.edu, e-mail: cffm@umn.edu.

Fixed and Flexible Cash Rental Arrangements for Your Farm. Midwest Plan Services, Iowa State University, Ames, IA. 1997. Publication number: NCR-75. Contact Midwest Plan Services, 122 Davidson Hall, Iowa State University, Ames, IA 50011-3080, phone: (800) 562-3618, on-line: www.mwpshq.org.

Holistic Management Financial Planning Software. Allan Savory Center. 2000. Contact the Allan Savory Center for Holistic Management, 1010 Tijeras NW, Albuquerque, NM 87102, phone: (505) 842-5252, on-line: www.holisticmanagement.org, e-mail: savorycenter@holisticmanagement.org.

Income Tax Management for Farmers. Midwest Plan Services, Iowa State University, Ames, IA. Revised 2002. Publication number: NCR-2. Contact Midwest Plan Services, 122 Davidson Hall, Iowa State University, Ames, IA 50011-3080, phone: (800) 562-3618, on-line: www.mwpshq.org, e-mail: mwps@iastate.edu.

In the Eyes of the Law: Legal Issues Associated with Direct Farm Marketing. Richard F. Prim and Kaarin K. Foede. University of Minnesota Extension Service. 2002. Product number: BU-07683. Contact the University of Minnesota Extension Service, 405 Coffey Hall, 1420 Eckles Ave., St. Paul, MN 55108-6068, phone: (800) 876-8636, e-mail: order@extension.umn.edu.

Managing Risk in Farming: Concepts, Research and Analysis. Joy Harwood, Richard Heifner, Keigh Coble, Janet Perry, and Agapi Somwaru. Market and Trade Economics Division and Resource Economics Division, Economic Research Service, USDA. 1999. Report number AER 774. Contact the USDA Order Desk, 5285 Port Royal Road, Springfield, VA 22161, phone: (800) 999-6779, web version: www.ers.usda.gov/publications/AER774/index.htm.

Monitoring Sustainable Agriculture with Conventional Financial Data. Dick Levins. Land Stewardship Project (LSP). 1996. Contact LSP, 2200 4th St., White Bear Lake, MN 55110, phone: (651) 653-0618, on-line: www.landstewardshipproject.org.

Mortgages and Contracts for Deed. Phillip L. Kunkel and Scott T. Larson. University of Minnesota Extension Service. 2002. University of Minnesota Extension, 405 Coffey Hall, 1420 Eckles Ave., St. Paul, MN 55108-6068, phone: (800) 876-8636, e-mail: order@extension.umn.edu

Pasture Rental Arrangements for Your Farm. Midwest Plan Services, Iowa State University, Ames, IA. 1997. Publication number: NCR-149. Contact Midwest Plan Services, 122 Davidson Hall, Iowa State University, Ames, IA 50011-3080, phone: (800) 562-3618, on-line: www.mwpshq.org, e-mail: mwps@iastate.edu.

Planning the Financial/Organizational Structure of Farm and Agribusiness Firms: What Are the Options? Michael Boehlje and David Lins. Midwest Plan Services. 1998 (revised). Publication number: NCR-568. Contact Midwest Plan Services, 122 Davidson Hall, Iowa State University, Ames, IA 50011-3080, phone: (800) 562-3618 on-line: www.mwpshq.org, e-mail: mwps@iastate.edu.

Profitable Organic Farming. Jon Newton. Iowa State Press. Second edition 2002. Contact Iowa State Press, PO Box 570, Ames, IA 50010-0570, phone: (800) 862-6657, www.isupress.com.

Projected Cash Flow Statement. Freddie L. Barnard. Department of Agricultural Economics, Purdue University. 1986. Publication number: EC-616. Contact Purdue University Cooperative Extension, 1140 Ag. Administration Bldg., West Lafayette, IN 47907, phone: (765) 494-8499, on-line: www.ces.purdue.edu/anr.

Quicken Software for Farm/Ranch Financial Records, annual updates, Oklahoma State University. Contact Oklahoma State University, Agriculture Economics Department, Attn: Damona Doye, 529 Ag Hall, Oklahoma State University, Stillwater, OK 74078, phone: (405) 744-9813, on-line: agecon.okstate.edu/quicken/instructions.html, e-mail: ddoye@okstate.edu.

Selling or Storing Grain in Minnesota: How Do the Laws Affect Me? Minnesota Department of Agriculture. Contact James Johnson, Agricultural Marketing Services Division, Minnesota Department of Agriculture, 90 West Plato Boulevard, Saint Paul, MN 55107, phone: (651) 297-2314, e-mail: james.m.johnson@state.mn.us, www.mda.state.mn.us, web version: www.mda.state.mn.us/grain/grainfaq.htm.

Tax Planning When Buying or Selling A Farm. Midwest Plan Services, Iowa State University, Ames, IA. 1997. Publication number: NCR-43. Contact Midwest Plan Services, 122 Davidson Hall, Iowa State University, Ames, IA 50011-3080, phone: (800) 562-3618, on-line: www.mwpshq.org mwps@iastate.edu.

Transferring Your Farm Business to the Next Generation. Jim Polson, Robert Fleming, Bernard Erven, and Warren Lee. Ohio State University Extension. 1996.

Bulletin number: 862. Contact Ohio State University Extension, 385 Kottman Hall, 2021 Coffey Rd., Columbus, OH 43210-1044, phone: (614) 292-1607, e-mail: pubs@postoffice.ag.ohio-state.edu.

Agencies, Organizations and Networks

Center for Farm Financial Management. Develops educational tools and software for farmers, agricultural lenders and educators that apply the principles and concepts of farm planning, financing, and analysis in a practical manner. Contact CFFM, 130 Classroom Office Building, 1994 Buford Avenue, St. Paul, MN 55108, phone: (612) 625-1964 or toll-free (800) 234-1111, on-line: www.cffm.umn.edu, e-mail: cffm@umn.edu.

Farm Business Management, Education Programs. Courses and individual instruction/consultation about long-range financial monitoring and planning. Contact Farm Business Management Education Programs, State Director John Murray, Rochester Community and Technical College, 851 30th Ave. SE, Rochester, MN 55904-3109, phone: (507) 280-3109, on-line: www.mgt.org/fbm.

Farm Credit Services. A network of independently owned and operated credit and financial services institutions that serve farmers, ranchers, agribusinesses of every size and income range across the country. To find local institutions, visit on-line at: www.farmcredit.com/.

Farm Service Agency. Offers resources and assistance in stabilizing farm income, helping farmers conserve land and water resources, providing credit to new or disadvantaged farmers and ranchers, and helping farm operations recover from the effects of disaster. For local offices, visit on-line at: www.fsa.usda.gov.

Great Lakes Grazing Network (GLGN). A coalition of farmers, researchers, extensionists, resource agency staff, environmentalists, and others organized to support and promote managed grazing systems for livestock production. Coordinates grazing-based activities, shares research, education, training, policy, and outreach efforts, and develops policies supportive of grazing-based farming systems within the Great Lakes region. For more information, visit GLGN on-line at: www.glgn.org/ or contact Tom Kriegl, University of Wisconsin, Center for Dairy Profitability, University of Wisconsin-Madison/Extension, 1675 Observatory Drive, Madison, Wisconsin 53706, phone: (608) 263-5665, e-mail: tskriegl@facstaff.wisc.edu.

Minnesota Certified Risk Management Consultants. Listing of risk management consultants by county. Contact the Minnesota Department of Agriculture, 90 West Plato Boulevard, Saint Paul, MN 55107, phone: (651) 297-1629, on-line: www.mda.state.mn.us.

Minnesota Department of Agriculture Sustainable Agriculture Loan Program. Loan program enabling farmers to adopt practices that will lead them to a more sustainable farming system. Loans given for capital purchases, which enhance the environmental and economic viability of the farm. For more information, contact Wayne Monsen, Grant and Loan Program Coordinator at (651) 282-2261 or the Sustainable Agriculture Loan Program, Minnesota Department of Agriculture, 90 West Plato Boulevard, St. Paul, MN 55107, phone: (651) 297-1629, on-line: www.mda.state.mn.us.

National Agricultural Risk Management Education Library. USDA initiative that helps farmers locate information, tools, and assistance on risk management-related topics. View the National Agricultural Risk Management Education Library on-line at: www.agrisk.umn.edu.

North American Farmers' Direct Marketing Association (NAFDMA). Organizes conferences, international farm tours, newsletters, and workshops about the profitability of direct marketing. Contact NAFDMA, 62 White Loaf Rd., Southampton, MA 01073, phone: (888) 884-9270, on-line: www.nafdma.com.

Rural Finance Authority (RFA). Provides low-interest financing for beginning farmers. Loan Comparison chart describing interest rates, loan amounts, and applicant requirements available from the Minnesota Department of Agriculure, 90 West Plato Boulevard, St. Paul, MN 55107, phone: (651) 297-1629, on-line: www.mda.state.mn.us, or contact Gary Blahosky, Senior Loan Officer, phone: (651) 296-4985, e-mail: gary.blahosky@state.mn.us.

Resources

Glossary

'he following glossary is a partial listing of terms used in he Business Planning Guide. Definitions for the glossary erms were drawn from a number of sources including: *Business Plan: A State of the Art Guide, FINPACK Manual, OCIA International's 2001 International Certification Standards, Marketing Dictionary, A Guide to Starting a Business in Minnesota,* and *USDA 2000 Fact Book*.

Account receivable: a current asset representing money due for services performed or merchandise sold on credit.

Accrual accounting: revenue and expenses are recorded in the period in which they are earned or incurred regardless of whether cash is received or disbursed in that period. This is the accounting basis that is generally required to be used to conform with generally accepted accounting principles (GAAP) in preparing financial statements for external users.

Advertising: how businesses inform and persuade potential and current customers using paid announcements carried by mass media such as newspapers, magazines, television and radio stations, and internet web sites.

Advertising reach: number of individuals or households exposed to an ad.

Asset: anything owned by an individual or a business, that has commercial or exchange value. Assets may consist of specific property or claims against others, in contrast to obligations due others.

Audit trail: a comprehensive system of documentation that verifies the integrity of organic products and ingredients from production through harvest, storage, transport, processing, handling and sales.

Balance sheet: an itemized list of assets and liabilities for the business to portray its net worth at a given moment in time—usually at the beginning of each year.

Break-even point: the volume point at which revenues and costs are equal; a combination of sales and costs that will yield a no profit/no loss operation.

Budget: an itemized list of all estimated revenue that a given business anticipates receiving along with a list of all estimated costs and expenses that will be incurred in obtaining the above mentioned income during a given period of time. A budget is typically for one business cycle, such as a year, or for several cycles.

Business continuation agreement: a written contract between the business' buyer and seller that describes how the business transfer will take place. This is also called a "buy/sell agreement."

Business plan: a written plan used to chart a new or ongoing business' strategies, sales projections, and key personnel in order to obtain financing or to provide a strategic foundation on which a business can grow.

Capital: the total amount of money or other resources owned or used to acquire future income or benefits.

Cash accounting: an accounting basis in which revenue and expenses are recorded in the period they are actually received or expended in cash. Use of the cash basis generally is not considered to be in conformity with generally accepted accounting principles (GAAP) and is therefore used only in selected situations, such as for very small businesses and (when permitted) for income tax reporting.

Cash flow statement: measures the business' ability to meet its obligations with internally generated cash.

Certification: a process used to ensure that each producer or handler of organic food or fiber meets industry certification standards for production, processing and handling.

Certification agent: any company, organization or government body that offers the service of organic certification.

Collaborative marketing group (CMG): a group of farmers who have agreed to work together over an extended period of time to collectively market the agricultural products they produce. A cooperative is the most common type of a CMG.

Common stock: the most frequently issued class of stock; usually it provides a voting right but is secondary to preferred stock in dividend and liquidation rights.

Competition: the contest between businesses for customers and sales.

Community Supported Agriculture (CSA): CSA organizations are similar to a cooperative in that you produce for members. CSA members purchase annual shares of production at the beginning of the year or season. In return, they receive weekly or bi-monthly deliveries of fruits, vegetables and/or livestock products.

Consumer good: products that are produced and sold to the final consumer.

Cooperative: an organization formed for the purpose of producing and marketing goods or products owned collectively by members who share in the benefits.

Corporation: a separate legal entity that is owned by one or more shareholders.

Crop rotation: the practice of alternating the species or families of annual or biennial crops grown on specific fields in a planned pattern or sequence so as to break weed, pest and disease cycles, and improve soil fertility and organic matter content.

Current assets: the cash and other assets that will be received, converted to cash, or consumed in production during the next 12 months. This generally includes cash and checking balances, crops held for sale or feed, livestock held for sale, prepaid expenses and supplies, the value of growing crops, accounts receivable, hedging account balances, and any other assets that can quickly be turned into cash.

Current liabilities: debts due and payable within one year from the date of the balance sheet. In addition to short term operating loans, this usually includes accounts payable, accrued interest and other accrued expenses, and government crop loans. By definition, the amount of principal due within 12 months on intermediate and long-term debts is also considered a current liability.

Custom work: specific farm operations performed under contract between a farmer and contractor. The contractor furnishes labor, equipment, and materials to perform the operation. Custom harvesting of grain, spraying and picking of fruit, and sheep shearing are examples of custom work.

Demographics: customer groups based on age, sex, race, religion, education, marital status, income and household size.

Depreciation: prorating the cost of a depreciable asset over its projected economic life to account for any decline in the asset's production value over time. Depreciation charges, in effect, reflect the funds that need to be set aside in order to replace the depreciating asset.

Direct marketing: marketing directly to customers without involving retailers, wholesalers, agents or other intermediaries; the easiest, fastest and least expensive contact with your business' target market.

Distribution: moving a product or service from producer to customer; taking orders, packing, inventory management, storage, transportation and follow-up service.

Earned net worth change: represents income that either contributed to or depleted the farm's net worth. The earned net worth change is calculated by adding nonfarm income to net farm income and then subtracting family living expenses, partner withdrawals, and taxes.

Equity: represents ownership or percentage of ownership in a business or items of value.

Expenses: daily costs incurred in running and maintaining a business.

Export broker: an entity that brings together foreign buyers with domestic manufacturers for a fee, generally providing few other services.

Export license: a government-issued legal permit to export merchandise.

Farm: As of 1997, the USDA defines a farm as any place from which $1,000 or more of agricultural products were produced and sold, or normally would have been sold during the year.

Farm Credit System (FCS): a system made up of cooperatively owned financial institutions in districts covering the United States and Puerto Rico that finance farm and farm-related mortgages and operating loans. Institutions within each district specialize in farmland loans and operating credit or lending to farmer-owned supply, marketing, and processing cooperatives. FCS institutions rely on the bond market as a source of funds.

Family farm: an agricultural business that (1) produces agricultural commodities for sale in such quantities so as to be recognized as a farm rather than a rural residence; (2) produces enough income (including off farm employment) to pay family and farm operating expenses, to pay debts, and to maintain the property; (3) is managed by the operator; (4) has a substantial amount of labor provided by the operator and family; and (5) may use seasonal labor during peak periods and a reasonable amount of full-time hired labor.

Financial feasibility: the ability of a business plan or investment to satisfy the financing terms and performance criteria agreed to by a borrower and a lender.

inancial risk: the risk associated with the use of orrowing and leasing; uncertainties about the ability to neet financial obligations.

iscal year: an accounting period of 12 months.

ixed costs: operating expenses that generally do not ary with business volume. Examples include rent, roperty taxes, and interest expense.

orage: vegetable matter, fresh or preserved, that is athered and fed to animals as roughage; includes alfalfa ay, corn silage, and other hay crops.

orward contracting: a method of selling crops before arvest by which the buyer agrees to pay a specified price o a grower for a portion (or all) of the grower's crops.

utures contract: an agreement between two entities, ne that sells and agrees to deliver and one that buys and grees to receive, a certain kind, quality, and quantity of roduct to be delivered during a specified delivery month t a specified price.

eneral partnership: one or more partners are jointly esponsible or liable for the debts of the partnership.

reen manure: a crop that is grown and then plowed into he soil or left to decompose for the purpose of soil mprovement.

rowth potential: the increased amount of money, xpansion, activity and other developments that are likely or a business based on product marketing, management kill, industry growth and other factors.

andler: any person engaged in the business of handling gricultural products.

dentity preserved product: a product that meets roduction, packaging, storage, and transportation equirements designed to preserve the genetic or physical dentity of the product.

mage advertising: an advertising strategy that builds wareness and interest in products through the use of a ame, term, sign, symbol, design or some combination. A rand and logo is used to identify the products of a usiness and distinguish them from competitors.

nspector: a person independent from the decision-naking process who is accredited to perform inspections or certification agents.

ntermediary: a business that helps buy, sell, assemble, tore, display and promote products; they help move roducts through the distribution channel. Intermediaries nclude retailers, wholesalers, distributors, brokers and ooperatives.

Intermediate assets: assets with a useful life of ten years or less, such as breeding livestock, machinery and equipment.

Intermediate liabilities: intermediate (five to seven years) debt obligations for loans on equipment, machinery, and breeding livestock.

Invoice: an itemized list of goods shipped, usually specifying the price and terms of sale.

Labeling: any written, printed, or graphic representation that is present on the label of a product, accompanies the product, or is displayed near the product at its point of sale.

Land: in accounting terms is the value of real estate minus the value of improvements, such as buildings.

Liability: a loan, expense or any other form of claim on the assets of a business that must be paid or otherwise honored by the business.

Liquidity: a business' ability to meet current obligations with cash or other assets that can be quickly converted to cash.

Long-term assets: assets with a useful life of more than ten years, such as farm land and buildings.

Long-term liabilities: long-term (eight years or more) debt obligations for buildings and equipment.

Market identity: the ability to create familiarity and loyalty for a product or business in the eyes of the customer through promotions, packaging, labeling, product name and other factors.

Marketing: the process through which a business creates and keeps customers.

Market niche: a particular appeal, identity or place in the market that a product or business has; what a business does well that is different or better than other competitors in the market.

Market segmentation: the separation of one large market into smaller markets or categories; by product, customer, geography or industry.

Market share: the percent of the target market that a business hopes to capture.

Market trends: factors that indicate where the market is headed; changes in customer needs or preferences, shifts in population, establishment of new industries in the area.

Natural: a substance derived from plant, animal or mineral source that has not undergone a synthetic process.

Net farm income: represents the returns to labor, management and equity capital invested in the business; what the farm will contribute to net worth growth over time. See Appendix B for net farm income calculation.

Net worth: the financial claim by owners on the total assets of a business, calculated as total assets minus total liabilities. Also called equity capital and owner's equity.

Off-farm income: wages and salaries from working for other farmers, plus nonfarm income, for all owner operator families (whether they live on a farm or not).

Operating expenses: the outlays incurred or paid by a business for all inputs purchased or hired that are used up in production during the accounting period.

Operating loan: a short-term loan (less than one year) to finance crop production, livestock production, inventories, accounts receivable, and other operating or short-term liquidity needs of a business.

Operations structure: pertains to the competitiveness, size, organization, production and resource management of the farm business.

Organic agriculture: a holistic production management system which promotes and enhances agro-ecosystem health, including biodiversity, biological cycles, and soil biological activity; emphasizes the use of management practices over the use of off-farm inputs and utilizes cultural, biological and mechanical methods as opposed to synthetic materials.

Organic conversion: the act of establishing organic management practices in accordance with industry standards.

Organic conversion period: the time between the start of organic management and certification of the crop or livestock production system or site as organic (also called transition period).

Packer: a type of handler, such as a produce packing operation, that receives raw agricultural products and packs the products for shipping. A produce packer may also store products and apply post-harvest materials. A meat packer converts live animals to carcass meats and possibly to primal cut or boxed meat and other fresh meat forms.

Partnership: an association of two or more persons to carry on, as co-owners, a business for profit.

Pasture: land used for grazing of livestock that is under management measures designed to maximize soil fertility, provide feed value, protect the environment from degradation, and support range land health.

Positioning: an action taken by a business to fill a meaningful and unique niche in the market.

Principal amount: the face-value of a loan that must be repaid at maturity, separate from interest.

Processing: cooking, baking, heating, drying, mixing, grinding, churning, separating, extracting, cutting, fermenting, slaughtering, eviscerating, preserving, dehydrating, freezing, dyeing, sewing, or otherwise manufacturing and packaging, including canning, and jarring, that is different from normal post-harvest packaging of crops.

Product: any commodity, finished consumer good, or service produced by the farm.

Product advertising: aims to increase sales directly and immediately for an advertised product.

Profitability: the relative profit performance of a business, enterprise, or other operating unit. Profitability comparisons occur over time, across peer groups, relative to projections, and relative to norms or standards.

Promotion: a marketing activity that aims to increase sales through specific product, image or total approach advertising. See product advertising, image advertising, total approach advertising.

Proprietorship: an unincorporated business owned and operated by a single individual.

Psychographics: customers' lifestyle characteristics, behavioral patterns, beliefs and values, attitudes about themselves, their families and society.

Rate of return on assets (ROA): the profitability measure representing the rate-of-return on business assets during an accounting period. ROA is calculated by dividing the dollar return to assets during the accounting period by the value of assets at the beginning of the period or the average value of assets over the period.

Rate of return on equity (ROE): the profitability measure representing the rate-of-return on the equity capital that owners have invested in a business. ROE is calculated by dividing the dollar return to equity capital during an accounting period by the value of equity capital at the beginning of the period or the average value of equity capital over the period.

Records: field maps, field logs, journals, calendars, harvest, storage and sales information, animal health reports, receipts, invoices, billing statements, bills of lading, inventory control reports, production reports, facility diagrams, process flow charts, questionnaires, affidavits, inspection reports, laboratory analysis reports, meeting minutes, personnel files, correspondence, photographs, and other materials. Records that pertain to organic certification include any information in written, visual, or electronic form that documents that the activities undertaken by producers, processors, handlers, inspectors, and certification agents comply with organic standards.

Repayment ability: the anticipated ability of a borrower to generate sufficient cash to repay a loan plus interest according to the terms established in the loan contract.

Retailer: a business intermediary, such as a grocery store, that may provide storage, logistical support, and advertising.

Retained earnings: the portion of net income that is retained within a business and added to net worth.

Risk: the possibility of adversity or loss; refers to uncertainty that matters.

S-Corporation: a type of corporation in which the owner holds 100 percent of the shares.

Segmentation: grouping customers into segments or subgroups that share distinct similarities. Marketers commonly segment by geographics, demographics, and psychographics.

Shipper: a handler that is located at growing or other shipping points. A shipper sells products that it has grown or packed under its own name. A shipper may sell on behalf of growers or other shippers.

Sole proprietorship: a business that is owned and controlled by one individual.

Solvency: the business condition of financial viability in which net worth is positive; value of total assets exceeds debts

Split operation: an operation that produces or handles nonorganic agricultural products in addition to agricultural products produced organically.

Standard of living: the measure of the quality of life in such areas as housing, food, education, clothing, and transportation.

Statement of cash flows: a financial statement presenting the cash receipts and cash payments over a specified period of time. The cash receipts and payments are separated into operating, investing, and financing activities.

Sustainable agriculture: an integrated system of plant and animal production practices having a site-specific application that will, over the long term, satisfy food and fiber needs, enhance environmental quality and natural resources, make the most efficient use of nonrenewable resources and on-farm resources, integrate natural biological cycles and controls, sustain the economic viability of farm operations, and enhance the quality of life.

Synthetic: a substance that is formulated or manufactured by a chemical process or by a process that chemically changes a substance extracted from naturally occurring plant, animal, or mineral sources, except for those substances created by naturally occurring biological processes.

Target market: particular segment(s) of the market that the product is directed toward; the initial customers that you hope to win over.

Total approach advertising: combines both image and product promotion strategies.

Transition period: the time between the start of organic management and certification of the crop or livestock production system or site as organic (also called organic conversion period).

Value-added: creating new uses for or additional value to raw agricultural commodities through marketing, processing, and production.

Vegetative cover: trees or perennial grasses, legumes, or shrubs with an expected lifespan of five years or more.

Warehouser: an operator who receives and stores products, does not take legal title to the products, and does not open product containers, or mix, combine, or otherwise handle the products while in custody.

Watershed: the total land area, regardless of size, above a given point on a waterway that contributes runoff water to the flow at that point. A major subdivision of a drainage basin. The United States is generally divided into 18 major drainage areas and 160 principal river drainage basins containing some 12,700 smaller watersheds.

Wetlands: land that is characterized by an abundance of moisture and that is inundated by surface or ground water often enough to support a prevalence of vegetation typically adapted for life in saturated soil conditions.

Wholesaler: a business intermediary who either buys products or takes possession and acts as a commission merchant.

Glossary

Appendices

Appendix A: Business Plan, Cedar Summit Farm

Appendix B: Farm Financial Standards Council Business Performance Measures (Sweet Sixteen)

Appendix C: Sample Job Description

Appendix D: Direct Labor Requirements for Traditional Crop and Livestock Enterprises

Appendices

Appendix A

Business Plan
Cedar Summit Farm

25816 Drexel Ave.

New Prague, MN 56071

Owners-Dave and Florence Minar

October 2, 2000

Executive Summary

Cedar Summit Farm will build a milk processing plant as a natural extension of our dairy business. We are located just north of New Prague and within 25 miles of the Minneapolis-St. Paul area including the suburbs of Edina, Minnetonka, Eden Prairie, Burnsville and Apple Valley. By capturing more of the consumer dollar, we can afford to bring our farm-oriented children into the business. We feel that our grass-fed cows produce a superior product that has much value to the health conscious. We value producer to consumer relationships. The past few years that we have direct marketed our meat products have shown us that consumers value knowing where their food comes from. This past spring we sent out 450 brochures to past customers.

We will distribute our products from delivery trucks and a storefront with a drive-up window that will be part of our processing plant. Our distribution will be home delivery, drop off sites at churches, co-op food stores and restaurants that cater to locally produced food. The plant and store will be located near the intersection of Scott Co. roads 2 and 15. Within 5 years we plan to have all of the milk we produce sold as Cedar Summit dairy products. We plan to process 15% of our milk production the first year, and we will need to borrow about $xxx,xxx (numbers excluded for confidentiality reasons) for buildings and equipment, and an additional $xxx,xxx for operating expenses. But our business will be profitable in the third year. All our milk will be processed at Cedar Summit Farm by the fifth year and we will turn a profit, after wages are paid, of $xxx,xxx.

We have children with many abilities and envision this business as a future for them and their families, and as a valued asset to our community.

Values

- Our most important value is health. Healthy people, healthy animals and a healthy environment make all endeavors possible.
- Extol Christian values in our relationship with our family, customers and neighbors.
- Strive for open, trusting communication with family, employees and customers.
- Because our health is directly tied to the health of the environment, we strive to produce healthy dairy and meat products by utilizing sustainable methods in their production.
- We value preserving our forests and grasslands for future generations to enjoy.
- It is important to be a contributing member of the community both socially and economically; our community values the esthetic beauty of seeing farm animals on the land.

Mission Statement

Cedar Summit Farm will provide clean, healthy, locally grown and safe meat and dairy products to our local community and within the 25-mile surrounding area. Our animals will be raised humanely in an environmentally sound manner. We will strive to educate consumers about the health benefits of grass-fed meat and milk products. We hope to be a model for other farmers that are looking for a way to be more profitable and sustainable.

Farm History

My Grandfather purchased what is now Cedar Summit Farm in 1935. When my parents married in 1938, they moved onto the farm. I was born and raised there.

Florence and I met at the University of Minnesota where we were both students. I graduated in 1963 with a B.S. in Agricultural Economics & Dairy Science, and in 1964 we were married. I farmed with my father after service in the U.S. Army and in 1966 accepted a position with Minnesota Valley Breeders as an Artificial Insemination Technician. Our family grew fast—Lisa was born in 1965, Chris in 1966, and Mike in 1967.

In 1969 we made the decision to return to the farm full-time. Having been raised there, I knew what we were getting into. I was the only son and felt an obligation to return to what my Grandfather started.

We built a new sixty-cow tie stall barn in 1971. Over the years we developed a registered Holstein herd that has received state and national recognition. We showed our animals at many shows and fairs.

The farm was originally 120 acres. We purchased an additional 80 acres in 1972, and another 18 acres more recently. We lease an additional 65 acres that adjoin our property. We also own a 160-acre farm at McGrath, MN that consists of 90 acres of improved pasture for young stock.

In 1974 we discontinued the use of pesticides, and started exploring alternative ways to combat pests. We knew it could be done, because it had been done in the past.

In 1977 we started our second family when Laura was born. Dan was to follow in 1980. In this time period more changes were made in our family. My father, who was my main source of help, died in 1979. Chris and Mike, who were 13 and 12, were now my main source of labor. We managed to get the work done with the help of Dan Kajer, a part-time helper, and still allow them time for sports and 4-H. In the mid-80's the older children graduated from high school and went to college. In 1986, our Dan was starting school and Florence found a full-time job in town. We hired Paul Kajer, Dan Kajer's younger brother who was still in school, to help. Paul stayed with us until 1991, when he left to start farming on his own. Laura and our Dan were old enough to help now, and we also hired John Nelson full-time.

By the late 1980's, we began to realize that we weren't making the progress that we should be making, and started asking ourselves some serious questions. Our debt load had remained static through the years because of equipment replacement costs and herd turnover. We were intrigued with the idea of improving animal health by allowing them to harvest their own feed for 7 months of the year. The idea, which we found exciting, was that all of our land, some of which adjoins Sand Creek, would be in permanent pasture grasses and thus would stop erosion. This would also improve the water and mineral cycles. We could see how it would improve our quality of life with less feed to harvest. We sold our milking herd and bred heifers in 1993, and started grazing with our young stock. This sale allowed us to pay off almost all of our loans. In 1994, we built a new milking parlor and started milking again.

Paul Kajer joined our operation again in 1997 and brought with him the nucleus of his herd. Paul is paid a percentage of the gross check with a bonus at the end of the year. He retains ownership of his herd and its growth.

We were told when we started grazing that there was a 7- year learning curve. This seems to be true, because after a few years of struggling, we were able to significantly reduce our debt load in 1999.

In 1994 we started a direct marketing retail meat business with pasture-raised chicken. We had some underutilized areas where we could raise chickens and the chickens we had been buying in the grocery store were becoming less and less appealing. We knew others felt the same way. We hired a marketing consultant to help us with a brochure and we raised 900 chickens. Our chickens sold out and we were on our way. This venture has evolved into a significant sideline. In 1998 Florence quit her job to help more at home. Over the past 5 years we have also included turkeys, hogs and steers.

It is a good feeling to be able to supply our community with high quality food and hope we can continue to do so in the future.

Current Situation

Cedar Summit Farm is managed as a partnership between Dave & Florence Minar and Paul Kajer. Paul is our herd manager and provides most of the labor for the dairy. Our son, Dan, relieves him on every other weekend and one night during the week. Dan is also going to college, studying marketing and business management. Josh, a high school student, also helps Paul milk on weekends. Dave needs to scale back his work in the dairy and devote more time to managing and marketing our direct market venture.

Our dairy has been the main source of revenue on our farm. During the 70's and 80's the farm usually sold about 1 million pounds of milk annually to a wholesale outlet. Last year the farm wholesaled 2 million pounds of milk (243,000 gallons) to a cheese factory. We have implemented a cross breeding program the past five years. We hope to develop a cow that is more compatible with our new grazing management, and will produce higher component milk that will meet our future needs. The farm dairy enterprise's return over direct expenses in 1999 was $xxx,xxx.

We currently raise 1500-2000 broilers in a free-range environment. These chickens are processed at an inspected facility and made available fresh to the public three times each summer. Frozen birds are available for sale, by appointment, until sold out. We are licensed food vendors through the Minnesota Department of Agriculture. Cedar Summit Farm works with the Minnesota Food Association's Community Food Project. We, along with several other poultry producers in our area, provide chickens for residents of low income housing units. Fresh turkeys for Thanksgiving have been a popular fall item. We have them processed for fresh pickup the day before Thanksgiving. There are already twenty people on the waiting list for Thanksgiving 2000. The poultry enterprise's return over direct expenses in 1999 was $x,xxx.

Our 50 hogs are raised outside in the fresh air and sunshine. This year they will be processed at a state inspected facility. They will be sold in "Quarter Packs". A quarter pack will equal one-quarter hog. These packs will contain fresh pork as well as ham and some sausage. The hog enterprise's return over direct expenses in 1999 was $xx,xxx.

Our popular "Beef Gourmet Packs" are the mainstay of our (steer) beef sales. The 30-pound burger packs are also a very good seller. Most of our burger comes from low-milk producing cows. We keep about 30% of our bull calves to raise for steers, this can be increased to keep up with sales.

We started the meat business because we didn't like supermarket chickens and thought others felt the same way. Cedar Summit Farm is located in Helena Township of Scott County, at the very southern edge of the Minneapolis-St. Paul Metro area. Our area of Helena Township is zoned for 10-acre lots. Many farms have been further subdivided into smaller lots, turning our area into a more urban-like setting. Our customers are moving in around us! Our targeted market is people who have experienced eating home-raised meat products, families with small children, and the health conscious.

Our main marketing strategy has been to publish a brochure every March, which includes order cards for all our products. Our daughter Lisa helps us, and we mailed 450 brochures this year to our customers of the past three years. We use newspaper ads, attend food and community expos, are licensed "Minnesota Grown" producers, and are listed in all of their publications. We have found that word of mouth is our best advertising. One marketing strategy that didn't work was putting signs in the metro area, as it netted us nothing.

Our marketing emphasis has been the production and sale of non-confined, grass-fed meat products, produced without the use of hormones or antibiotics. We prefer that our customers come to the farm to pick up their meat products. Our brochure states; "Many consumers are generations removed from farming and have no clear idea where their food is grown. You can be an important link in the effort to create a food system in which consumers have a real connection to the farm. Every one has their own doctor, dentist and banker. The Minars at Cedar Summit Farm want to be your farmer."

We have made an effort to keep a good relationship with our bank. We bring a budget and operating statement to our banker early in the year. The competition among our local banks for our business has allowed us to borrow money at a very low interest rate.

Our net farm income in 1999 was $xxx,xxx. The rate of return on farm assets was 14% and the rate of return on farm equity was 24.6%.

Vision

The future looks bright! Cedar Summit Farm is still a diversified livestock enterprise after ten years. We have listened to our customers and have adjusted our product line to suit their needs. All of our products are sold at our farm store, farmers' markets, CSAs, church drop-off spots, food co-ops or delivered to homes and restaurants within a 25-mile radius of the farm. Included in our product line are a large variety of dairy and meat products. The customer base at Cedar Summit Farm has grown to the point that we must ally with neighboring sustainable producers. The fact that the farm is almost totally surrounded by homes has played a part in this growth.

Goals

Our goal is to build a small milk processing plant and retail center, with a drive-up window, on our farm. This building will be built on our property near the intersection of Scott Co. roads 2 and 15. We must obtain a conditional use permit and secure financing. A brochure detailing our proposed milk processing plant and retail center will be published by June 1, 2000. This will be for county and township officials and neighbors informing them of our plans. Cedar Summit Farm will process and retail all of our dairy products to local customers (25-mile radius) within 5 years, and continue to expand our local meat business.

Cedar Summit Farm will provide full or part-time employment to any family member who desires to work in the family business. It is our desire to provide educational opportunities and benefits such as health insurance and a 401K plan.

We will market products that we feel good about, and distribute them locally when possible. Excess product will be donated to food shelves. We will package and market our products in the most economical and environmentally sound way possible.

Cedar Summit Farm will produce extra value products that will enhance the local economy, purchase supplies locally as much as possible, and take pride in a superior product.

Marketing

The marketing book *The Long Boom* by Schwartz, Leyden and Hyatt, says that people like the power that choice gives them. The more standardized and homogenized our food becomes, the more it makes us crave the unusual and non-commonplace. They also say that 10 percent of the market would be made up of people seeking a radically different product. Our grass-fed cows do produce a different product. Grass-fed cows produce higher amounts of Omega-3 and conjugated linoleic acid in their meat and milk then grain-fed cows. These two fatty acids fight cancer, promote lean muscle mass in humans, and have many other health benefits. In the Minneapolis-St. Paul Metro area, 10 percent equates to 200,000 potential customers. Many customers come to our farm and tell us they are so glad that we are here; we get many new customers each year by word of mouth. There is enthusiasm for consumer to producer relationships; people are passionate to know where their food comes from. In order to bring families to our farm we have an open house in the spring; we are looking at having a tour each fall.

Our target market is upper middle class families with young children, people who have experienced eating home-raised meat products, the health conscious, and fine restaurants. We will be marketing a wide range of high-quality dairy products, priced between organic and supermarket prices.

These will be distributed in a small, used, repainted refrigerated van. We will continue the use of professional looking promotional material to add credibility to our endeavor. A customer marketing brochure detailing our prices and products will be ready by Sept.1, 2000 when we are ready to start our home delivery canvassing.

Distribution

Along with our retail center and drive-up, we will establish home delivery routes, drop off sites at churches, co-op food stores and restaurants. These will be established before production begins. Other distribution places will be farmers' markets.

Our retail center will be attached to the production facility with a glassed area to view processing. It will be open according to customer demand. There will also be an outside cooler for customers to access before and after hours, operated on the honor system. We will have a drive-up window so parents won't have to leave their car to buy milk and other products.

We will canvas neighborhoods before production begins to establish economically feasible delivery routes. We will begin with New Prague and surrounding area. People that show an interest outside our 25-mile radius will be asked to find drop sites at churches and other locations that have facilities for cold and frozen foods.

Upper end restaurants have shown interest in local and sustainably produced food. These businesses use large amounts of cream and butter. Co-op food stores have also shown an interest in our products.

Products

Fluid milk will be sold in gallons and half gallons as skim, 1%, 2%,and whole milk. Cream will be sold in pints, butter in 1-pound solid blocks and buttermilk in quarts. In the future we plan to make ice cream, yogurt and soft cheeses. We will have hard cheeses made for us from our milk until we can learn the art. Meat products that we sell now will be available also.

Competition

We know of no farmer in our area that is processing and selling his own dairy products. Our other sources of competition are grocery stores, Meyer Bros. Home Delivery and Schwans. Meyer Bros. buys milk and resells it, and Schwans will affect us only with ice cream. We have some local competition with our meat products, but we still sell out.

Human Resources

Paul Kajer is our herd manager and is in charge of milking and general welfare of the dairy herd. Paul was raised on a dairy farm near New Prague and grew up taking care of dairy animals. Paul worked for us during high school, and for a while after he graduated, until he started farming on his own. Paul, like most other young farmers, had a hard time starting on his own so he moved his herd in with ours in 1997 and became our herdsman.

Tammy Kajer (Paul's wife), will work in the processing plant, the store, do accounting and help with marketing.

Lisa White is our graphic designer. Lisa does our brochures and promotion material.

Bob White (Lisa's husband), is our artist and marketing advisor.

Chris Minar probably won't be involved in our venture. Chris is an Aeronautical/ Medical Engineer and head of his company's research and development department. We have used his engineering and management expertise.

Linda Minar (Chris' wife) has an associate degree in accounting. Linda will work in accounting, promotions and the store as her work permits.

Mike Minar will be our processing manager. Mike graduated with a degree in Fishery and Wildlife Management and Biology.

Merrisue Minar has a degree in business administration and is willing to manage home deliveries, work in the store, and help with accounting and promotions.

Laura Ganske will drive the delivery truck, help with processing, manage the store and work in marketing and promotions.

Eric Ganske (Laura's husband), is our computer guru. He will host the Web site and keep it updated, be our technical support and work in the store when his job allows.

Dan Minar is in business school right now taking business management and marketing. Dan will be the business manager in due time. He must learn the business from the ground up first. While he is in school he will be involved in building the plant, working in the plant and store, making deliveries, marketing and all other aspects of the business.

All of our children and their spouses have worked at one time on the farm, and therefore, have a working knowledge of farming.

Operations

Our dairy herd size will remain at about 150 cows, as this is all our land base will allow. We hope to start building construction by late summer and have it completed by Oct. 31, 2000. We will purchase used equipment for the plant if possible. We hope to have all the equipment installed by Dec. 15, 2001. We hope to begin milk processing by Dec. 30, 2001.

The milk will be hauled to the plant with a bulk tank trailer and pumped into a raw milk storage tank. It will then move to a batch pasteurizer and be pasteurized. Next it will be separated into skim milk and cream, and then some cream will be added back to make the assorted milk products. The rest of the cream will be made into ice cream and butter. The buttermilk from the butter will be mixed with chocolate or cultured and bottled as buttermilk. We plan to process three days a week.

Our retail store will be open according to our customers' demand. We will have a cooler outside with dairy products to be bought on the honor system, and we will have a drive-up window so parents will not have to leave their car.

We will purchase a refrigerated delivery truck by June 1, 2001. This will be used for meat and dairy product deliveries. Home delivery routes, drop-off sites, restaurants and food co-op schedules will be established by Dec. 1, 2001. Our billing system will be developed by Dec. 1, 2001.

We plan to build a kiosk and have it operational by the summer of 2002, for the sale of ice cream cones. This kiosk will travel to town celebrations and fairs as a moneymaker and an advertisement for our products. This would possibly be a good place for Dan to put his business schooling to use. Hopefully, it will be a place for our grandchildren to make some money in the summer, when they are older and learn to work together.

Financing

We plan to borrow money to build and equip our proposed milk processing plant and retail center. We also need operating capital to finance our operation for the first two years.

The Appendices to the Minars' Business Plan (Project Cost Budget, Five Year Cash Flow Plan, Financial Analysis of Current Operation: 1998-2000, Tax Statements from Current Operation: 1998-2000, and Resumes for Management Team Members) have not been included for confidentiality reasons.

Appendix B: Farm Financial Standards Council Business Performance Measures (Sweet Sixteen)

The following calculations and descriptions were adapted from the 2000 Farm Business Management Report for Central and West Central Minnesota.

Liquidity

Current Ratio: Calculated as (total current farm assets) / (total current farm liabilities). This measure of liquidity reflects the extent to which current farm assets, if sold tomorrow, would pay off current farm liabilities.

Working Capital: Calculated as (total current farm assets) – (total current farm liabilities). This measure represents the short-term operating capital available from within the business.

Solvency

Debt-to-Asset Ratio: Calculated as (total farm liabilities) / (total farm assets). This represents the bank's share of your business. A higher ratio is an indicator of greater financial risk and lower borrowing capacity.

Equity-to-Asset Ratio: Calculated as (farm net worth) / (total farm assets). This measure of solvency compares farm equity to total farm assets.

Debt-to-Equity Ratio: Calculated as (total farm liabilities) / (farm net worth). This measure compares the bank's ownership to your ownership of the business.

Profitability

Rate of Return on Assets: Calculated as [(net farm income) + (farm interest) – (value of operator labor and management)] / (average value of farm assets). This measure represents the average "interest" rate being earned on all investments in the business (your investment and that of your creditors).

Rate of Return on Equity: Calculated as [(net farm income) – (value of operator labor and management)] / (average farm net worth). This measure represents the "interest" rate being earned by your investment in the farm. This return can be compared to the return on your investments if equity were invested somewhere else, outside the business.

Operating Profit Margin: Calculated as (return on farm assets) / (value of farm production), where return on farm assets equals (net farm income from operation) + (farm interest expense) – (opportunity return to labor and management). This measure of

Appendices

profitability shows the operating efficiency of the business. Low expenses relative to the value of farm production result in a healthy operating profit margin.

Net Farm Income: Calculated as (gross cash farm revenue) – (total cash farm expense) + (inventory changes) + (depreciation and other capital adjustments, including gains/losses from the sale of capital assets). This measure represents profitability or the farm's return to labor, management and equity.

Repayment capacity

Term Debt Coverage Ratio: Calculated as [(net farm operating income) + (net nonfarm income) + (depreciation) + (scheduled interest on term debt and capital leases) – (family living and taxes paid)] / (scheduled principal and interest payments on term debt and capital leases). This measure of repayment capacity tells whether the business produced enough cash to cover all intermediate and long-term debt payments.

Capital Replacement Margin: Calculated as the value of (net farm income) + (net nonfarm income) + depreciation – (family living expenses, taxes paid, scheduled payments on term debt). This measure describes the amount of money left over after all operating expenses, taxes, family living costs, and scheduled debt payments have been made.

Efficiency

Asset Turnover Rate: Calculated as the (gross farm revenue) / (average farm assets). This measures the efficiency of using capital. A high level of production in proportion to the level of capital investment yields a high (or efficient) asset turnover rate.

Operating Expense Ratio: Calculated as the value of [(total farm operating expenses)–(depreciation) – (farm interest)] / (gross farm revenue). This measure reflects the proportion of farm revenues used to pay operating expenses, not including principal or interest.

Interest Expense Ratio: Calculated as (farm interest) / (gross farm revenue). This measure of financial efficiency shows how much of gross farm revenue is used to pay for borrowed capital.

Depreciation Expense Ratio: Calculated as (depreciation and other capital adjustments) / (gross farm revenue). This measure indicates what proportion of farm revenue is needed to maintain the capital used by your business.

Net Farm Income from Operations Ratio: Calculated as (net farm income from operations) / (gross farm revenue). This measure of financial efficiency compares profit to gross farm revenue. It shows how much is left after all farm expenses, except for the return to unpaid operator and family labor, management and capital, are paid.

Appendix C: Sample Job Description [1]

I. General

Business/farm name: ____________________

Address: ____________________

____________________ Phone: (   ) ____________

II. Position title: ____________________

Summary description of position: ____________________

____

III. Major duties, responsibilities, and authority:

____

____

____

____

IV. Minor/other duties:

____

____

V. Supervision necessary:

A. Amount: None ____ Minimal ____ Considerable ____ Close ____

B. Manager/Supervisor ____________________

VI. Normal work hours/overtime: ____________________

____

____

VII. Work environment: ____________________

____

____

VIII. Advancement/promotion possibilities: ____________________

____

____

IX. Qualifications required/desired:

	Required	Desired
1. Formal education/training:		
2. Work experience:		
3. Skills/knowledge:		
4. Personal characteristics:		
5. Physical attributes:		
6. Flexibility (time, task):		
7. Other:		

X. Wage rate:

Beginning: $__________ Per __________; Range ____________________

Bonus, incentive programs (if any): ____________________

____

XI. Benefits provided/housing: ____________________

____

____

XII. Provisions for time off/vacation/sick leave: ____________________

____

____

____

[1] This form excerpted with permission from: *Acquiring and Managing Resources for the Farm Business*. Part IV in the Six Part Series: *Business Management for Farmers*. Kenneth Thomas. Midwest Plan Service. February 2001. NCR-610D.

Appendix D: Direct Labor Requirements for Traditional Crop and Livestock Enterprises [2]

Enterprise		Unit	Annual Hours of Labor Per Unit		
			Average	High Mechanization	Low Mechanization
Corn, grain		1 acre	3.5	2.0	7.00
Soybeans		1 acre	3.5	2.0	7.0
Wheat		1 acre	1.5	0.7	4.5
Oats		1 acre	1.5	0.7	4.0
Corn silage		1 acre	6.0	3.0	20.0
Hay harvesting	0.5-1.2 tons/acre	1 ton	3.0	2.0	6.0
	Over 1.2 tons/acre	1 ton	2.0	1.0	4.0
Silage harvesting	1.0 -7.4 tons/cutting	1 ton	0.6	0.3	2.0
	Over 7.5 tons/cutting	1 ton	0.3	0.1	1.0
Dairy herd	10-24 cows	1 cow	115	90	140
	25-49 cows	1 cow	90	65	115
	50-99 cows	1 cow	75	55	100
Beef cow herd, calf sold	1-15 cows	1 cow	52	20	40
	15-39 cows	1 cow	15	12	25
	40-100 cows	1 cow	10	8	16
Beef cow herd, calf fed	1-15 cows	1 cow	40	30	60
	15-39 cows	1 cow	25	20	40
	40-100 cows	1 cow	20	15	30
Feeder cattle, long fed[3]	1-40 head	1 feeder	15	10	25
	40-119 head	1 feeder	10	7	17
	120-200 head	1 feeder	8	5	13
Feeder cattle, short fed[3]	1-40 head	1 feeder	10	8	18
	40-119 head	1 feeder	10	8	18
	120-200 head	1 feeder	5	3	10
Sheep, farm flock[3]	1-25 ewes	1 ewe	7	5	10
	25-49 ewes	1 ewe	5	3	7
	50-100 ewes	1 ewe	4	2	6
Hogs	15-39 litters	1 litter	23	15	35
	40-99 litters	1 litter	18	10	30
	100 litters or more	1 litter	15	8	25
Feeder pigs	1-100 hogs	1 pig	2.2	1.6	1.4
	100-249 hogs	1 pig	1.0	0.7	0.5
	250-500 hogs	1 pig	4.5	3.0	2.7
Poultry	> 2,000 hens	100 hens	40	20	80

2 Source: *Farm Management Manual.* University of Illinois Cooperative Extension Service. AE-4473

3 Includes time for harvesting hay and straw and hauling manure in addition to more time for caring for livestock.